The
of the Novels and Selected Writings
of Daniel Defoe

The FORTUNATE MISTRESS

Volume I

The Famous ROXANA.

Frontispiece of the first edition of "The Fortunate Mistress . . . or Roxana" (1724)
The British Museum copy of this book does not contain the frontispiece, and no other copy could be traced in England. The present reproduction was made from material kindly supplied by Messrs. Constable, who utilized for their edition of this book, a copy of the first edition which is no longer available.

The FORTUNATE
MISTRESS or A
HISTORY of the LIFE

and Vast Variety of Fortunes of
Mademoiselle de Beleau, afterwards call'd
The Countess *de Wintselsheim*,
in Germany.
Being the Person known by the Name of the LADY
ROXANA, in the Time of King *Charles* II.

Volume I

OXFORD: BASIL BLACKWELL
Publisher to the SHAKESPEARE HEAD PRESS
of STRATFORD-UPON-AVON
1927

FIRST PUBLISHED BY THE
SHAKESPEARE HEAD PRESS IN 1927
REPRINTED IN GREAT BRITAIN BY
PHOTO OFFSET 1974 BY
WILLIAM CLOWES & SONS, LIMITED,
LONDON, BECCLES AND COLCHESTER

DISTRIBUTED IN THE USA BY
ROWMAN & LITTLEFIELD
TOTOWA, NEW JERSEY

ISBN 0-87471-500-8

THE FORTUNATE MISTRESS: OR, A HISTORY
OF THE LIFE AND VAST VARIETY OF FORTUNES
OF MADEMOISELLE DE BELEAU, ... London:
printed for T. Warner *at the* Black-Boy *in* Paternoster-
Row; W. Meadows *at the* Angel *in* Cornhil; W. Pepper
at the Crown,*etc.,was first published on the* 14 *March,*1724,
in one octavo volume, (Frontispiece, Title, and Preface 3
leaves,and pages 407). *It had as a frontispiece a picture of the*
Lady Roxana, in her drawing-room. W.Wilson *in his ad-*
mirable Memoirs of the Life and Times of Daniel Defoe
(3 vols. 1830) *quotes some remarks of his early friend Charles*
Lamb, that Defoe " *left out the best part of* Roxana *in subse-*
quent editions, from a foolish hyper-criticism of his friend
Southerne." (vide Vol. III, page 429). *This tradition is re-*
peated again a little later in the same volume, where we are
told that Defoe was persuaded by his friend Southerne to leave
out the whole of the story relating to Roxana's daughter,
Susannah; but Wilson *does not say that he ever saw such an*
edition, and admits that most of the subsequent editions do con-
tain the story. It is interesting to note that Godwin's tragedy of
Fawkener (*to which Chas. Lamb contributed the prologue*)
was based upon the Susannah episode in The Fortunate
Mistress.

The first edition was apparently the only one published dur-
ing the life-time of Defoe. An edition appeared in 1735, *under*
the title of The Life and Adventures of Roxana, the Fortunate Mistress, or most unhappy Wife. *Another edition,*
printed for H.Slater,*in* Clement's Lane,*was issued in* 1742,
with another slight variation in the title, but with the text of
the original edition. In 1745, *there appeared a new impres-*
sion in duodecimo, with a continuation of Roxana's life until
the time of her death, written in imitation of the style of Defoe,
and this additional matter is retained in several subsequent
editions, but with the omission, in some cases, of certain passages

in the first edition. The edition, printed for H. Owen, *in* White-Fryars, *in* 1755, *is noticeable for the fact that it is divided into chapters, and is embellished with copper-plates. Other editions appeared in* 1765, 1774, *and* 1775. *The last was printed for Frances Noble, and is a sadly mutilated edition.*

The present text is a careful reprint of the first edition, with the exception of a few obvious printer's errors, which have been silently corrected.

THE PREFACE

THE *History of this* Beautiful Lady *is to speak for itself: If it is not as Beautiful as the Lady herself is reported to be; if it is not as diverting as the Reader can desire, and much more than he can reasonably expect; and if all the most diverting Parts of it are not adapted to the Instruction and Improvement of the Reader, the* Relator says, *it must be from the Defect of his Performance; dressing up the Story in worse Cloaths than the* Lady, *whose Words he speaks, prepar'd it for the World.*

He takes the Liberty to say, That this Story differs from most of the Modern Performances of this Kind, tho' some of them have met with a very good Reception in the World: I say, *It differs from them in this Great and Essential Article,* Namely, *That the Foundation of This is laid in Truth of Fact; and so the Work is not a Story but a History.*

The Scene is laid so near the Place where the Main Part of it was transacted, that it was necessary to conceal Names and Persons; lest what cannot be yet entirely forgot in that Part of the Town shou'd be remember'd, and the Facts trac'd back too plainly, by the many People yet living, who wou'd know the Persons by the Particulars.

It is not always necessary that the Names of Persons shou'd be discover'd, though the History may be many Ways useful; and if we shou'd be always oblig'd to name the Persons or not to relate the Story, the Consequence might be only this, That many a pleasant and delightful History wou'd be Buried in the Dark, and the World be depriv'd both of the Pleasure and the Profit of it.

The Writer *says, He was particularly acquainted with this Lady's First Husband, the Brewer, and with his Father; and also with his Bad Circumstances; and knows that first Part of the Story to be Truth.*

This may, he hopes, be a Pledge for the Credit of the rest, tho' the Latter Part of her History lay Abroad, and cou'd not so well be vouch'd as the First; yet, as she has told it herself, we have the less Reason to question the truth of that Part also.

In the Manner she has told the Story, it is evident she does not insist upon her Justification in any one Part of it; much less does she recommend her Conduct, or indeed any Part of it, except her Repentance, to our Imitation: On the contrary, she makes frequent Excursions in a just censuring and condemning her own Practice: How often does she reproach herself in the most passionate Manner; and guide us to just Reflections in the like Cases?

It is true She met with unexpected Success in all her wicked Courses; but even in the highest Elevations of her Prosperity she makes frequent Acknowledgments, That the Pleasure of her Wickedness was not worth the Repentance; and that all the Satisfaction she had, all the Joy in the View of her Prosperity, no, nor all the Wealth she rowl'd in; the Gaiety of her Appearance; the Equipages, and the Honours, she was attended with, cou'd quiet her Mind, abate the Reproaches of her Conscience, or procure her an Hour's Sleep, when just Reflections kept her waking.

The Noble Inferences that are drawn from this one Part, are worth all the rest of the Story; and abundantly justify (as they are the profess'd Design of) the Publication.

If there are any Parts in her Story which being oblig'd to relate a wicked Action, seem to describe it too plainly, the Writer *says, all imaginable Care has been taken to keep clear of Indecencies and immodest Expressions; and 'tis hop'd you will find nothing to prompt a vicious Mind, but everywhere much to discourage and expose it.*

Scenes of Crime, can scarce be represented in such a Manner but some may make a Criminal Use of them; but when Vice is painted in its Low-priz'd Colours, 'tis not to make People in love with it, but to expose it; and if the Reader makes a wrong Use of the Figures, the Wickedness is his own.

In the mean-time the Advantages of the present Work are so great, and the Virtuous Reader has room for so much Improvement, that we make no Question, the Story, however meanly told, will find a Passage to his best Hours, and be read both with Profit and Delight.

The FORTUNATE MISTRESS or A History of the Life, etc.

I WAS Born, *as my Friend, told me*, at the City of Poi-
tiers, in the Province, or County of Poitou in *France*,
from whence I was brought to *England* by my Parents,
who fled for their Religion about the Year 1683, when
the Proteſtants were banish'd from *France* by the Cruelty
of their Persecutors.

I, who knew little or nothing of what I was brought
over hither for, was well-enough pleas'd with being
here. *London*, a large and gay City, took with me mighty
well, who from my being a Child lov'd a crowd and to see
a great many fine Folks.

I retain'd nothing of *France*, but the language: My
Father and Mother, being People of better Fashion than
ordinarily the People call'd Refugees at that Time were,
and having fled early, while it was easy to secure their Effects, had, before their coming over, remitted considerable Sums of Money, or, *as I remember*, a considerable
Value in *French* brandy, Paper, and other Goods; and
these selling very much to Advantage here, my Father
was in very good Circumſtances at his coming over, so
that he was far from applying to the reſt of our Nation
that were here for Countenance and Relief: On the contrary, he had his Door continually throng'd with miser-
ble Objeɛts of the poor ſtarving Creatures, who at that

Time fled hither for Shelter on Account of Conscience, *or something else.*

I have indeed, heard my Father say, That he was pester'd with a great-many of those, who, *for any Religion they had,* might e'en have ſtay'd where they were, but who flock'd over hither in Droves for what they call in *English,* a livelihood; hearing with what Open Arms the REFUGEES were receiv'd in *England,* and how they fell readily into Business, being, by the charitable Assiſtance of the People in *London,* encourag'd to Work in their Manufactures, in *Spittle-Fields, Canterbury,* and other Places, and that they had a much better Price for their Work, than in *France, and the like.*

My Father, *I say, told me,* That he was more peſter'd with the Clamours of these People, than of those who were truly REFUGEES and fled in Diſtress, *merely for Conscience.*

I was about ten Years old when I was brought over hither, where, *as I have said,* my Father liv'd in very good Circumſtances and died in about eleven Years more; in which time, as I had accomplish'd myself for the sociable Part of the World, so I had acquainted myself with some of our *English* Neighbours, as is the Cuſtom in *London;* and as, while I was Young, I had pick'd up three or four Play-fellows and Companions, suitable to my Years; so as we grew bigger, we learnt to call one-another Intimates and Friends; and this forwarded very much the finishing me for Conversation, and the World.

I went to *English* Schools, and, being young, I learnt the *English* Tongue perfectly well, with all the Cuſtoms of the English Young-Women; so that I retain'd nothing of the *French,* but the Speech; nor did I so much as keep any Remains of the *French* Language tagg'd to my Way of Speaking, *as most Foreigners do*, but spoke what we call Natural *English*, as if I had been born here.

Being to give my own Character , I must be excused to give it as impartially as possible, and as if I was speaking of another-body; *and the Sequel will lead you to judge whether I flatter my self or no.*

I was (*speaking of myself as about Fourteen Years of Age*) tall, and very well made; sharp as a Hawk in Matters of common Knowledge; quick and smart in Discourse; apt to be Satyrical; full of Repartee, and a little too forward in Conversation; or, as we call it in *English*, BOLD, tho' perfectly Modest in my Behaviour. Being *French* Born, I danced, *as some say*, naturally, loved it extremely, and sang well also; and so well, that, *as you will hear*, it was afterwards some Advantage to me: With all these Things, I wanted neither Wit, Beauty, nor Money. In this Manner I set out into the World, having all the Advantages that any Young Woman cou'd desire, to recommend me to others, and form a Prospect of happy Living to myself.

At about Fifteen Years of Age my Father gave me, *as he call'd it in* French, 25,000 Livres, *that is to say*, two Thousand Pounds Portion, and married me to an Eminent Brewer in the City; *pardon me if I conceal his Name, for tho' he was the Foundation of my Ruin, I cannot take so severe a Revenge upon him.*

With this Thing call'd a Husband I liv'd eight Years in good Fashion, and for some Part of the Time, kept a Coach; *that is to say*, a kind of Mock-Coach; for all the Week the Horses were kept at Work in the Dray-Carts, but on *Sunday* I had the Privilege to go Abroad in my Chariot, either to Church, or otherwise, as my Husband and I cou'd agree about it; which, *by the way*, was not very often: But of that hereafter.

Before I proceed in the History of the Marry'd Part of my Life, you must allow me to give as impartial an Account of my Husband as I have done of myself: He was a jolly, handsome Fellow, as any Woman need wish for a companion; tall, and well made; rather a little too large, but not so as to be ungentile; he danc'd well, which, *I think* was the first thing that brought us together: He had an old Father who manag'd the Business carefully, so that he had little of that Part lay on him but now-and-then to appear and show himself; and he took the Advantage of it, for he troubl'd himself very little about it, but went Abroad, kept Company, hunted much, and lov'd it exceedingly.

After I have told you that he was a Handsome Man and a good Sportsman, I have indeed, said all; and unhappy was I—like other young People of our Sex, I chose him for being a handsome, jolly Fellow, as I have said; for he was otherwise a weak, empty-headed, untaught Creature as any Woman could ever desire to be coupled with: And here I must take the Liberty, whatever I have to reproach myself with in my after-Conduct, to turn to my Fellow-Creatures, the Young Ladies of this Country, and speak to them by way of Precaution, If you have any Regard to your future Happiness; any View of living comfortably with a Husband; any Hope of preserving your Fortunes, or restoring them after any Disaster, Never, Ladies, marry a Fool; any Husband rather than a Fool; with some other Husbands you may be unhappy, but with a Fool you will be miserable; with another Husband you *may*, I say, be unhappy, but with a Fool you *must*; nay, if he wou'd, he cannot make you easie; everything he does is so awkward, everything he says is so empty, a Woman of any Sence cannot but be surfeited and sick of him twenty times a-Day: What is more shocking, than for a Woman to bring a handsome, comely Fellow of a Husband, into Company, and then be oblig'd to Blush for him every time she hears him speak; To hear other Gentlemen talk Sence and he able to say nothing? And so look like a Fool; or, which is worse, hear him talk Nonsense, and be laugh'd at for a fool.

In the next Place, there are so many Sorts of Fools, such an infinite Variety of Fools, and so hard it is to know the Worst of the Kind, that I am oblig'd to say, No Fool, Ladies, at all, no kind of Fool; whether a mad Fool, or a sober Fool, a wise Fool, or a silly Fool, take anything but a Fool; *nay*, be anything, be even an Old Maid, the worst of Nature's Curses, rather than take up with a Fool.

But to leave this a-while, for I shall have Occasion to speak of it again; my Case was particularly hard, for I had a Variety of foolish Things complicated in this unhappy Match.

First, and which I must confess is very unsufferable, he was a conceited Fool, *Tout Opiniâtre*; everything he said was Right, was Best, and was to the Purpose, whoever was in Company and whatever was advanc'd by others, tho' with the greatest Modesty imaginable; and yet when he came to defend what he had said by Argument and Reason, he would do it so weakly, so emptily, and so nothing to the Purpose, that it was enough to make anybody that heard him sick and asham'd of him.

Secondly, He was positive and obstinate, and the most positive in the most simple and inconsistent Things such as were intollerable to bear.

These two Articles, if there had been no more, qualified him to be a most unbearable Creature for a Husband; and so it may be suppos'd at first Sight, what a kind of

Life I led with him: However, I did as well as I could, and
held my Tongue, which was the only Victory I gain'd
over him; for when he would talk after his own empty
rattling Way with me, and I would not answer, or enter
into Discourse with him on the Point he was upon, he
would rise up in the greatest Passion imaginable, and go
away; which was the cheapest way I had to be deliver'd.

I could enlarge here much upon the Method I took to
make my life passable and easie with the most incorrigible
Temper in the World; but it is too long and the Articles
too trifling: I shall mention some of them as the Circumstances I am to relate, shall necessarily bring them in.

After I had been Married about four Years, my own
Father died, my Mother having been dead before; he lik-
ed my Match so ill, and saw so little Room to be satisfied
with the Conduct of my Husband, that tho' he left me
5000 Livres, and more at his Death, yet he left it in the
Hands of my Elder Brother, who, running on too rashly
in his Adventures as a Merchant, fail'd, and lost not only
what he had, but what he had for me too; as you shall hear
presently.

Thus I lost the last Gift of my Father's Bounty by having a Husband not fit to be trusted with it; there's one of
the Benefits of marrying a Fool!

Within two Years after my own Father's Death my
Husband's Father also died, and, as I thought, left him a
considerable Addition to his Estate; the whole Trade of
the Brewhouse, which was a very good one, being now his
own.

But this Addition to his Stock was his Ruin, for he had
no Genius to Business; he had no Knowledge of his Accounts; he bustled a little about it indeed, at first, and put
on a Face of Business, but he soon grew slack; It was be-

low him to inspect his Books, he committed all that to his Clerks and Book-Keepers; and while he found Money in Cash to pay the Malt-Man and the Excise, and put some in his Pocket, he was perfectly easie and indolent, let the main Chance go how it would.

I foresaw the Consequences of this, and attempted several times to persuade him to apply himself to his Business; I put him in Mind how his Customers complain'd of the Neglect of his Servants on one hand, and how abundance Broke in his Debt, on the other hand, for want of the Clerk's Care to secure him, *and the like*; but he thrust me by, either with hard Words or fraudulently with representing the Cases otherwise than they were.

However, to cut short a dull Story, which ought not to be long, he began to find his Trade sunk, his Stock declin'd, and that, in short, he could not carry on his Business; and once or twice his Brewing Utensils were extended for the Excise; and the last Time he was put to great extremities to clear them.

This alarm'd him, and he resolv'd to lay down his Trade; which indeed I was not sorry for; foreseeing that if he did not lay it down in Time, he would be forc'd to do it another Way, namely, as a Bankrupt. Also, I was willing he should draw out while he had something left, lest I should come to be stript at Home, and be turn'd out of Doors with my Children; for I had now five Children by him: the only Work (perhaps) that Fools are good for.

I thought myself happy when he got another Man to take his Brewhouse clear off his Hands; for, paying down a large Sum of Money, my Husband found himself a clear Man, all his Debts paid, and with between Two and Three Thousand Pound in his Pocket; and being now obliged to remove from the Brewhouse, we took a House at ———,

a Village about two Miles out of Town; and happy I
thought myself, all things consider'd, that I was got off
clear, upon so good Terms, and had my handsome Fellow had but one Cap full of Wit, I had been ſtill well
enough.

I propos'd to him either to buy some Place with the
Money or with Part of it, and offer'd to join my Part to it,
which was then in Being and might have been secur'd; so
we might have liv'd tolerably, at leaſt, during his Life.
But as it is the Part of a Fool to be void of Council, so he
negleƈted it, liv'd on as he did before, kept his Horses and
Men, rode every Day out to the Foreſt a-hunting, and
nothing was done all this while; but the money decreas'd
apace, and I thought I saw my ruin haſtening on without
any possible Way to prevent it.

I was not wanting with all that Perswasions and En-
treaties could perform, but it was all fruitless; representing to him how faſt our Money waſted, and what would
be our Condition when it was gone, made no Impression
on him; but like one ſtupid, he went on, not valuing all
that Tears and Lamentations could be suppos'd to do;
nor did he abate his Figure or Equipage, his Horses or
Servants, even to the laſt, till he had not a Hundred
Pound left in the whole World.

It was not above three Years that all the Ready-Money
was thus spending off; yet he spent it, as I may say, foolishly too, for he kept no valuable Company neither; but
generally with Huntsmen and Horse-Coursers, and Men
meaner than himself, which is another Consequence of a
Man's being a Fool; such can never take delight in Men
more wise and capable than themselves; and that makes
them converse with Scoundrels, drink Belch with Porters,
and keep Company always below themselves.

This was my wretched Condition, when one Morning my Husband told me he was sensible he was come to a miserable Condition and he would go and seek his fortune somewhere or other; he had said something to that purpose several times before that, upon my pressing him to consider his Circumstances and the Circumstances of his Family before it should be too late: But as I found he had no Meaning in anything of that Kind, as indeed he had not much in anything he ever said; so I thought they were but Words of Course now: When he said he wou'd be gone, I us'd to wish secretly, and even say in my Thoughts, *I wish you wou'd, for if you go on thus you will starve us all.*

He stayed, however, at home all that Day, and lay at home that Night; early the next Morning he gets out of Bed, goes to a Window which look'd out towards the Stables, and sounds his *French* Horn, as he call'd it, which was his usual Signal to call his Men to go out a-hunting.

It was about the latter end of *August*, and so was light yet at five a-Clock, and it was about that Time that I heard him and his two Men go out and shut the Yard-Gates after them. He said nothing to me more than as usual when he us'd to go out upon his Sport; neither did I rise, or say anything to him that was material, but went to sleep again after he was gone, for two Hours or thereabouts.

It must be a little surprising to the Reader to tell him at once, that after this I never saw my Husband more; but to go further, I not only never saw him more, but I never heard from him, or of him, neither of any or either of his two Servants or of the Horses, either what became of them, where or which Way they went, or what they did, or intended to do, no more than if the Ground had open'd and swallowed them all up, and no-body had known it, except as hereafter.

I was not for the firſt Night or two at all surpriz'd, no, nor very much the firſt Week or two, believing that if anything evil had befallen them I should soon enough have heard of that; and also knowing that as he had two Servants and three horses with him, it would be the ſtrangeſt Thing in the World that anything could befal them all, but that I muſt some time or other hear of them.

But you will easily allow that as Time ran on a Week, two Weeks, a Month, two Months, and so on, I was dreadfully frighted at laſt, and the more when I looked into my own Circumſtances and consider'd the Condition in which I was left; with five Children and not one Farthing Subsiſtence for them, other than about seventy Pound in Money and what few Things of Value I had about me, which, tho' considerable in themselves, were yet nothing to feed a Family, and for a length of Time too.

What to do I knew not, nor to whom to have recourse; to keep in the House where I was, I could not, the Rent being too great; and to leave it without his Order, if my Husband should return, I could not think of that neither; so that I continued extremely perplex'd, melancholy, and discouraged to the laſt Degree.

I remain'd in this dejeƈted Condition near a Twelvemonth. My Husband had two Siſters, who were married and liv'd very well, and some other near Relations that I knew of, and I hop'd would do something for me; and I frequently sent to these, to know if they could give me any Account of my vagrant Creature; but they all declar'd to me in Answer, that they knew nothing about him; and, after frequent sending, began to think me troublesome, and to let me know they thought so too, by their treating my Maid with very slight and unhandsome Returns to her Enquiries.

This grated hard and added to my Affliction, but I had no recourse but to my Tears, for I had not a Friend of my own left me in the World; I should have observ'd that it was about half a Year before this Elopement of my Husband, that the disaster I mention'd above befell my Brother; who Broke, and that in such bad Circumstances, that I had the mortification to hear not only that he was in Prison, but that there would be little or nothing to be had by Way of Composition.

Misfortunes seldom come alone: This was the Forerunner of my Husband's Flight, and as my Expectations were cut off on that Side, my Husband gone, and my Family of Children on my Hands, and nothing to subsist them, my Condition was the most deplorable that Words can express.

I had some Plate and some Jewels, as might be supposed, my Fortune and former Circumstances consider'd, and my Husband, who had never stayed to be distress'd, had not been put to the Necessity of rifling me, as Husbands usually do in such Cases: But as I had seen an End of all the Ready-Money during the long Time I had liv'd in a state of Expectation for my Husband, so I began to make away one Thing after another, till those few Things of Value which I had, began to lessen apace, and I saw nothing but Misery and the utmost Distress before me, even to have my Children starve before my Face; I leave any one that is a Mother of Children, and has liv'd in Plenty and good Fashion, to consider and reflect what must be my Condition: As to my Husband, I had now no Hope or Expectation of seeing him any more; and indeed, if I had, he was the Man, of all the Men in the

World the least able to help me, or to have turn'd his hand to the gaining one Shilling towards lessening our Distress. He neither had the Capacity or the Inclination; he could have been no Clerk, for he scarce wrote a legible Hand; he was so far from being able to write Sence, that he could not make Sence of what others wrote; he was so far from understanding good *English*, that he could not spell good *English*. To be out of all Business was his Delight, and he would stand leaning against a Post for half an Hour together, with a Pipe in his Mouth, with all the Tranquillity in the World, smoaking, *like* Dryden's *countryman that Whistled as he went, for want of Thought*; and this even when his Family was, as it were, starving, that little he had wasting, and that we were all bleeding to Death, he not knowing, and as little considering, where to get another Shilling when the last was spent.

This being his Temper, and the Extent of his Capacity, I confess I did not see so much loss in his parting with me as at first I thought I did; though it was hard and cruel to the last Degree in him not giving me the least Notice of his Design; and indeed, that which I was most astonish'd at, was, that seeing he must certainly have intended this Excursion some few Moments at least, before he put it in Practice, yet he did not come and take what little Stock of Money we had left; or at least, a Share of it, to bear his Expense for a little while; but he did not; and I am morally certain he had not five Guineas with him in the World, when he went away: All that I cou'd come to the Knowledge of, about him, was, that he left his Hunting-Horn, which he called the *French* Horn, in the Stable, and his Hunting Saddle, went away in a handsome Furniture, as they call it, which he used sometimes to Travel with, having an embroidered Housing, a Case of Pistols, and other

things belonging to them; and one of his Servants had
another Saddle with Pistols, though plain, and the other
a long Gun; so that they did not go out as Sportsmen, but
rather as Travellers. What Part of the World they went
to I never heard for many Years.

As I have said, I sent to his Relations, but they sent me
short and surly Answers; nor did any one of them offer to
come to see me or to see the Children, or so much as to
enquire after them, well perceiving that I was in a Condition that was likely to be soon troublesome to them: But
it was no Time now to dally with them or with the World:
I left off sending to them, and went myself among them;
laid my Circumstances open to them, told them my whole
Case and the Condition I was reduc'd to, begg'd they
would advise me what Course to take, laid myself as low
as they could desire, and intreated them to consider that I
was not in a Condition to help myself, and that without
some Assistance, we must all inevitably perish: I told
them that if I had had but one Child, or two Children, I
would have done my Endeavour to have work'd for them
with my Needle, and should only have come to them to
beg them to help me to some Work, that I might get our
Bread by my Labour; but to think of one single Woman
not bred to work, and at a Loss where to get Employment, to get the Bread of five Children, that was not possible, some of my Children being young too, and none of
them big enough to help one another.

It was all one; I receiv'd not one Farthing of Assistance
from any-body was hardly ask'd to sit down at the two
Sister's Houses, nor offer'd to Eat or Drink at two more
near Relations. The Fifth, an Ancient Gentlewoman,
Aunt-in-Law to my Husband, a Widow, and the least
able also of any of the rest, did, indeed ask me to sit down,

gave me a Dinner, and refresh'd me with a kinder Treatment than any of the rest; but added the melancholy Part, viz. That she would have help'd me, but that indeed, she was not able; which, however, I was satisfied was very true.

Here I reliev'd myself with the constant Assistant of the afflicted, I mean Tears; for, relating to her how I was received by the other of my Husband's Relations, it made me burst into Tears, and I cry'd vehemently for a great while together, till I made the good old Gentlewoman cry too several times.

However, I came home from them all without any Relief, and went on at home till I was reduc'd to such inexpressible Distress, that it is not to be describ'd: I had been several times after this at the old Aunt's, for I prevail'd with her to promise me to go and talk with the other Relations; at least, that if possible she could bring some of them to take on the Children, or to contribute something towards their Maintenance; and to do her Justice, she did use her Endeavour with them, but all was to no Purpose, they would do nothing, at least that Way: I think, with much Entreaty, she obtain'd by a kind of Collection among them all, about eleven or twelve Shillings in Money, which, tho' it was a present Comfort, was yet not to be nam'd as capable to deliver me from any Part of the Load that lay upon me.

There was a poor Woman that had been a kind of a Dependent upon our Family, and who I had often, among the rest of the Relations, been very kind to; my Maid put it into my Head one Morning to send to this poor Woman and to see whether she might not be able to help, in this dreadful Case.

I must remember it here, to the Praise of this poor Girl,

my Maid, that tho' I was not able to give her any Wages, and had told her so, nay, I was not able to pay her the Wages that I was in Arrears to her, yet she would not leave me; nay, and as long as she had any Money, when I had none, she would help me out of her own; for which, tho' I acknowledg'd her Kindness and Fidelity, yet it was but a bad Coin that she was paid in at laſt, as will appear in its Place.

AMY (for that was her Name) put it into my Thoughts to send for this poor Woman to come to me, for I was now in great Diſtress, and I resolv'd to do so; but juſt the very Morning that I intended it, the old Aunt, with the poor Woman in her Company, came to see me; the good old Gentlewoman was, it seems, heartily concern'd for me, and had been talking again among those People, to see what she could do for me, but to very little Purpose.

You shall judge a little of my present Diſtress by the Poſture she found me in: I had five little Children, the Eldeſt was under ten Years old, and I had not one Shilling in the House to buy them Viƈtuals, but had sent *Amy* out with a Silver Spoon to sell it and bring home something from the Butcher's, and I was in a Parlour, sitting on the Ground with a great Heap of old Rags, Linen, and other things about me, looking them over to see if I had anything among them that would Sell or Pawn for a little Money, and had been crying ready to burſt myself to think what I should do next.

At this Junƈture they knock'd at the Door, I thought it had been *Amy*, so I did not rise up, but one of the Children open'd the Door, and they came direƈtly into the Room where I was, and where they found me in that Poſture and crying vehemently, as above; I was surprized at their coming, you may be sure, especially seeing the Person I had but juſt before resolved to send for: But when they saw me, how I look'd, for my Eyes were swell'd with crying, and what a Condition I was in as to the House, and the Heaps of Things that were about me, and especially when I told them what I was doing and on what Occasion, they sat down, like *Job*'s three Comforters, and said not one Word to me for a great while, but both of them cry'd as faſt and as heartily as I did.

The Truth was, there was no Need of much Discourse in the Case, the Thing spoke for itself; they saw me in Rags and Dirt, who was but a little before riding in my Coach; thin, and looking almoſt like one Starv'd, who was before fat and beautiful: The House, that was before handsomely furnish'd with Pictures and Ornaments, Cabinets, Pier-Glasses, and everything suitable, was now ſtripp'd and naked, moſt of the Goods having been seiz'd by the Landlord for Rent or sold to buy Necessaries; in a word, all was Misery and Diſtress, the Face of Ruin was everywhere to be seen; we had eaten up almoſt everything, and little remain'd, unless, like one of the pitiful Women of *Jerusalem*, I should eat up my very Children themselves.

After these two good Creatures had sat, as I say, in Silence some time, and had then look'd about them, my Maid *Amy* came in and brought with her a small Breaſt of Mutton and two great Bunches of Turnips, which she intended to ſtew for our Dinner: As for me, my Heart was so overwhelm'd at seeing these two Friends, for such they were, tho' poor, and at their seeing me in such a Condition, that I fell into another violent Fit of Crying; so that, in short, I could not speak to them again for a great while longer.

During my being in such an Agony, they went to my

Maid *Amy* at another Part of the same Room, and talk'd
with her. *Amy* told them all my Circumstances, and set
them forth in such moving Terms and so to the Life, that
I could not upon any Terms have done it like her myself;
and, in a Word, affected them both with it in such a manner, that the old Aunt came to me, and tho' hardly able to
speak for Tears: Look ye, Cousin, said she in a few Words,
Things must not stand thus; some Course must be taken,
and that forthwith; pray where were these Children born?
I told her the Parish where we liv'd before; that four of
them were born there and one in the House where I now
was, where the Landlord, after having seiz'd my Goods
for the Rent past, not then knowing my Circumstances,
had now given me leave to live for a whole Year more
without any Rent, being moved with Compassion; but
that this Year was now almost expired.

Upon hearing this Account, they came to this Resolution: That the Children should be all carried by them to
the Door of one of the Relations mention'd above, and be
set down there by the Maid *Amy*, and that I, the Mother,
should remove for some Days, shut up the Doors, and be
gone; that the People should be told, That if they did not
think fit to take some Care of the Children, they might
send for the Church-wardens if they thought that better;
for that they were born in that Parish and there they must
be provided for; as for the other Child which was born in
the Parish of ———, that was already taken care of by the
Parish-Officers there; for indeed they were so sensible of
the Distress of the Family, that they had at first Word
done what was their Part to do.

This was what these good Women propos'd, and bade
me leave the rest to them. I was at first sadly afflicted at
the Thoughts of parting with my Children, and especially

at that terrible thing their being taken into the Parish keeping; and then a hundred terrible things came into my Thoughts, *viz.* of Parish-Children being Starv'd at Nurse, of their being ruin'd, let grow crooked, lam'd, and the like, for want of being taken care of; and this sank my very Heart within me.

But the Misery of my own Circumstances hardened my Heart against my own Flesh and Blood; and when I consider'd they must inevitably be Starv'd, and I too, if I continued to keep them about me, I began to be reconcil'd to parting with them all, anyhow and anywhere, that I might be freed from the dreadful Necessity of seeing them all perish and perishing with them myself: So I agreed to go away out of the House and leave the Management of the whole Matter to my Maid *Amy* and to them; and accordingly I did so, and the same Afternoon they carried them all away to one of their *Aunts*.

Amy, a resolute Girl, knock'd at the Door with the Children all with her, and bade the Eldest, as soon as the Door was open, run in, and the rest after her: She set them all down at the Door before she knock'd, and when she knock'd she stayed till a Maid-Servant came to the Door; Sweetheart, said she, pray go in and tell your Mistress, here are her little Cousins come to see her from ———, naming the Town where we liv'd; at which the maid offer'd to go back: Here, child, says *Amy*, take one of 'em in your Hand, and I'll bring the rest, so she gives her the least, and the Wench goes in mighty innocently with the Little One in her Hand; upon which *Amy* turns the rest in after her, shuts the Door softly, and marches off as fast as she cou'd.

Just in the Interval of this, and even while the Maid and her Mistress were quarrelling, for the Mistress rav'd and scolded at her like a Mad-Woman, and had order'd her to go and stop the Maid *Amy* and turn all the Children out of the Doors again; but she had been at the Door and *Amy* was gone, and the Wench was out of her Wits, and the Mistress too: I say, just at this Juncture came the poor old Woman, not the Aunt, but the other of the two that had been with me, and knocks at the Door; the aunt did not go, because she had pretended to Advocate for me, and they would have suspected her of some Contrivance; but as for the other Woman, they did not so much as know that she had kept up any Correspondence with me.

Amy and she had concerted this between them, and it was well enough contriv'd that they did so. When she came into the House, the Mistress was fuming and raging like one Distracted, and calling the Maid all the foolish Jades and Sluts that she could think of, and that she would take the Children and turn them all out into the Streets. The good poor Woman, seeing her in such a Passion, turn'd about as if she would be gone again, and said Madam, I'll come again another time, I see you are engag'd. No, no, Mrs. ——, says the Mistress, I am not much engaged; sit down: This sensless Creature here has brought in my Fool of a Brother's whole House of Children upon me, and tells me that a Wench brought them to the Door, and thrust them in, and bade her carry them to me; but it shall be no Disturbance to me, for I have order'd them to be set in the Street without the Door, and so let the Church-Wardens take Care of them, or else make this dull Jade carry them back to —— again and let her that brought them into the World, look after them if she will; what does she send her brats to me for?

The last indeed had been the best of the two, says the Poor Woman, if it had been to be done, and that brings me to tell you my Errand, and the Occasion of my coming, for I came on purpose about this very Business, and to have prevented this being put upon you, if I could; but I see I am come too late.

How do you mean too late? says the Mistress. What, have you been concern'd in this Affair, then? What, have you helped bring this Family-Slur upon us? I hope you do not think such a thing of me, Madam, says the poor Woman; but I went this Morning to —— to see my old Mistress and Benefactor, for she had been very kind to me, and when I came to the Door I found all fast lock'd and bolted, and the House looking as if nobody was at Home.

I knock'd at the Door, but no-body came, till at last some of the Neighbours' Servants call'd to me and said, There's nobody lives there, Mistress, what do you knock for? I seemed surpriz'd at that; What, no-body live there! *said* I; what d'ye mean? Does not Mrs. —— live there? The answer was, No, she is gone; at which I parly'd with one of them, and ask'd her what was the Matter. Matter, says she, why, 'tis matter Enough; the poor Gentlewoman has liv'd there all alone, and without anything to subsist her, a long time, and this Morning the Landlord turn'd her out of doors.

Our of doors! says I; what, with all her children! poor Lambs, what is become of them? Why, truly nothing worse, *said they*, can come to them than staying here, for they were almost starv'd with Hunger; so the Neighbours seeing the poor Lady in such Distress, for she stood crying, and wringing her Hands over her Children like one distracted, sent for the Church-Wardens to take care of the Children; and they when they came, took the Youngest, which was born in this Parish, and have got it a very good Nurse and taken Care of it; but as for the other four, they had sent them away to some of their Father's Relations, who were very substantial people and who, besides that, liv'd in the parish where they were born.

I was not so surpriz'd at this as not presently to foresee that this Trouble would be brought upon you or upon Mr. ——, so I came immediately to bring you word of it, that you might be prepared for it and might not be surpriz'd, but I see they have been too nimble for me, so that I know not what to advise; the poor Woman, it seems, is turned out of Doors into the Street; and another of the Neighbours there told me that when they took her Children from her she swoon'd away, and when they recover'd her out of that, she ran distracted, and is put into a Mad-House by the Parish, for there is no-body else to take any Care of her.

This was all acted to the Life by this good, kind, poor Creature; for tho' her Design was perfectly good and charitable, yet there was not one Word of it true in Fact; for I was not turn'd out of Doors by the Landlord, nor gone distracted; it was true indeed that at parting with my poor Children, I fainted, and was like one Mad when I came to myself and found they were gone; but I remained in the House a good while after that; as you shall hear.

While the poor Woman was telling this dismal Story, in came the Gentlewoman's Husband, and though her Heart was harden'd against all Pity, who was really and nearly related to the Children, for they were the Children of her own Brother, yet the good Man was quite soften'd with the dismal Relation of the Circumstances of the Family; and when the poor Woman had done, he said to his wife, This is a dismal Case, my Dear, indeed, and something must be done: His Wife fell a-raving at him. What!

says she, do you want to have four Children to keep? Have we not Children of our own? Would you have these Brats come and eat up my Children's Bread? No, no, let 'em go to the Parish, and let them take Care of them; I 'll take Care of my own.

Come, come, my dear, *says the Husband,* Charity is a Duty to the Poor, and *He that gives to the Poor, lends to the Lord*; let us lend our Heavenly Father a little of our Children's Bread, as you call it; it will be a Store well laid up for them, and will be the beſt Security that our Children shall never come to want Charity or be turn'd out of Doors as these poor innocent Creatures are.

Don't tell me of Security, *says the Wife*; 'tis a good Security for our Children, to keep what we have together, and provide for them, and then 'tis time enough to help to keep other Folks' Children. Charity begins at home.

Well, my Dear, *says he again,* I only talk of putting out a little Money to Intereſt; our Maker is a good Borrower, never fear making a bad Debt there, Child, I 'll be Bound for it.

Don't banter me with your Charity and your Allegories, *says the Wife angrily*; I tell you they are my Relations, not yours, and they shall not rooſt here, they shall go to the Parish.

All your Relations are my Relations now, *says the good Gentleman very calmly,* and I won't see your Relations in Diſtress and not pity them, any more than I would my own; indeed, my Dear, they shan't go to the Parish; I assure you none of my Wife's Relations shall come to the Parish, if I can help it.

What! will you take four Children to keep? *says the wife.*

No, no, my Dear, says he, there's your Siſter ——, I 'll

go and talk with her; and your Uncle ———, I 'll send for him and the rest; I 'll warrant you when we are all together we will find Ways and Means to keep four poor little Creatures from Beggary and Starving, or else it will be very hard; we are none of us in so bad Circumstances but we are able to spare a Mite for the Fatherless; don't shut up your Bowels of Compassion against your own Flesh and Blood: Could you hear these poor innocent Children cry at your Door for hunger and give them no Bread?

Prithee, why need they cry at our Door? says she, 'tis the business of the Parish to provide for them. They shan't cry at our Door; if they do, I'll give them nothing. Won't you? *says he*; but *I* will. Remember that dreadful Scripture is directly against us, Prov. 2 1. 1 3; Whoso stoppeth his Ears at the cry of the Poor, he also shall cry himself, but shall not be heard.

Well, well, *says she*, you must do what you will, because you pretend to be Master; but if I had my Will, I would send them where they ought to be sent, I would send them from whence they came.

Then the poor Woman put in and said, But, Madam, that is sending them to starve indeed; for the Parish has no Obligation to take Care of 'em, and so they would lie and perish in the Street.

Or be sent back again, *says the husband*, to our Parish in a Cripple-Cart by the Justice's Warrant, and so expose us and all the Relations to the last Degree among our Neighbours, and among those who knew the good Old Gentleman their Grandfather, who liv'd and flourish'd in this Parish so many Years and was so well belov'd among all People, and deserved it so well.

I don't value that one farthing, not I, *says the Wife*, I'll keep none of them.

Well, my dear, *says her Husband*, but *I* value it, for I won't have such a Blot lie upon the Family and upon your Children; he was a worthy, ancient, and good Man, and his Name is respected among all his Neighbours; it will be a Reproach to you that are his Daughter, and to our Children, that are his Grand-Children, that we should let your Brother's Children perish, or come to be a Charge to the Public, in the very Place where your Family once flourished. Come, say no more, I'll see what can be done.

Upon this he sends and gathers all the Relations together at a Tavern hard by, and sent for the four little Children that they might see them; and they all at first Word agreed to have them taken Care of; and because his Wife was so furious that she would not suffer one of them to be kept at Home, they agreed to keep them all together for a while. So they committed them to the poor Woman that had manag'd the Affair for them, and enter'd into Obligations to one another to supply the needful Sums for their Maintenance; and not to have one separated from the rest, they sent for the Youngest from the Parish where it was taken in, and had them all brought up together.

It would take up too long a Part of this Story to give a particular account with what a charitable Tenderness this good Person, who was but Uncle-in-Law to them, managed that affair; how careful he was of them, went constantly to see them, and to see that they were well provided for, cloth'd, put to School, and at last put out in the World for their Advantage; but 'tis enough to say he acted more like a Father to them than an Uncle-in-Law, tho' all along much against his Wife's Consent, who was of a Disposition not so tender and compassionate as her Husband.

You may believe I heard this with the same Pleasure

which I now feel at the relating it again, for I was terribly frighted at the Apprehensions of my Children being brought to Misery and Diſtress, as those muſt be who have no Friends but are left to Parish Bencvolcnce.

I was now, however, entering on a new Scene of Life. I had a great House upon my Hands, and some Furniture left in it, but I was no more able to maintain myself and my Maid *Amy* in it than I was my five Children; nor had I anything to subſiſt with, but what I might get by work-ing, and that was not a Town where much Work was to be had.

My Landlord had been very kind indeed after he came to know my Circumſtances, though before he was ac-quainted with that Part, he had gone so far as to seize my Goods, and to carry some of them off too.

But I had lived three Quarters of a year in his House after that and had paid him no Rent, and, which was worse, I was in no Condition to pay him any; However, I observ'd he came oftner to see me, look'd kinder upon me, and spoke more friendly to me, than he us'd to do; particularly the laſt two or three times he had been there, he observ'd, *he said*, how poorly I liv'd, how low I was re-duc'd, and the like, told me it griev'd him for my sake; and the laſt time of all he was kinder ſtill, told me he came to Dine with me, and that I should give him leave to Treat me; so he called my Maid *Amy*, and sent her out to buy a joint of Meat; he told her what she should buy, but nam-ing two or three things, either of which she might take; the Maid, a cunning Wench, and faithful to me, as the Skin to my Back, did not buy anything out-right, but brought the Butcher along with her, with both the things that she had chosen, for him to please himself; the one was a large very good Leg of Veal, the other a Piece of the

Fore-Ribs of Roasting Beef; he look'd at them, but bade me chaffer with the Butcher for him, and I did so, and came back to him, and told him what the Butcher demanded for either of them, and what each of them came to; so he pulls out 11s. 3d., which they came to together, and bade me take them both, the rest, he said, would serve another time.

I was surpriz'd, you may be sure, at the Bounty of a Man that had but a little while ago been my Terror, and had torn the Goods out of my House like a Fury; but I consider'd that my Distresses had mollified his Temper, and that he had afterwards been so compassionate as to give me Leave to live Rent-free in the House a whole Year.

But now he put on the Face, not of a Man of Compassion only, but of a Man of Friendship and Kindness, and this was so unexpected, that it was surprizing. We chatted together, and were, as I may call it, Cheerful, which was more than I could say I had been for three Years before; he sent for Wine and Beer too, for I had none; poor *Amy* and I had drank nothing but Water for many Weeks, and indeed, I have often wonder'd at the faithful Temper of the poor Girl, for which I but ill requited her at last.

When *Amy* was come with the Wine, he made her fill a Glass to him, and with the Glass in his Hand he came to me, and kiss'd me, which I was, I confess, a little surpriz'd at, but more, at what follow'd; for he told me, That as the sad Condition which I was reduc'd to had made him pity me, so my Conduct in it, and the Courage I bore it with, had given him a more than ordinary Respect for me, and made him very thoughtful for my Good; that he was resolv'd for the present to do something to relieve me, and to employ his Thoughts in the meantime, to see if he

could, for the future, put me into a Way to support myself.

While he found me change Colour, and look surpriz'd
at his Discourse, for so I did to be sure, he turns to my
Maid *Amy*, and looking at her, he says to me, I say all this,
Madam, before your Maid, because both she and you shall
know that I have no ill Design, and that I have in meer
Kindness resolved to do something for you, if I can; and
as I have been a Witness of the uncommon honesty and
fidelity of Mrs. *Amy* here, to you in all your Distresses, I
know she may be trusted with so honest a Design as mine
is; for, I assure you, I bear a proprotion'd Regard to your
Maid too, for her Affection to you.

Amy made him a Curtsie, and the poor Girl looked so
confounded with Joy, that she could not speak, but her
Colour came and went, and every now and then she
blush'd as red as Scarlet, and the next Minute look'd as
pale as Death: Well, having said this, he sat down, made
me sit down, and then drank to me, and made me drink
two Glasses of Wine together; for, *says he*, you have
Need of it; and so indeed I had: When he had done
so, Come, *Amy*, says he, with your mistress's Leave you
shall have a Glass too; so he made her drink two Glasses
also, and then rising up; And now, *Amy*, says he, go and
get Dinner; and you, Madam, *says he* to me, go up and
dress you, and come down and smile and be merry, adding, I'll make you easy if I can; and in the meantime, he
said, he would walk in the Garden.

When he was gone, *Amy* chang'd her Countenance indeed and look'd as merry as ever she did in her Life.
Dear Madam, says she, what does this Gentleman mean?
Nay, *Amy*, said I, he means to do us Good, you see, don't
he? I know no other Meaning he can have, for he can get

nothing by me: I warrant you, Madam, says she, he'll
ask you a Favour by and by. No, no, you are mistaken,
Amy, I dare say, *said I*; you heard what he said, didn't you?
Ay, says *Amy*, it's no matter for that, you shall see what he
will do after Dinner: Well, well, *Amy*, says I, you have
hard Thoughts of him; I cannot be of your Opinion; I
don't see anything in him yet that looks like it: As to that,
Madam, says *Amy*, I don't see anything of it yet neither;
but what should move a Gentleman to take Pity of us as
he does? Nay, *says I*, that's a hard thing too, that we should
judge a Man to be wicked because he's charitable, and
vicious because he's kind. O, Madam, says *Amy*, there's
abundance of Charity begins in that Vice, and he is not so
unacquainted with things as not to know that Poverty is
the strongest incentive; a Temptation against which no
Virtue is powerful enough to stand out; he knows your
Condition as well as you do: Well, and what then? Why,
then he knows too that you are young and handsome, and
he has the surest Bait in the World to take you with.

Well, *Amy*, said I, but he may find himself mistaken
too in such a thing as that: Why, Madam, says *Amy*, I
hope you won't deny him if he should offer it.

What d'ye mean by that, Hussy? *said I*. No, I'd starve
first.

I hope not, Madam, I hope you would be wiser; I'm
sure if he will set you up, as he talks of, you ought to deny
him nothing; and you will starve if you do not consent,
that's certain.

What! consent to lie with him for Bread? *Amy*, said I,
how can you talk so?

Nay, Madam, says *Amy*, I don't think you wou'd for
anything else; it would not be Lawful for anything else,

but for Bread, Madam. Why, nobody can starve; there's no bearing that, I'm sure.

Ay, *says I*, but if he would give me an Estate to live on, he should not lye with me, I assure you.

Why, look you, Madam, if he would but give you enough to live easie upon, he should lye with me for it with all my Heart.

That's a Token, *Amy*, of inimitable Kindness to me, *said I*, and I know how to value it; but there's more Friendship than Honesty in it, *Amy*.

Oh, Madam, says *Amy*, I'd do anything to get you out of this sad Condition; as to Honesty, I think Honesty is out of the Question when Starvation is the Case; are not we almost starv'd to Death?

I am indeed, *said I*, and thou art for my sake; but to be a Whore, *Amy*!—and there I stopt.

Dear Madam, says *Amy*, if I will starve for your sake, I will be a Whore, or anything for your sake; why, I would die for you if I were put to it.

Why, that's an Excess of Affection, *Amy*, said I, I never met with before; I wish I may be ever in Condition to make you some Returns suitable: But, however, *Amy*, you shall not be a Whore to him, to oblige him to be kind to me; no, *Amy*, nor I won't be a Whore to him, if he would give me much more than he is able to give me, or do for me.

Why Madam, says *Amy*, I don't say I will go and ask him; but I say if he should promise to do so and so for you, and the Condition was such that he would not serve you unless I would let him lye with me, he should lie with me as often as he would, rather than you should not have his Assistance; but this is but Talk, Madam, I don't see any need of such Discourse, and you are of Opinion that there will be no need of it.

Indeed, so I am, *Amy*; but, *said I*, if there was, I tell you again I'd die before I would consent, or before you should consent for my sake.

Hitherto I had not only preserv'd the Virtue itself, but the virtuous inclination and Resolution; and had I kept myself there, I had been happy, tho' I had perished of meer Hunger; for, without queſtion, a Woman ought rather to die, than to proſtitute her Virtue and Honour, let the Temptation be what it will.

But to return to my Story; he walk'd about the Garden, which was indeed all in Disorder, and overrun with Weeds, because I had not been able to hire a Gardener to do any-thing to it, no, not so much as to dig up Ground enough to sow a few Turnips and Carrots for Family-Use: After he had view'd it, he came in and sent *Amy* to fetch a poor Man, a Gardener that us'd to help our Man-Servant, and carry'd him into the Garden, and order'd him to do several things in it to put it into a little Order; and this took him up near an Hour.

By this time I had dress'd me as well as I could, for tho' I had good Linnen left ſtill, yet I had but a poor Head-Dress, and no Knots but old Fragments, no Necklace, no Ear-Rings; all those things were gone long ago for meer Bread.

However, I was tight and clean, and in better Plight than he had seen me in a great while, and he look'd ex-tremely pleased to see me so, for he said I looked so dis-consolate and so afflicted before, that it griev'd him to see me; and he bade me pluck up a good Heart, for he hop'd to put me in a Condition to live in the World, and be be-holden to nobody.

I told him that was impossible, for I must be beholden to him for it, for all the Friends I had in the world would not, or could not, do so much for me as that he spoke of. Well, Widow, says he (so he call'd me, and so indeed I was in the worst Sence that desolate Word cou'd be us'd in), if you are beholden to me, you shall be beholden to nobody else.

By this time Dinner was ready and *Amy* came in to lay the Cloth, and indeed it was happy there was none to Dine but he and I, for I had but six Plates left in the House and but two Dishes; however, he knew how things were, and bade me make no Scruple about bringing out what I had, he hop'd to see me in a better Plight, he did not come, *he said*, to be Entertain'd, but to Entertain me and Comfort and Encourage me: Thus he went on, speaking so chearfully to me and such chearful things, that it was a Cordial to my very Soul, to hear him speak.

Well, we went to Dinner, I'm sure I had not eat'n a good Meal hardly in a Twelvemonth, at least not of such a Joint of Meat as the Loin of Veal was; I ate indeed very heartily, and so did he, and he made me drink three or four Glasses of Wine, so that, in short, my Spirits were lifted up to a Degree I had not been us'd to; and I was not only cheerful but merry, and so he press'd me to be.

I told him I had a great deal of Reason to be merry, seeing he had been so kind to me, and had given me Hopes of recovering me from the worst Circumstances that ever Woman of any sort of fortune was sunk into; that he cou'd not but believe that what he had said to me, was like Life from the Dead; that it was like recovering one Sick from the Brink of the Grave; how I should ever make him a Return any way suitable, was what I had not yet had time to think of; I cou'd only say that I should never forget it

while I had Life, and should be always ready to acknowledge it.

He said that was all he desir'd of me, that his Reward
would be, the Satisfaction of having rescued me from
Misery; that he found he was obliging one that knew
what Gratitude meant; that he would make it his Business to make me compleatly easie first or last, if it lay in
his Power; and in the meantime he bade me consider of
anything that I thought he might do for me, for my Advantage and in order to make me perfectly easy.

After we had talk'd thus he bade me be cheerful; come
says he, lay aside these melancholy things and let us be
merry. *Amy* waited at the Table, and she smil'd and
laugh'd and was so merry she could hardly contain it, for
the Girl lov'd me to an Excess hardly to be describ'd; and
it wa such an unexpected thing to hear any one talk to her
Mistress, that the Wench was beside herself almost; and
as soon as Dinner was over, *Amy* went upstairs and put on
her Best Clothes too, and came down dressed like a Gentlewoman.

We sat together talking of a thousand Things, of what
had been and what was to be, all the rest of the Day, and
in the Evening he took his Leave of me with a thousand
Expressions of Kindness and Tenderness and true Affection to me, but offer'd not the least of what my Maid
Amy had suggested.

At his going away, he took me in his Arms, protested
an honest Kindness to me, said a thousand kind things to
me, which I cannot now recollect, and, after kissing me
twenty times, or thereabouts, put a Guinea into my Hand,
which he said was for my present Supply, and told me,
that he would see me again, before 'twas out : also, he gave
Amy Half a Crown.

When he was gone, Well, *Amy said I,* are you convinc'd now that he is an honest as well as a true Friend,
and that there has been nothing, not the least Appearance
of anything of what you imagin'd, in his Behaviour: Yes,
says *Amy,* I am, but I admire at it; he is such a Friend as
the world sure has not abundance of to show.

I am sure, *says I,* he is such a Friend as I have long
wanted, and as I have as much Need of as any Creature in
the World has or ever had; and, in short, I was so overcome with the Comfort of it that I sat down and cry'd for
Joy a good-while, as I had formerly cry'd for Sorrow.
Amy and I went to Bed that Night (for *Amy* lay with me)
pretty early, but lay chatting almost all Night about it, and
the Girl was so transported that she got up two or three
times in the Night and danc'd about the Room in her
Shift; in short, the Girl was half distracted with the Joy
of it, a Testimony still of her violent Affection for her
Mistress, in which no servant ever went beyond her.

We heard no more of him for two Days, but the third
Day he came again; then he told me, with the same Kindness, that he had order'd me a supply of Household-
Goods for the furnishing the House; that in particular he
had sent me back all the Goods that he had seiz'd for Rent,
which consisted indeed of the best of my former Furniture; and now, says he, I'll tell you what I have had in my
Head for you for your present Supply, and that is, *says he,*
that the House being well furnish'd, you shall let it out
to lodgings for the Summer Gentry, says he, by which
you will easily get a good, comfortable Subsistence, especially seeing you shall pay me no Rent for two years, nor
after neither, unless you can afford it.

This was the first View I had of living comfortably indeed, and it was a very probable Way, I must confess;

seeing we had very good Conveniences, six Rooms on a
Floor, and three Stories high: While he was laying down
the Scheme of my Management, came a Cart to the Door
with a Load of Goods, and an Upholsterer's Man to put
them up; they were chiefly the Furniture of two Rooms
which he had carried away for his two Years' Rent, with
two fine Cabinets and some Pier-Glasses, out of the Parlour, and several other valuable things.

These were all restor'd to their Places, and he told me
he gave them me freely, as a Satisfaction for the Cruelty
he had us'd me with before; and the Furniture of one
Room being finish'd and set up, he told me he would furnish one Chamber for himself, and would come and be
one of my Lodgers if I would give him leave.

I told him, he ought not to ask me Leave, who had so
much right to make himself welcome; so the House began to look in some tollerable Figure and clean; the Garden also, in about a Fortnight's Work began to look something less like a Wilderness than it us'd to do; and he
order'd me to put up a Bill for Letting Rooms, reserving
one for himself to come to as he saw Occasion.

When all was done to his Mind, as to placing the
Goods, he seem'd very well pleas'd, and we din'd together again of his own providing, and the Upholsterer's
Man gone; after Dinner he took me by the Hand. Come
now, Madam, says he, you must show me your House
(for he had a-Mind to see everything over again). No, sir,
said I, but I'll show you your House, if you please; so we
went up thro' all the Rooms, and in the Room which was
appointed for himself, *Amy* was doing something. Well,
Amy, says he, I intend to Lye with you to Morrow Night.
To Night, if you please, sir, says *Amy* very innocently; *your
Room is quite ready:* Well, *Amy, says he,* I am glad you are

so willing : No, says *Amy*, I mean your Chamber is ready
to-Night; and away she ran out of the Room, asham'd
enough, for the Girl meant no Harm, whatever she had
said to me in private.

However, he said no more then; but when *Amy* was
gone he walk'd about the Room and look'd at everything,
and taking me by the Hand, he kiss'd me and spoke a
great many kind, affectionate things to me indeed; as of
his Measures for my Advantage, and what he wou'd do
to raise me again in the World; told me that my Afflictions
and the Conduct I had shown in bearing them to such an
Extremity had so engag'd him to me, that he valued me
infinitely above all the Women in the World; that though
he was under such Engagements that he cou'd not Marry
me (his Wife and he had been parted for some Reasons,
which make too long a Story to intermix with mine), yet
that he wou'd be everything else that a Woman could ask
in a Husband. And with that he kiss'd me again and took
me in his Arms, but offer'd not the least uncivil Action to
me, and told me he hop'd I would not deny him all the
Favours he should ask, because he resolv'd to ask nothing
of me but what it was fit for a Woman of Virtue and Modesty, for such he knew me to be, to yield.

I confess the terrible Pressure of my former Misery,
the Memory of which lay heavy upon my Mind, and the
surprising Kindness with which he had deliver'd me, and
withal, the Expectations of what he might still do for me,
were powerful things, and made me have scarce the Power to deny him anything he wou'd ask; however, I told
him thus, with an Air of Tenderness too, that he had done
so much for me, that I thought I ought to deny him nothing, only I hop'd and depended upon him that he would
not take the Advantage of the infinite Obligations I was

under to him, to desire anything of me, the yielding to which would lay me lower in his Esteem than I desir'd to be; that as I took him to be a Man of Honour, so I knew he could not like me the better for doing anything that was below a Woman of Honesty and Good Manners to do.

He told me, that he had done all this for me without so much as telling me what Kindness or real Affection he had for me; that I might not be under any Necessity of yielding to him in anything, for want of Bread: and he would no more oppress my Gratitude now, than he would my Necessity before, nor ask anything, supposing he would stop his Favours, or withdraw his Kindness, if he was deny'd; it was true, he said, he might tell me more freely his Mind now, than before, seeing I had let him see that I accepted his Assistance, and saw that he was sincere in his Design of serving me; that he had gone thus far to show me that he was kind to me, but that now he would tell me, that he lov'd me, and yet wou'd demonstrate that his Love was both honourable, and that what he shou'd desire was what he might honestly ask and I might honestly grant.

I answer'd that, within those two Limitations, I was sure I ought to deny him nothing, and I should think myself not ungrateful only, but very unjust if I shou'd; so he said no more, but I observed he kiss'd me more and took me in his Arms in a kind of familiar Way, more than usual and which once or twice put me in Mind of my maid *Amy*'s Words; and yet I must acknowledge, I was so overcome with his Goodness to me in those many kind things he had done, that I not only was easie at what he did and made no Resistance, but was inclin'd to do the like, whatever he offer'd to do: But he went no further than what I have said, nor did he offer so much as to sit down on the Bed-side with me, but took his Leave, said he lov'd me tenderly, and would convince me of it by such Demonstrations as should be to my Satisfaction: I told him I had a great deal of Reason to believe him; that he was full Master of the whole House, and of me, as far as was within the Bounds we had spoken of, which I believ'd he would not break; and asked him if he would not lodge there that Night.

He said he cou'd not well stay that Night, Business requiring him in *London*, but added, smiling, that he wou'd come the next day and take a Night's lodging with me. I press'd him to stay that Night, and told him I should be glad a Friend so valuable should be under the same Roof with me; and indeed I began at that time not only to be much oblig'd to him, but to love him too, and that in a Manner that I had not been acquainted with myself.

Oh let no Woman slight the Temptation that being generously deliver'd from Trouble is to any Spirit furnished with Gratitude and just Principles; This gentleman had freely and voluntarily deliver'd me from Misery, from Poverty, and Rags; he had made me what I was, and put me into a Way to be even more than I ever was, namely, to live happy and pleas'd, and on his Bounty I depended: What could I say to this Gentleman when he press'd me to yield to him, and argued the Lawfullness of it? But of that in its Place.

I press'd him again to stay that Night, and told him it was the first completely happy Night that I had ever had in the House in my Life, and I should be very sorry to have it be without his Company, who was the Cause and Foundation of it all; that we would be innocently merry, but that it could never be without him; and, in short, I courted him so, that he said he cou'd not deny me, but he wou'd take his horse and go to *London*, do the Business he had to do, which, it seems, was to pay a Foreign Bill that was due that Night, and would else be protested; and that he wou'd come back in three Hours at farthest and Sup with me; but bade me get nothing there, for since I was resolv'd to be merry, which was what he desir'd above all things, he wou'd send me something from *London*, and we will make it a Wedding Supper, my Dear, *says he*, and with that Word, took me in his Arms, and kiss'd me so vehemently, that I made no question but he intended to do everything else that *Amy* had talk'd of.

I started a little at the Word *Wedding*. What do you mean? to call it by such a Name? *says I*; adding, We will have a supper, but t'other is impossible as well on your side as mine; he laughed. Well, says he, you shall call it what you will, but it may be the same thing, for I shall satisfy you, it is not so impossible as you make it.

I don't understand you, said I; have not I a Husband, and you a Wife?

Well, well, says he, we will talk of that after Supper. So he rose up, gave me another Kiss, and took his Horse for *London*.

This kind of Discourse had fir'd my Blood, I confess, and I knew not what to think of it; it was plain now that he intended to lye with me, but how he would reconcile it to a legal thing like a Marriage, that I cou'd not imagine: We had both of us us'd *Amy* with so much Intimacy and trusted her with everything, having such unexampled Instances of her Fidelity, that he made no Scruple to kiss me, and say all these things to me before her, nor had he car'd one Farthing, if I would have let him Lay with me, to have had *Amy* there too all Night. When he was gone,

Well, *Amy*, says I, what will all this come to now? I am all in a Sweat at him: Come to, Madam, says *Amy*, I see what it will come to; I muſt put you to-Bed to-Night together: Why you wou'd not be so impudent, you Jade you, *says I*, wou'd you? Yes, I wou'd, says she, with all my Heart, and think you both as honeſt as ever you were in your lives.

What ails the Slut to talk so? *said I*. Honeſt! how can it be honeſt? Why, I'll tell you, Madam, says *Amy*; I sounded it as soon as I heard him speak, and it is very true too; he calls you Widow, and such indeed you are; for as my Maſter has left you so many Years, he is dead to be sure; at leaſt he is dead to you; he is no Husband, you are, and ought to be free to marry who you will; and his Wife being gone from him, and refuses to lye with him, then he is a single Man again, as much as ever; and though you cannot bring the Laws of the Land to join you together, yet one refusing to do the Office of a Wife, and the other of a Husband, you may certainly take one another fairly.

Nay, *Amy*, *says I*, if I cou'd take him fairly, you may be sure I'd take him above all the Men in the World; It turn'd the very Heart within me, when I heard him say he lov'd me; how cou'd it do otherwise when you know what a Condition I was in before, despis'd and trampled on by all the World; I cou'd have taken him in my Arms and kiss'd him as freely as he did me, if it had not been for Shame.

Ay, and all the reſt too, says *Amy*, at the firſt word; I don't see how you can think of denying him anything; has he not brought you out of the Devil's Clutches, brought you out of the blackeſt Misery that ever poor Lady was reduc'd to? Can a Woman deny such a Man anything?

Nay, I don't know what to do, *Amy*, says I; I hope he

won't desire anything of that Kind of me, I hope he won't attempt it; if he does, I know not what to say to him.

Not ask you! says *Amy*; depend upon it, he will ask you, and you will grant it, too; I'm sure my Miſtress is no Fool; come, pray, Madam, let me go air you a clean Shift; don't let him find you in foul Linnen the Wedding-Night.

But that I know you to be a very honeſt Girl, *Amy, says I*, you would make me abhor you; why, you argue for the Devil, as if you were one of his Privy-Counsellors.

It's no matter for that, Madam, I say nothing but what I think; you own you love this Gentleman, and he has given you sufficient Teſtimony of his Affeᴄtion to you; your Conditions are alike unhappy, and he is of Opinion that he may take another Woman, his firſt Wife having broke her Honour, and living from him, and that, tho' the Laws of the Land will not allow him to marry formally, yet, that he may take another Woman into his Arms, provided he keeps true to the other Woman as a Wife; nay, he says it is usual to do so, and allow'd by the Cuſtom of the Place, in several Countries abroad; and, I muſt own, I'm of the same Mind, else 'tis in the Power of a Whore, after she has jilted and abandoned her Husband, to confine him from the Pleasure as well as Convenience of a Woman all Days of his Life, which wou'd be very unreasonable; and, as times go, not tollerable to all People; and the like on your side, Madam.

Had I now had my Sences about me, and had my Reason not been overcome by the powerful Attraᴄtion of so kind, so beneficent a Friend; had I consulted Conscience and Virtue, I shou'd have repelled this *Amy*, however faithful and honeſt to me in other things, as a Viper and Engine of the Devil; I ought to have remembered that

neither he or I, either by the Laws of God or Man, cou'd
come together upon any other Terms than that of notori-
ous Adultery. The ignorant Jade's argument, That he
had brought me out of the Hands of the Devil, by which
she meant the Devil of Poverty and Distress, shou'd have
been a powerful Motive to me, not to plunge myself into
the Jaws of Hell and into the Power of the real Devil, in
recompense for that Deliverance; I shou'd have look'd
upon all the Good this Man had done for me, to have been
the particular Work of the Goodness of Heaven, and that
goodness shou'd have mov'd me to a Return of Duty and
humble Obedience; I shou'd have received the Mercy
thankfully, and applied it soberly, to the Praise and Honour of my Maker; whereas by this wicked Course, all the
Bounty and Kindness of this Gentleman, became a Snare
to me, was a meer Bait to the Devil's Hook; I receiv'd his
Kindness at the dear Expence of Body and Soul, mort-
gaging Faith, Religion, Conscience, and Modesty for (as
I may call it) a Morsel of Bread; or, if you will, ruin'd my
Soul from a Principle of Gratitude, and gave myself up to
the Devil, to show myself grateful to my Benefactor: I
must do the Gentleman that Justice, as to say, I verily believe that he did nothing but what he thought was Lawful; and I must do that Justice upon myself, as to say, I
did what my own Conscience convinc'd me at the very
Time I did it, was horribly unlawful, scandalous, and
abominable.

But Poverty was my Snare, dreadful Poverty! The
Misery I had been in, was great, such as wou'd make the
Heart tremble at the Apprehensions of its Return, and I
might appeal to any that has had any Experience of the
World, whether one so entirely destitute as I was, of all
manner of all Helps, or Friends, either to support me, or

to assist me to support myself, could withstand the Proposal; not that I plead this as a Justification of my Conduct, but that it may move the Pity, even of those that abhor the Crime.

Besides this, I was young, handsome, and with all the Mortifications I had met with, was vain, and that not a little; and as it was a new thing, so it was a pleasant thing, to be courted, caress'd, embrac'd, and high Professions of Affection made to me by a Man so agreeable and so able to do me good.

Add to this, that if I had ventured to disoblige this Gentleman, I had no Friend in the World to have Recourse to; I had no Prospect, no, not of a Bit of Bread; I had nothing before me, but to fall back into the same Misery, that I had been in before.

Amy had but too much Rhetorick in this Cause; She represented all those Things in their proper Colours; she argued them all with her utmost Skill, and at last the Merry Jade, when she came to Dress me, Look ye, Madam, *said she*, if you won't consent, tell him you'll do as *Rachel* did to *Jacob*, when she could have no Children— put her Maid to Bed to him; tell him you cannot comply with him, but there's *Amy*, he may ask her the Question, she has promised me she won't deny you.

And would you have me say so, *Amy? said I.*

No, madam, but I would really have you do so, besides, you are undone if you do not; and if my doing it would save you from being undone, as I said before, he shall if he will; if he asks me I won't deny him, not I; Hang me if I do, *says Amy*.

Well, I know not what to do, *says I* to *Amy*.

Do! *says Amy*, Your Choice is fair and plain; here you may have a handsome, charming Gentleman, be rich, live

pleasantly, and in Plenty; or refuse him, and want a Dinner, go in Rags, live in Tears; in short, beg and ſtarve;
you know this is the Case, Madam, *says Amy*; I wonder
how you can say you know not what to do.

Well, *Amy, says I*, the Case is as you say, and I think
verily I muſt yield to him; but then, *said I, moved by Conscience*, don't talk any more of your Cant, of its being Lawful that I ought to Marry again, and that he ought to
Marry again, and such Stuff as that; 'tis all Nonsense,
says I, Amy, there's nothing in it, let me hear no more of
that; for if I yield 'tis in vain to mince the Matter, I am a
Whore, *Amy*, neither better nor worse, I assure you.

I don't think so, Madam, by no means, *says Amy*, I
wonder how you can talk so; and then she ran on with her
Argument of the Unreasonableness that a Woman should
be oblig'd to live single, or a man to live single in such
Cases, as before: Well, *Amy, said I*, come let us dispute
no more, for the longer I enter into that Part, the greater
my Scruples will be; but if I let it alone, the Necessity of
my present Circumſtances is such, that I believe I shall
yield to him, if he should importune me much about it,
but I should be glad he would not do it at all, but leave me
as I am.

As to that, Madam, you may depend, *says Amy*, he ex-
pects to have you for his Bedfellow to-Night. I saw it
plainly in his Management all Day, and at laſt he told you
so too, as plain, I think, as he cou'd. Well, well, *Amy, said
I*, I don't know what to say; if he will, he muſt, I think, I
don't know how to resiſt such a man that has done so
much for me: I don't know how you should, *says Amy*.

Thus *Amy* and I canvass'd the business between us;
the Jade prompted the Crime, which I had but too much
Inclination to commit; that is to say, not as a Crime, for I

had nothing of the Vice in my Conſtitution; my Spirits were far from being high; my Blood had no Fire in it, to kindle the Flame of Desire, but the Kindness and good Humour of the Man, and the Dread of my own Circum-ſtances concurr'd to bring me to the Point, and I even resolv'd, before he ask'd, to give up my Virtue to him, whenever he should put it to the Queſtion.

In this I was a double Offender, whatever he was; for I was resolved to commit the Crime, knowing and owning it to be a crime; he, if it was true as he said, was fully per-suaded it was Lawful, and in that Perswasion he took the Measures and us'd all the Circumlocutions which I am going to speak of.

About two hours after he was gone, came a *Leaden-Hall* Basket-Woman, with a whole Load of good Things for the Mouth; the Particulars are not to the Purpose; and brought Orders to get Supper by Eight o'Clock; however, I did not intend to begin to dress anything, till I saw him; and he gave me time enough, for he came be-fore Seven; so that *Amy*, who had gotten one to help her, got everything ready in Time.

We sat down to Supper about Eight, and were indeed very merry; *Amy* made us some Sport, for she was a Girl of Spirit and Wit; and with her Talk she made us laugh very often, and yet the Jade manag'd her wit with all the good Manners imaginable.

But to shorten the Story; after Supper he took me up into his Chamber, where *Amy* had made a good Fire, and there he pull'd out a great many Papers and spread them upon a little Table, and then took me by the Hand, and after kissing me very much he enter'd into a Discourse of his Circumſtances, and of mine, how they agreed in seve-ral things exaƈtly; for Example, that I was abandon'd of

a husband in the Prime of my Youth and Vigour, and he
of a Wife in his Middle-Age; how the End of Marriage
was deftroyed by the Treatment we had either of us receiv'd, and it wou'd be very hard that we should be ty'd
by the Formality of the Contract where the Essence of it
was deftroy'd: I interrupted him, and told him, There
was a vaft Difference between our Circumftances, and
that in the moft essential Part, namely, That he was Rich
and I was Poor, that he was above the World, and I infinitely below it; that his Circumftances were very easie,
mine miserable, and this was an Inequality the moft essential that could be imagined: As to that, my dear, *says*
he, I have taken such Measures as shall make an Equality
ftill; and with that, he showed me a Contract in Writing,
wherein he engag'd himself to me; to cohabit conftantly
with me; to provide for me in all Respects as a Wife; and
repeating in the Preamble a long account of the Nature
and Reason of our living together, and an Obligation in
the Penalty of 7000. l. never to abandon me; and at laft
showed me a Bond for 500. l. to be paid to me, or to my
Assigns within three Months after his Death.

He read over all these things to me, and then in a moft
moving, affectionate Manner, and in Words not to be
answered, *he said*, Now, my Dear, is this not sufficient?
Can you object anything againft it? If not, as I believe
you will not, then let us debate this Matter no longer;
with that he pull'd out a silk Purse, which had three-score
Guineas in it, and threw them into my Lap, and concluded
all the reft of his Discourse with Kisses and Proteftations
of his Love; of which, indeed, I had abundant Proof.

Pity, human Frailty, you that read of a Woman reduc'd
in her Youth and Prime to the utmoft Misery and Distress, and rais'd again, as above, by the unexpected and

surprising Bounty of a Stranger; I say, pity her if she was not able, after all these things, to make any more Resistance.

However, I stood out a little longer still, I asked him how he could expect that I cou'd come into a Proposal of such Consequence, the very first Time it was moved to me, and that I ought (if I consented to it) to capitulate with him, that he should never upbraid me with Easiness and consenting too soon: *He said*, No, but on the contrary, he would take it as a Mark of the greatest Kindness I could show him; then he went on to give Reasons why there was no Occasion to use the ordinary Ceremony of Delay; or to wait a reasonable Time of Courtship, which was only to avoid Scandal; but, as this was private, it had nothing of that Nature in it; that he had been courting me some time, by the best of Courtship, viz. doing Acts of Kindness to me; and he had given Testimonies of his sincere Affection to me by Deeds, not by flattering Trifles, and the usual Courtship of Words, which were often found to have very little Meaning; that he took me not as a Mistress, but as his Wife; and protested, it was clear to him he might lawfully do it, and that I was perfectly at Liberty; and assur'd me by all that it was possible for an Honest Man to say, that he would treat me as his Wife, as long as he liv'd; in a Word, he conquer'd all the little Resistance I intended to make; He protest'd he loved me above all the World, and begg'd I would for once believe him; that he had never deceiv'd me, and never would, but would make it his Study to make my Life comfortable and happy, and to make me forget the Misery I had gone through: I stood still a-while and said nothing, but seeing him eager for my Answer, I smil'd, and looking up at him, And must I, then, *says I*, say Yes, at first asking?

Muſt I depend upon your Promise? Why, then, *said I*, upon the Faith of that Promise, and in the Sence of that inexpressible Kindness you have shown me, you shall be oblig'd, and I will be wholly yours to the End of my Life; and with that I took his Hand which held me by the Hand, and gave it a Kiss.

And thus, in Gratitude for the Favours I receiv'd from a Man, was all Sence of Religion, and Duty to God, all Regard to Virtue and Honour, given up at once, and we were to call one another Man and Wife, who in the Sence of the laws of both God and our Country were no more than two Adulterers, in short, a Whore and a Rogue; nor, as I have said above, was my Conscience silent in it, tho' it seems, his was; for I sinned with open Eyes, and thereby had a double Guilt upon me; as I always said, his Notions were of another Kind, and he either was before of the Opinion, or argued himself into it now, that we were both Free, and might lawfully Marry.

But I was quite of another Side, nay, and my Judgment was right, but my Circumſtances were my Temptation; the Terrors behind me look'd blacker than the Terrors before me; and the dreadful Argument of wanting Bread, and being run into the horrible Diſtresses I was in before, maſter'd all my Resolution, and I gave myself up, as above.

The reſt of the Evening we spent very agreeably to me; he was perfectly good-humour'd and was at that time very merry; then he made *Amy* dance with him, and I told him I would put *Amy* to Bed to him; *Amy* said, with all her Heart; she never had been a Bride in her Life; in short, he made the Girl so merry, that had he not been to lie with me the same Night, I believe he would have play'd the fool with *Amy* for half an Hour, and the Girl would

no more have refus'd him that I intended to do; yet be-
fore, I had always found her a very modeſt Wench, as any
I ever saw in all my Life, but, in short, the Mirth of that
Night, and a few more such afterwards, ruined the Girl's
Modeſty for ever, as shall appear by and by in its Place.

So far does fooling and toying sometimes go, that I
know nothing a young Woman has to be more cautious
of; so far had this innocent girl gone in jeſting between
her and I, and in talking that she would let him lye with
her, if he would but be kinder to me, that at laſt she let
him lie with her in earneſt; and so empty was I now of all
principle, that I encourag'd the doing it almoſt before my
Face.

I say but too juſtly, that I was empty of Principle, because, as above, I had yielded to him, not as deluded to
believe it Lawful, but as overcome by his Kindness, and
terrify'd at the Fear of my own misery if he should leave
me; so with my Eyes open, and with my Conscience, as I
may say, awake, I sinn'd, knowing it to be a Sin but having no Power to resiſt; When this had thus made a Hole
in my Heart, and I was come to such a height as to trans-
gress againſt the Light of my own Conscience, I was then
fit for any Wickedness, and Conscience left off speaking,
where it found it cou'd not be heard.

But to return to our Story; having consented, as above
to his Proposal, we had not much more to do; he gave me
my Writings, and the Bond for my Maintenance during
his Life and for 500 l. after his Death; and so far was he
from abating his Affeƈtion to me afterwards, that two
Year after we were thus, as he call'd it, marry'd, he made
his Will, and gave me a Thousand Pound more, and all
my Household-Stuff, Plate, &c., which was considerable
too.

Amy put us to-Bed, and my new Friend, I cannot call
him Husband, was so well pleas'd with *Amy* for her Fidelity and Kindness to me, that he paid her all the Arrears
of her Wages that I owed her, and gave her five Guineas
over, and had it gone no further, *Amy* had richly deserv'd
what she had, for never was a Maid so true to a Mistress
in such dreadful Circumstances as I was in; nor was what
follow'd more her own Fault than mine, who led her almost into it at first, and quite into it at last; and this may
be a further Testimony what a hardness of crime I was
now arriv'd to, which was owing to the Conviction that
was from the beginning, upon me, that I was a Whore,
not a Wife, nor cou'd I ever frame my Mouth to call him
Husband, or to say my Husband when I was speaking of
him.

We liv'd, surely, the most agreeable Life, the grand
Exception only excepted, that ever Two liv'd together;
he was the most obliging, Gentlemanly man, and the most
tender of me, that ever Woman gave herself up to; nor
was there ever the least interruption to our mutual Kindness, no, not to the last Day of his Life: but I must bring
Amy's Disaster in at once, that I may have done with her.

Amy was dressing me one Morning, for now I had two
Maids, and *Amy* was my Chamber-Maid; Dear madam,
says Amy, what! a'n't you with Child yet? No, *Amy, says I,*
nor any Sign of it. *Law*, Madam, *says Amy*, what have
you been doing? Why, you have been Marry'd a Year
and a Half; I warrant you, Master would have got me
with-Child twice in that time: it may be so, *Amy, says I,*
let him try, can't you: No, *says Amy*, you'll forbid it now;
before, I told you he shou'd with all my Heart, but I won't
now, now he's all your own: Oh, *says I, Amy*, I'll freely
give you my Consent, it will be nothing at-all to me; nay,

I'll put you to Bed to him myself one Night or other if
you are willing: No, madam, no, *says Amy*, not now he's
yours.

Why, you Fool you, *says I*, don't I tell you I'll put you
to Bed to him myself.

Nay, nay, *says Amy*, if you put me to-Bed to him, that's
another Case; I believe I shall not rise again very soon.

I'll venture that, *Amy, said I.*

After Supper that Night, and before we were risen
from Table, *I said to him, Amy* being by, Hark ye, Mr.
———, do you know that you are to lye with *Amy* to-Night?
No, not I, *says he*; but turns to *Amy*, Is it so, *Amy? says he*.
No, sir, *says she*. Nay, don't say no, you Fool; did not I
promise to put you to-Bed to him? But the Girl said no
ſtill, and it pass'd off.

At Night, when we came to go to-Bed, Amy came into
the Chamber to undress me, and her Maſter slipt into
bed firſt; then I began and told him all that *Amy* had said
about my not being with-Child, and of her being with-
Child twice in that time: Ay, Mrs. *Amy, says he*, I believe
so too; Come hither and we'll try. But *Amy* did not go:
Go, you fool, *says I*, can't you; I freely give you both
Leave. But *Amy* would not go. Nay, you Whore, *says I*,
you said if I wou'd put you to-Bed you would with all
your Heart: and with that I sat her down, pull'd off her
Stockings and Shoes, and all her Cloaths, Piece by Piece,
and led her to the Bed to him: *Here*, says I, *try what you
can do with your maid* Amy: She pull'd back a little, wou'd
not let me pull off her Cloaths at firſt, but it was hot Weather, and she had not many Cloaths on, and particularly,
no Stays on; and at laſt, when she see I was in earneſt, she
let me do what I wou'd; so I fairly ſtript her, and then I
threw open the Bed, and thruſt her in.

I need say no more; this is enough to convince anybody that I did not think him my Husband, and that I had cast off all Principle, and all Modesty, and had effectually stifled Conscience.

Amy, I dare say, began now to repent, and would fain have got out of Bed again, but he said to her, Nay, *Amy*, you see your mistress has put you to Bed, 'tis all her doing, you must blame her; so he held her fast, and the Wench being naked in the Bed with him, 'twas too late to look back, so she lay still and let him do what he wou'd with her.

Had I look'd upon myself as a Wife, you cannot suppose I would have been willing to have let my Husband lye with my Maid, much less before my Face, for I stood by all the while; but as I thought myself a Whore, I cannot say but that it was something design'd in my Thoughts, that my maid should be a Whore too, and should not reproach me with it.

Amy, however, less vicious than I, was grievously out of Sorts the next Morning, and cry'd and took on most vehemently; that she was ruin'd and undone, and there was no pacifying her; she was a Whore, a Slut, and she was undone! undone! and cry'd almost all day. I did all I could to pacify her. A whore! says I; well, and am not I a whore as well as you? No, no, *says Amy*, no, you are not, for you are marry'd. Not I, *Amy*, *says I*, I do not pretend to it; he may Marry you to-Morrow if he will, for anything I cou'd do to hinder it; I am not Marry'd, I do not look upon it as anything: Well, all did not pacify *Amy*, she cried two or three Days about it; but it wore off by Degrees.

But the case differ'd between Amy and her Master, exceedingly; for *Amy* retain'd the same kind Temper she

always had; but on the contrary he was quite alter'd, for
he hated her heartily, and could, I believe, have kill'd her
after it; and he told me so, for he thought this a vile Action, whereas what he and I had done he was perfectly
easie in, thought it just, and esteemed me as much his
Wife as if we had been Marry'd from our Youth, and had
neither of us known any other; nay, he lov'd me, I believe,
as entirely as if I had been the Wife of his Youth; nay, he
told me, it was true in one Sence, that he had two Wives,
but that I was the Wife of his Affection, the other the
Wife of his Aversion.

I was extremely concern'd at the Aversion he had tak-
en to my Maid *Amy*, and used my utmost Skill to get it
alter'd; for tho' he had indeed debauch'd the Wench, I
knew that I was the principal Occasion of it, and as he was
the best-humour'd Man in the World, I never gave him
over till I prevail'd with him to be easie with her; and as I
was now become the Devil's Agent, to make others as
wicked as myself, I brought him to lie with her again
several times after that, till at last, as the poor Girl said, so
it happened, and she was really with-Child.

She was terribly concern'd at it, and so was he too: Come,
my dear, *says I*, when *Rachel* put her Handmaid to Bed to
Jacob she took the Children as her own; don't be uneasie,
I'll take the Child as my own; had not I a hand in the Fro-
lick of putting her to-Bed to you? It was my fault, as much
as yours; so I call'd Amy and encourag'd her too, and
told her that I would take Care of the Child and her too,
and added the same Argument to her. For, *says I, Amy*, it
was all my Fault; did not I drag your Cloaths off your
Back and put you to-Bed to him: Thus I, that had, indeed, been the Cause of all the Wickedness between
them, encourag'd them both when they had any Re-

morse about it, and rather prompted them to go on with it than to repent of it.

When *Amy* grew big she went to a place I had provided for her, and the Neighbours knew nothing but that *Amy* and I were parted; she had a fine Child indeed, a Daughter, and we had it nurs'd, and *Amy* came again in about half a Year, to live with her old Miſtress. But neither my Gentleman nor *Amy* either, car'd for playing that Game over again; for, as he said, the jade might bring him a House-Full of children to keep.

We liv'd as merrily, and as happily, after this as cou'd be expeſted, considering our Circumſtances; I mean as to the pretended Marriage, *&c.* and as to that, my Gentleman had not the leaſt Concern about him for it; but as much as I was harden'd, and that was as much as I believe ever any wicked Creature was, yet I could not help it; there was and would be, Hours of Intervals and of dark Refleſtions which came involuntarily in, and thruſt in Sighs into the middle of all my Songs, and there would be, sometimes, a heaviness of Heart which intermingl'd itself with all my Joy, and which would often fetch a Tear from my Eye; and let others pretend what they will, I believe it impossible to be otherwise with anybody; there can be no subſtantial satisfaſtion in a Life of known Wickedness; Conscience will, and does, often break in upon them at particular times, let them do what they can to prevent it.

But I am not to preach, but to relate, and whatever loose Refleſtions were, and how often soever those dark intervals came on, I did my utmoſt to conceal them from him, ay, and to suppress and smother them too in myself, and to outward Appearance we liv'd as cheerfully and as agreeably as it was possible for any Couple in the World to live.

After I had thus liv'd with him something above two Year, truly I found my-self with Child too. My Gentleman was mightily pleas'd at it, and nothing could be kinder than he was in the Preparations he made for me, and for my Lying-in, which was, however, very private, because I cared for as little Company as possible, nor had I kept up my neighbourly Acquaintance, so that I had nobody to invite upon such an Occasion.

I was brought to-Bed very well (of a Daughter too, as well as *Amy*), but the Child died at about six Weeks old; so all that Work was to do over again, that is to say, the Charge, the Expence, the Travel, *&c.*

The next Year I made him amends, and brought him a Son, to his great Satisfaction; it was a charming Child and he did very well: After this, my Husband, as he call'd himself, came to me one Evening and told me, he had a very difficult Thing happen'd to him, which he knew not what to do in, or how to resolve about, unless I would make him easy; this was, that his Occasions requir'd him to go over to *France* for about two Months.

Well, my Dear, *says I*, and how shall I make you easy?

Why, by consenting to let me go, *says he*; upon which Condition I'll tell you the Occasion of my going, that you may judge of the Necessity there is for it on my Side; then to make me easy in his going, he told me he would make his Will before he went, which should be to my full Satisfaction.

I told him, the last part was so kind, that I could not decline the first Part, unless he would give me Leave to add, that if it was not for putting him to an extraordinary Expence I would go over along with him.

He was so pleased with this Offer, that he told me he would give me full Satisfaction for it, and accept of it too;

so he took me to *London* with him the next Day, and there he made his WILL, and shew'd it to me, seal'd it before proper Witnesses, and then gave it to me to keep: In this will he gave a thousand Pounds to a Person that we both knew very well, in Trust, to pay it, with the Interest from the Time of his Decease, to me or my Assigns; then he Will'd the Payment of my Jointure, as he call'd it, viz. his Bond of a Hundred Pounds, after his Death, also he gave me all my Household-Stuff, Plate, &c.

This was a most engaging thing for a Man to do to one under my Circumstances; and it would have been hard, as I told him, to deny him anything, or to refuse to go with him anywhere; so we settled everything as well as we cou'd, left *Amy* in Charge of the House, and for his other Business, which was in Jewels, he had two Men he en-trusted, whom he had good Security for, and who man-ag'd for him and corresponded with him.

Things being thus concerted, we went away to *France*, arriv'd safe at *Calais*, and by easy Journeys came in eight Days more to *Paris*, where we lodg'd in the House of an *English* Merchant of his Acquaintance and were very courteously entertain'd.

My Gentleman's Business was with some Persons of the First Rank, and to whom he had sold some Jewels of very good Value, and receiv'd a great Sum of Money in Specie, and, as he told me privately, he gain'd 3000 Pis-toles by his Bargain, but would not suffer the most inti-mate Friend he had there, to know what he had receiv'd, for it is not so safe a thing in *Paris*, to have a great Sum of Money in keeping, as it might be in *London*.

We made this Journey much longer than we intended; and my Gentleman sent for one of his Managers in *London*, to come over to us to *Paris* with some Diamonds, and sent him back to *London* again, to fetch more; then other Business fell into his Hands so unexpectedly, that I began to think we should take up our constant Residence there, which I was not very averse to, it being my Native Country, and I spoke the Language perfectly well; so we took a good House in *Paris*, and liv'd very well there; and I sent for *Amy* to come over to me; for I liv'd gallantly, and my Gentleman was, two or three times going to keep me a Coach, but I declin'd it, especially at *Paris*; but as they have those Conveniences by the Day there, at a certain Rate, I had an Equipage provided for me whenever I pleas'd, and I lived here in a very good Figure, and might have liv'd higher if I pleas'd.

But in the middle of all this Felicity a dreadful disaster befel me, which entirely unhing'd all my Affairs and threw me back into the same state of Life that I was in before; with this one happy Exception, however, that whereas before I was Poor even to Misery, now I was not only provided for, but very Rich.

My Gentleman had the Name in Paris for a very rich Man, and indeed he was so, tho' not so immensely rich as People imagin'd; but that which was fatal to him, was that he generally carried a shagreen Case in his Pocket, especially when he went to Court, or to the Houses of any of the Princes of the Blood, in which he had Jewels of very great Value.

It happen'd one day, that being to go to *Versailles* to wait upon the Prince of ———, he came up into my Chamber in the Morning, and laid out his Jewel-Case, because he was not going to show any Jewels, but to get a Foreign Bill accepted, which he had receiv'd from *Amsterdam*; so when he gave me the Case, *he said*, My Dear, I think I need not carry this with me, because, it may be, I may not

come back till Night, and it is too much to venture: I return'd then, My Dear, you shan't go: Why? *says he*: because as they are too much for you, so you are too much
for me to venture, and you shall not go, unless you will
promise me not to ſtay, so as to come back in the Night.

I hope there's no Danger, said he, seeing I have nothing about me of any Value; and therefore, leſt I should,
take that too, *says he*, and gives me his Gold Watch, and a
rich Diamond, which he had in a Ring, and always wore
on his Finger.

Well, but, *my Dear*, says I, you make me more uneasie
now than before; for if you apprehend no Danger, why
do you use this Caution? and if you apprehend there is
Danger, why do you go at all?

There is no Danger, *says he*, if I do not ſtay late, and I
do not design to do so.

Well, but promise me, then, that you won't, *says I*, or
else I cannot let you go.

I won't indeed, my Dear, *says he*, unless I am oblig'd
to it; I assure you I do not intend it; but if I shou'd, I am
not worth robbing now; for I have nothing about me, but
about six Piſtoles in my little Purse, and that little Ring,
showing me a small Diamond Ring, worth about ten or
twelve Piſtoles, which he put upon his Finger, in the
room of the rich one he usually wore.

I ſtill press'd him not to ſtay late, and he said he wou'd
not. But if I am kept late, *says he*, beyond my Expeᴄ̄ta-
tion, I'll ſtay all Night, and come next Morning. This
seemed a very good Caution, but ſtill my Mind was very
uneasie about him, and I told him so, and entreated him
not to go; I told him I did not know what might be the
reason, but that I had a ſtrange Terror upon my Mind
about his going, and that, if he did go, I was perswaded

some Harm wou'd attend him; he smiled, and return'd, Well, my Dear, if it should be so, you are now richly provided for; all that I have here, I give to you; and with that he takes up the Casket or Case, Here, *says he*, Hold your hand, there is a good Estate for you, in this Case; if anything happens to me, 'tis all your own, I give it you for yourself; And with that he put the Casket, the fine Ring, and his Gold Watch all into my Hands, and the Key of his Scrutore besides, adding, And in my Scrutore there is some Money; 'tis all your own.

I stared at him as if I was frighted, for I thought all his Face looked like a Death's-Head; and then immediately I thought I perceiv'd his Head all Bloody, and then his Cloaths look'd Bloody, too; and immediately it all went off, and he look'd as he really did. Immediately I fell a-crying and hung about him, My Dear, *said I*, I am frighted to Death; you shall not go; depend upon it, some Mischief will befall you; I did not tell him how my vapourish Fancy had represented him to me; that, I thought, was not proper; besides, he would only have laugh'd at me, and wou'd have gone away with a Jest about it: But I press'd him seriously not to go that Day, or, if he did, to promise me to come Home to *Paris* again by Day-light: He look'd a little graver then, than he did before; told me, he was not apprehensive of the least Danger; but if there was, he would either take Care to come in the Day, or, as he had said before, wou'd stay all Night.

But all these Promises came to nothing; for he was set upon in the open Day, and robb'd by three Men on Horseback, mask'd, as he went; and one of them, who, it seems, rifled him, while the rest stood to stop the Coach, stabb'd him into the body with a Sword, so that he died immediately: He had a Footman behind the Coach, who

they knock'd down with the Stock or But-end of a Cara-
bine: They were suppos'd to kill him, because of the Dis-
appointment they met with, in not getting his Case or
Casket of Diamonds, which they knew he carry'd about
him; and this was suppos'd, because after they had kill'd
him, they made the Coachman drive out of the Road, a
long-Way over the Heath, till they came to a convenient
Place, where they pull'd him out of the Coach and search'd
his Cloaths more narrowly, than they could do while he
was alive.

But they found nothing but his little Ring, six Piſtoles,
and the Value of about seven Livres in small Moneys.

This was a dreadful Blow to me; tho' I cannot say I
was so surpriz'd as I should otherwise have been; for all
the while he was gone, my Mind was oppress'd with the
Weight of my own Thoughts; and I was as sure that I
should never see him any more, that I think nothing could
be like it; the Impression was so ſtrong, that, I think, nothing could make so deep a Wound, that was imaginary;
and I was so dejeᵭed and disconsolate, that when I receiv'd the News of his Disaſter, there was no room for
any extraordinary Alteration in me: I had cry'd all that
Day, eat nothing, and only waited, as I might say, to receive the dismal News, which I had brought to me about
Five a-Clock in the Afternoon.

I was in a ſtrange Country, and, tho' I had a pretty many
my Acquaintances, had but very few Friends that I could
consult on this Occasion; all possible Enquiry was made
after the Rogues, that had been thus barbarous, but nothing could be heard of them; nor was it possible, that
the Footman could make any Discovery of them, by his
Description; for they knock'd him down immediately, so
that he knew nothing of what was done afterwards; the

Coachman was the only Man that cou'd say any thing, and all his Account amounted to no more than this, that one of them had Soldier's Cloaths, but he cou'd not remember the Particulars of his Mounting so as to know what Regiment he belong'd to; and as to their Faces, that he could know nothing of, because they had all of them Masks on.

I had him Buried as decently as the Place would permit a Protestant Stranger to be Buried, and made some of the Scruples and Difficulties on that Account, easy, by the help of Money to a certain Person, who went impudently to the Curate of the Parish *St. Sulpuis* in *Paris*, and told him, that the Gentleman that was kill'd was a Catholic; that the Thieves had taken from him a Cross of Gold, set with Diamonds, worth 6000 Livres, that his Widow was a Catholic, and had sent by him 60 Crowns to the Church of —— for Masses to be said, for the Repose of his Soul: Upon all which, *tho' not one Word of it was true*, he was buried with all the Ceremonies of the *Roman* Church.

I think I almost cry'd myself to Death for him, for I abandon'd myself to all the Excesses of Grief; and indeed I lov'd him to a Degree inexpressible; and considering what Kindness he had shown me at first, and how tenderly he had us'd me to the last, what cou'd I do less?

Then the Manner of his Death was terrible and frightful to me, and, above all, the strange Notices I had of it; I had never pretended to the Second Sight or anything of that Kind, but certainly, if any one ever had such a thing, I had it at this time; for I saw him as plainly in all those terrible Shapes as above, *First*, as a Skeleton, not Dead only, but rotten and wasted; *Secondly*, as kill'd, and his Face bloody; and *Thirdly*, his Cloaths bloody; and all within the Space of one Minute, or indeed of a very few Moments.

These things amaz'd me, and I was a good-while as one ſtupid; however, after some time, I began to recovcr, and look into my Affairs; I had the Satisfaćtion not to be left in Diſtress, or in danger of Poverty; on the contrary, besides what he had put into my Hands fairly, in his Lifetime, which amounted to a very considerable Value, I found above seven Hundred Piſtoles in Gold, in his Scrutore, of which he had given me the Key; and I found Foreign-Bills accepted, for about 12,000 Livres; so that, in a Word, I found myself possessed of almoſt ten Thousand Pounds Sterling, in a very few Days after the Disaſter.

The firſt thing I did upon this Occasion, was to send a Letter to my Maid, as I ſtill called her, *Amy*; wherein I gave her an Account of my Disaſter; how, my Husband, as she call'd him(*for I never call'd him so*), was murther'd; and as I did not know how his Relations, or his Wife's Friends, might aćt upon that Occasion, I order'd her to convey away all the Plate, Linnen, and other things of Value, and to secure them in a Person's Hands that I direćted her to, and then to sell, or dispose the Furniture of the House, if she could; and so, without acquainting anybody with the Reason of her going, withdraw; sending notice to his Head Manager at *London*, that the House was quitted by the Tennant, and they might come and take Possession of it for the Executors. *Amy* was so dext'rous, and did her Work so nimbly, that she gutted the House, and sent the Key to the said Manager almoſt as soon as he had Notice of the Misfortune that befell their Maſter.

Upon their receiving the surprising News of his Death, the Head Manager came over to *Paris*, and came to the House. I made no scruple of calling myself Madame ———, the widow of Monsieur ———, the *English* Jeweller; and as I spoke French naturally, I did not let him know, but that I was his Wife, married in *France*, and that I had not heard that he had any Wife in *England*, but pretended to be surpriz'd, and exclaim'd against him for so base an Action; and that I had good friends in *Poictou*, where I was Born, who would take Care to have justice done me in *England*, out of his Estate.

I should have observ'd that as soon as the News was public of a Man being murther'd, and that he was a Jeweller, Fame did me the Favour as to publish, presently, that he was robb'd of his Casket of Jewels, which he always carry'd about him; I confirm'd this, among my daily Lamentations, for his Disaster, and added, that he had with him a fine Diamond Ring, which he was known to wear frequently about him, valued at 100 Pistoles, a Gold Watch, and a great Quantity of Diamonds of inestimable Value, in his Casket; which Jewels he was carrying to the Prince of———, to show some of them to him; and the Prince own'd that he had spoken to him to bring some such Jewels, to let him see them. But I sorely repented this Part afterwards, as you shall hear.

This Rumour put an End to all Enquiry after his Jewells, his Ring, or his Watch; and as for the 700 Pistoles, that I secur'd: For the Bills which were in hand, I own'd I had them; but that, as, *I said*, I brought my husband 30000 Livres Portion, I claimed the said Bills, which came to not above 12,000 Livres, for my *amende*; and this, with the Plate and the Household-Stuff, was the principal of all his Estate which they could come at; as to the foreign bill which he was going to *Versailles* to get accepted, it was really lost with him; but his Manager, who

had remitted the Bill to him by Way of *Amsterdam*, bringing over the second Bill, the Money was sav'd, as they
call'd it, which would, otherwise, have been also gone:
the thieves who robb'd and murther'd him were, to be
sure, afraid to send any-body to get the Bill accepted; for
that would undoubtedly have discover'd them.

By this time my Maid *Amy* was arriv'd, and she gave
me an Account of her Management and how she had secur'd every thing, and that she had quitted the House,
and sent the Key to the Head-Manager of his Business,
and let me know how much she had made of every thing,
very punctually and honestly.

I should have observ'd in the Account of his dwelling
with me so long at ――――, that he never pass'd for any
thing there but a Lodger in the House, and tho' he was
Landlord, that did not alter the Case; so that at his Death,
Amy coming to quit the house and give them the Key,
there was no affinity between that, and the Case of their
Master who was newly kill'd.

I got good Advice at *Paris* from an eminent Lawyer, a
Counsellor of the Parliament there, and, laying my Case
before him, he directed me to make a Process in Dower
upon the Estate, for making good my new Fortune upon
Matrimony, which accordingly I did; and, upon the
whole, the Manager went back to *England*, well satisfied,
that he had gotten the unaccepted Bills of Exchange,
which was for 2 500 l. with some other things, which together, amounted to 17,000 Livres; and thus I got rid of
him.

I was visited with great Civility on this sad occasion,
of the Loss of my Husband, as they thought him, by a
great many Ladies of Quality; and the Prince of――――, to
whom it was reported he was carrying the Jewels, sent

his Gentleman with a very handsome Compliment of Condolence to me; and his Gentleman, whether with or without Order, hinted as if His Highness did intend to have visited me himself, but that some Accident, which he made a long story of, had prevented him.

By the Concourse of Ladies and others, that thus came to visit me, I began to be much known: and as I did not forget to set myself out with all possible Advantage, considering the Dress of a Widow, which in those days was a moſt frightful thing; I say, as I did thus from my own Vanity, for I was not ignorant that I was very handsome; I say, on this Account I was soon made very publick, and was known by the name of *La belle veuve de Poictou,* or The pretty widow of *Poictou*: As I was very well pleas'd to see myself thus handsomely us'd in my Affliction, it soon dry'd up all my Tears; and tho' I appeared as a Widow, yet, as we say in *England,* it was of a Widow comforted: I took Care to let the ladies see, that I knew how to receive them; that I was not at a Loss how to Behave to any of them; and, in short, I began to be very popular there; But I had an Occasion afterwards which made me decline that kind of Management, as you shall hear presently.

About four Days after I had receiv'd the Compliments of Condolence from the Prince of ——, the same Gentleman he had sent before, came to tell me that His Highness was coming to give me a Visit; I was indeed surpriz'd at that, and perfectly at a Loss how to Behave: However, as there was no Remedy, I prepar'd to receive him as well as I could; it was not many Minutes after, but he was at the Door, and came in, introduc'd by his own Gentleman, as above, and after by my Woman *Amy.*

He treated me with abundance of Civility, and condol'd handsomely the Loss of my Husband, and likewise

the Manner of it; he told me, he understood he was coming to *Versailles*, to himself, to show him some Jewels;
that it was true, that, he had discours'd with him about
jewels, but cou'd not imagine how any Villains shou'd
hear of his coming at that time with them; that he had not
order'd him to attend with them at *Versailles*, but told
him, that he would come to *Paris* by such a Day, so that
he was no way accessory to the Disaster: I told him grave-
ly, I knew very well that all His Highness had said of that
Part, was true; that these Villains knew his Profession,
and knew, no doubt, that he always carry'd a Casket of
Jewels about him, and that he always wore a Diamond
Ring on his Finger, worth a hundred Pistoles, which Report had magnified to five Hundred; and that if he had
been going to any other Place, it wou'd have been the
same thing: After this, His Highness rose up to go, and
told me he had resolv'd, however, to make me some Reparation; and with these Words, put a silk Purse into my
Hand, with a hundred Pistoles, and told me, he would
make me a further Compliment of a small Pension, which
his Gentleman would inform me of.

You may be sure I behav'd with a due Sence of so much
Goodness, and offer'd to kneel to kiss his Hand, but he
took me up, and saluted me, and sat down again (*tho' before, he made as if he was going away*), making me sit down
by him.

He then began to talk with me more familiarly; told
me he hoped I was not left in bad Circumstances; that
Mr. —— was reputed to be very Rich, and that he had
gain'd lately great Sums by some Jewels; and he hop'd
he said, that I had still a Fortune agreeable to the Condition I had liv'd in before.

I reply'd, with some tears, which I confess, were a little

forc'd, that I believed if Mr. —— had liv'd we should have been out of Danger of Want, but that it was impossible to Estimate the Loss which I had sustain'd, besides that of the Life of my Husband; that by the Opinion of those that knew something of his Affairs, and of what Value the Jewels were which he intended to have shown to *His Highness*, he could not have less about him than the value of a hundred Thousand Livres; that it was a fatal Blow to me, and to his whole Family, especially that they should be lost in such a Manner.

His Highness return'd, with an air of Concern, that he was very sorry for it; but he hoped if I settled in *Paris*, I might find Ways to restore my fortune; at the same time he complimented me upon my being very handsome, *as he was pleas'd to call it*, and that I could not fail of Admirers: I stood up and humbly thank'd *his Highness*, but told him, I had no Expectations of that Kind; that I thought I should be oblig'd to go over to *England* to look after my Husband's Effects there, which I was told, were considerable; but that I did not know what Justice a poor Stranger wou'd get among them; and as for *Paris*, my Fortune being so impair'd, I saw nothing before me, but to go back to *Poictou*, to my Friends, where some of my Relations, I hop'd, might do something for me, and added that one of my Brothers was an *Abbot* at ——, near *Poictiers*.

He stood up and, taking me by the Hand, led me to a large Looking-Glass, which made up the Pier in the Front of the Parlour; Look there, Madam, *said he*; Is it fit that Face, pointing to my Figure in the Glass, should go back to *Poictou*? No, Madam, *says he*, Stay, and make some Gentleman of Quality happy, that may, in return, make you forget all your Sorrows; and with that, he took

me, in his Arms, and kissing me twice, told me he wou'd
see me again, but with less Ceremony.

Some little time after this, but the same Day, his Gentleman came to me again, and with great Ceremony and
Respect, deliver'd me a Black Box ty'd with a Scarlet Ri-
band and seal'd with a noble Coat of Arms, which I suppose was the Prince's; there was in it a Grant from his
Highness, or an Assignment, I know not which to call it,
with a Warrant to his Banker to pay me Two thousand
Livres a Year, during my stay in *Paris*, as the Widow of
Monsieur —— the Jeweller, mentioning the horrid
Murther of my late Husband, as the Occasion of it, as
above.

I receiv'd it with great Submission, and Expressions
of being infinitely oblig'd to his Master, and of my showing myself on all Occasions *his Highness*'s most obedient
Servant; and after giving my most humble Duty to *his
Highness*, with the utmost Acknowledgments of the Obligation, *&c.*, I went to a little Cabinet, and taking out
some Money, which made a little Sound in taking it out,
offer'd to give him five Pistoles.

He drew back, but with the greatest Respect, and told
me he humbly thank'd me, but that he durst not take a
Farthing; that *his Highness* wou'd take it so ill of him, he
was sure, he would never see his Face more; but that he
wou'd not fail to acquaint his Highness what Respect I
had offer'd; and added, I assure you, Madam, you are
more in the good Graces of my Master, the Prince of
——, than you are aware of, and I believe you will hear
more of him.

Now I began to understand him, and resolv'd, if his
Highness did come again, he should see me under no
Disadvantages if I could help it: I told him if *his Highness*

did me the Honour to see me again, I hoped he would not let me be so surpriz'd as I was before; that I would be glad to have some little Notice of it, and would be oblig'd to him if he would procure it me: he told me, he was very sure that when *his Highness* intended to visit me, he should be sent before, to give me notice of it; and that he would give me as much Warning of it, as possible.

He came several times after this, on the same Errand, that is, about the Settlement, the Grant, requiring several things yet to be done, for making it payable, without going every time to the Prince again for a fresh Warrant; the Particulars of this part I did not understand; but as soon as it was finish'd, which was above two Months, the Gentleman came one Afternoon, and said *his Highness* design'd to visit me in the Evening, but desir'd to be admitted without Ceremony.

I prepar'd not my Rooms only, but myself, and when he came in, there was no-body appear'd in the House but his Gentleman, and my maid *Amy*; and of her I bid the Gentleman acquaint *his Highness*, that she was an *English* Woman; that she did not understand a Word of *French*, and that she was one also that might be trusted.

When he came into my Room, I fell down at his Feet, before he could come to salute me, and with Words that I had prepar'd, full of Duty and Respect, thank'd him for his Bounty and Goodness to a poor desolate Woman, oppress'd under the Weight of so terrible a Disaster, and refus'd to rise till he would allow me the Honour to kiss his Hand.

Levez-vous donc, says the Prince, taking me in his Arms, I design more Favours for you, than this Trifle; and going on, he added, You shall, for the future, find a Friend where you did not look for it; and I resolve to let you see how kind I can be, to one who is to me the most agreeable Creature on Earth.

I was dress'd in a kind of half-Mourning, had turn'd off my Weeds, and my Head, *tho' I had yet no Ribands or Lace*, was so dress'd as fail'd not to set me out with Advantage enough, for I began to understand his Meaning; and the Prince protest'd I was the most beautiful Creature upon Earth; *and where have I liv'd*, says he; *and how ill have I been serv'd, that I should never, till now, be shew'd the finest Woman in* France?

This was the Way, in all the World, the most likely to break in upon my Virtue, if I had been Mistress of any, for I was now become the vainest Creature upon Earth, and particularly, of my Beauty; which, as other people admir'd, so I became every Day more foolishly in Love with myself, than before.

He said some very kind Things to me after this, and sat down with me, for an Hour, or more; when getting up and calling his Gentleman by his Name, he threw open the Door. *Au Boir*, says he; upon which, his Gentleman immediately brought up a little Table cover'd with a fine Damask Cloth, the Table no bigger than he cou'd bring in his two Hands; but upon it was set two Decanters, one of Champagne, and the other of Water, six Silver Plates, and a Service of fine Sweet-Meats in fine *China* Dishes, on a Sett of Rings standing up about twenty Inches high, one above another; below was three roasted Partridges, and a Quail; as soon as his Gentleman had set it all down he order'd him to withdraw; now, *says the Prince*, I intend to Sup with you.

When he sent away his Gentleman, I stood up and offered to wait on *his Highness*, while he Eat, but he positively refus'd, and told me No; To-morrow you shall be the Widow of Monsieur——the Jeweller, but to-Night you shall be my Miſtress; therefore sit here, *says he*, and Eat with me, or I will get up and serve.

I would then have called up my Woman, *Amy*, but I thought that would not be proper neither; so I made my Excuse, that since *his Highness* wou'd not let his own Servant wait, I wou'd not presume to let my Woman come up, but if he wou'd please to let me wait, it would be my Honour to fill *his Highness*'s Wine; but, as before, he would by no means allow me, so we sat and Eat together.

Now, Madam, *says the Prince*, give me leave to lay aside my Charaçter, let us talk together with the Freedom of Equals. My Quality sets me at a Diſtance from you, and makes you ceremonious; your Beauty exalts you to more than an Equality; I muſt then treat you, as Lovers do their Miſtresses, but I cannot speak the Language; 'tis enough to tell you, how agreeable you are to me, how I am surpriz'd at your Beauty, and resolve to make you happy and to be happy with you.

I knew not what to say to him for a good-while, but blush'd and, looking up towards him, said I was already made happy, in the Favour of a Person of such Rank, and had nothing to ask of *his Highness* but that he would believe me infinitely oblig'd.

After he had Eaten, he poured the Sweet-Meats into my Lap, and the Wine being out he call'd his Gentleman again, to take away the Table, who at firſt, only took the Cloth, and the Remains of what was to Eat, away; and laying another Cloth, set the Table on one side of the Room, with a noble Service of Plate upon it, worth at leaſt 200 Piſtoles; then having set the two Decanters again upon the Table, fill'd as before, he withdrew, for I found the Fellow underſtood his business very well, and his Lord's Business too.

About half an Hour after, the Prince told me that I offered to wait a little before; that if I would now take the Trouble he would give me leave to give him some Wine; so I went to the Table, fill'd a Glass of Wine, and brought it to him, on a fine Salver, which the Glasses ſtood on, and brought the Bottle, or Decanter for Water, in my other Hand, to mix it as he thought fit.

He smil'd and bid me look on that Salver, which I did, and admir'd it much, for it was a very fine one indeed: You may see, *says he*, I resolve to have more of your Company, for my servant shall leave you that Plate for my Use. I told him I believ'd *his Highness* wou'd not take it ill, that I was not Furnish'd fit to Entertain a Person of his Rank, and that I would take great Care of it, and value myself infinitely upon the Honour of *his Highness*'s Visit.

It now began to grow late, and he began to take Notice of it; but, *says he*, I cannot leave you; have you not a spare Lodging for one Night? I told him I had but a homely Lodging to Entertain such a Gueſt; he said something exceedingly kind on that Head, but not fit to repeat; adding that my company would make him amends.

About Midnight he sent his Gentleman on an Errand, after telling him, aloud, that he intended to ſtay here all Night. In a little time his Gentleman brought him a Night-Gown, Slippers, two Caps, a Neckcloth, and a Shirt, which he gave me to carry into his Chamber, and sent his Man home; and then, turning to me, said, I shou'd do him the Honour to be his Chamberlain of the Household, and his Dresser also. I smil'd, and told him I would do myself the honour to wait on him upon all Occasions.

About One in the morning, while his Gentleman was yet with him, I begg'd leave to withdraw, supposing he would go to-Bed; but he took the Hint, and said, I'm not going to-Bed yet, pray let me see you again.

I took this time to undress me, and to come in a new Dress, which was in a manner *une Déshabillé*, but so fine, and all about me so clean, and so agreeable, that he seem'd surpriz'd. I thought, says he, you could not have dressed to more Advantage than you had done before; but now, *says he*, you Charm me a thousand times more, if that be possible.

It is only a loose Habit, my lord, said I, that I may the better wait on *your Highness*; he pulls me to him; You are perfectly obliging, *says he*; and sitting on the Bed-Side, *says he*, Now you shall be a Princess and know what it is to oblige the gratefullest Man alive; and with that he took me in his Arms. . . . I can go no further in the Particulars of what pass'd at that time, but it ended in this, that, in short, I lay with him all Night.

I have given you the whole Detail of this Story, to lay it down as a black Scheme of the Way how Unhappy Women are ruin'd by Great Men; for tho' Poverty and Want is an irresistible Temptation to the Poor, Vanity and Great Things are as irresistible to others; to be courted by a Prince, and by a Prince who was first a Benefactor, then an Admirer, to be call'd handsome, the finest Woman in *France*, and to be treated as a Woman fit for the Bed of a Prince: these are Things a Woman must have no Vanity in her, nay, no Corruption in her, that is not overcome by it; and my Case was such, that, as before, I had enough of both.

I had now no Poverty attending me; on the contrary, I was Mistress of Ten Thousand Pounds before the Prince did anything for me; had I been Mistress of my Resolution; had I been less obliging and rejected the first Attack, all had been safe; but my Virtue was lost before, and the Devil, who had found the Way to break-in upon me by one Temptation, easily master'd me now, by another; and I gave myself up to a Person who, tho' a Man of high Dignity, was yet the most tempting and obliging that ever I met with in my life.

I had the same Particular to insist upon here with the Prince, that I had with my Gentleman before; I hesitated much at consenting, at first asking, but the Prince told me, Princes did not court like other Men, that they brought more powerful Arguments, and he very prettily added, that they were sooner repuls'd than other Men, and ought to be sooner comply'd with, intimating, tho' very genteely, that after a Woman had positively refus'd him once, he cou'd not, like other Men, wait with Importunities, and Stratagems, and laying long Sieges; but as such Men as he Storm'd warmly, so, if repuls'd, they made no second Attacks; and indeed, it was but reasonable; for as it was below their Rank, to be long battering a Woman's Constancy, so they ran greater Hazards in being expos'd in their Amours than other Men did.

I took this for a satisfactory Answer, and told *his Highness*, that I had the same Thoughts, in respect to the Manner of his Attacks, for that his Person and his Arguments were irresistible; that a Person of his Rank, and a Munificence so unbounded, cou'd not be withstood; that no Virtue was Proof against him, except such, as was able too, to suffer Martyrdom; that I thought it impossible I could be overcome, but that now I found it was impossible I shou'd not be overcome; that so much Goodness, joined with so much Greatness, wou'd have conquer'd a Saint;

and that I confess'd he had the Victory over me, by a Merit infinitely superior to the Conquest he had made.

He made me a most obliging Answer; told me, abundance of fine things, which still flatter'd my vanity, till at last I began to have Pride enough to believe him, and fancy'd myself a fit Mistress for a Prince.

As I had thus given the Prince the last Favour, and he had all the Freedom with me, that it was possible for me to grant, so he gave me Leave to use as much Freedom with him, another Way, and that was, to have every thing of him I thought fit to command; and yet I did not ask of him with an Air of Avarice, as if I was greedily making a Penny of him, but I manag'd him with such Art, that he generally anticipated my Demands; he only requested of me, that I would not think of taking another House, as I had intimated to *his Highness*, that I had intended, not thinking it good enough to receive his Visits in; but, he said, my House was the most convenient that could possibly be found in all *Paris*, for an Amour, especially for him; having a Way out into Three Streets, and not overlook'd by any Neighbours, so that he could pass and repass, without Observation; for one of the Back-ways open'd into a narrow dark Alley, which Alley was a Thorow-fare, or Passage, out of one Street into another; and any Person that went in or out by the Door, had no more to do, but to see that there was no body following him in the Alley before he went in at the Door: This Request I knew was reasonable, and therefore I assur'd him, I would not change my Dwelling, seeing *his Highness* did not think it too mean for me to receive him in.

He also desir'd me that I wou'd not take any more Servants, or set up any Equipage, at least for the present; for that it would then be immediately concluded, I had been left very Rich, and then I should be thronged with the Impertinence of Admirers, who would by attracted by the Money, as well as by the Beauty of a young Widow, and he shou'd be frequently interrupted in his Visits; or that the World would conclude I was maintained by somebody, and wou'd be indefatigable to find out the Person; so that he should have Spies peeping at him every time he went out or in, which it would be impossible to disappoint; and that he shou'd presently have it talk'd over all the Toilets in *Paris* that the Prince de —— had got the Jeweller's Widow for a Mistress.

This was too just to oppose; and I made no Scruple to tell *his Highness*, that since he had stoop'd so low as to make me his own, he ought to have all the Satisfaction in the World, that I was all his own; that I would take all the measures he should please to direct me, to avoid the impertinent Attacks of others; and that, if he thought fit I would be wholly within-Doors, and have it given out that I was oblig'd to go to *England*, to solicit my Affairs there, after my Husband's Misfortune, and that I was not expected there again for at least a Year or two: This he lik'd very well; only, *he said*, that he would by no means have me confin'd, that it would injure my Health, and that I should then take a Country-House in some Village, a good-way off of the City, where it should not be known who I was; and that I should be there sometimes, to divert me.

I made no Scruple of the Confinement, and told *his Highness*, no Place could be a Confinement where I had such a Visitor; and so I put off the Country-House, which would have been to remove myself further from him, and have less of his Company, and I made the House be, as it were, shut up; *Amy*, indeed, appear'd, and when

any of the Neighbours and Servants enquir'd, she answered in broken *French*, that I was gone to *England*, to look
after my Affairs; which presently went current through
the Streets about us: For, you are to note, that the People
of *Paris*, especially the Women, are the most busy and
impertinent Enquirers into the Conduct of their Neighbours, especially that of a Single Woman, that are in the
World; tho' there are no greater Intriguers in the Uni-
verse than themselves; and perhaps that may be the Reason of it, for it is an old but a sure Rule; that

> When deep Intrigues are close and shy,
> The G U I L T Y are the first that spy.

Thus *his Highness* had the most easie, and yet the most
undiscoverable Access to me, imaginable, and he seldom
fail'd to come two or three Nights in a Week, and sometimes stay'd two or three Nights together: Once he told
me, he was resolv'd I should be weary of his Company,
and that he would learn to know what it was to be a Prisoner; so he gave out among his Servants that he was
gone to ——, where he often went a-Hunting, and that he
should not return under a Fortnight; and that Fort-night
he stay'd wholly with me, and never went out of my Doors.

Never Woman, in such a Station liv'd a Fortnight in
so complete a fullness of Humane Delight; for, to have
the entire Possession of one of the most accomplish'd
Princes in the World, and of the politest, best bred Man;
to converse with him all Day, and, *as he profess'd*, charm
him all Night; what could be more inexpressibly pleasing, and especially, to a Woman of a vast deal of Pride, as
I was?

To finish the Felicity of this Part, I must not forget,
that the Devil had play'd a new Game with me, and pre-

vail'd with me to satisfy myself with this Amour, as a lawful thing; that a Prince of such Grandeur, and Majeſty; so infinitely superior to me; and one who had made such a Introduction by an unparallel'd Bounty, I could not resiſt; and therefore, that it was very Lawful for me to do it, being at that time perfectly single, and unengag'd to any other Man; as I was, moſt certainly, by the unaccountable Absence of my firſt Husband, and the Murther of my Gentleman, who went for my second.

It cannot be doubted but that I was the easier to persuade myself of the Truth of such a Doctrine as this, when it was so much for my Ease, and for the Repose of my Mind, to have it be so.

> In Things we wish, 'tis easie to deceive;
> What we would have, we willingly believe.

Besides, I had no Casuiſts to resolve this Doubt; the same Devil that put this into my Head, bade me go to any of the *Romish* Clergy, and, under the Pretence of Confession, ſtate the Case exactly, and I should see they would either resolve it to be no Sin at all, or absolve me upon the easieſt Penance; This I had a ſtrong Inclination to try, but I know not what Scruple put me off it, for I could never bring myself to like having to do with those Prieſts; and tho' it was ſtrange that I, who had thus proſtituted my Chaſtity, and given up all sense of Virtue, in two such particular Cases, living a Life of open Adultery, should scruple anything; yet so it was, I argued with myself, that I could not be a Cheat in anything that was eſteem'd Sacred, that I could not be of one Opinion, and then pretend myself to be of another; nor could I go to Confession, who knew nothing of the Manner of it, and should betray myself to the Prieſt to be a Hugonot, and then might come into Trouble; but, in short, tho' I was a Whore, yet I was a Proteſtant Whore, and could not aᵭ as if I was Popish, upon any Account whatsoever.

But, I say, I satisfy'd myself with the surprizing Occasion, that, as it was all irresiſtible, so it was all lawful; for that Heaven would not suffer us to be punish'd for that which it was not possible for us to avoid; and with these Absurdities I kept Conscience from giving me any considerable Diſturbance in all this Matter, and I was as perfeᵭly easie as to the Lawfulness of it, as if I had been marry'd to the Prince, and had had no other Husband: So possible is it for us to roll ourselves up in Wickedness, till we grow invulnerable by Conscience; and that Centinel, once doz'd, sleeps faſt, not to be awaken'd while the Tide of Pleasure continues to flow, or till something dark and dreadful brings us to ourselves again.

I have, I confess, wondered at the Stupidity that my intelleᵭual Part was under all that while; what lethargic Fumes doz'd the Soul; and how it was possible that I, who in the Case before, where the Temptation was many ways more forcible, and the Arguments ſtronger, and more irresiſtible, was yet under a continued Inquietude on account of the wicked Life I led, could now live in the moſt profound Tranquility and with an uninterrupted Peace, nay, even rising up to Satisfaᵭion, and Joy, and yet in a more palpable State of Adultery than before; for before, my Gentleman who call'd me Wife, had the Pretence of his Wife being parted from him, refusing to do the Duty of her Office as a Wife to him; as for me, my circumſtances were the same; but as for the Prince, as he had a fine and extraordinary Lady, or Princess, of his own; so he had had two or three Miſtresses more besides me, and made no scruple of it at all.

However, I say, as to my own Part, I enjoyed myself in perfect Tranquility, and as the Prince was the only Deity I worshipp'd, so I was really his idol; and however it was with his Princess, I assure you, his other Mistresses found a sensible Difference; and tho' they could never find me out, yet I had good Intelligence, that they guess'd very well that their Lord had got some new Favourite that robbed them of his Company, and perhaps, of some of his usual Bounty too: And now I must mention the Sacrifices he made to his idol, and they were not a few, I assure you.

As he lov'd like a Prince, so he rewarded like a Prince; for tho' he declined my making a Figure, as above, he let me see, that he was above doing it for the saving the Expence of it, and so he told me, and that he would make it up in other things: First of all, he sent me a Toilet, with all the Appurtenances of Silver, even so much as the Frame of the Table; and then for the House, he gave me the Table or Side-Board of Plate I mention'd above, with all things belonging to it, of massy Silver; so that, in short, I could not, for my Life, study to ask him for any thing of *Plate* which I had not.

He could then accommodate me in nothing more but Jewels and Clothes, or money, for Cloaths; He sent his Gentleman to the Mercers, and bought me a Suit, or whole Piece, of the finest Brocaded Silk, figur'd with Gold, and another with Silver, and another of Crimson, so that I had three Suits of Cloaths such as the Queen of *France* would not have disdain'd to have worn at that time; yet I went out no-where; but as these were for me to put on, when I went out of Mourning, I dress'd myself in them, one after another, always when *his Highness* came to see me.

I had no less than five several Morning Dresses be-sides these, so that I need never be seen twice in the same Dress; to these he added several Parcels of fine Linnen, and of lace, so much, that I had no room to ask for more, or indeed for so much.

I took the liberty once, in our Freedoms to tell him he was too Bountiful, and that I was too chargeable to him for a Mistress, and that I would be his faithful Servant, at less Expense to him; and that he not only left me no room to ask him for anything, but that he supply'd me with such a Profusion of good things, that I scarce could wear them, or use them, unless I kept a great Equipage, which he knew was no way convenient for him or for me; he smiled, and took me in his Arms, and told me he was re-solv'd, while I was his, I should never be able to ask him for any-thing, but that he would be daily asking new Fa-vours of me.

After we were up, for this Conference was in Bed, he desir'd I would dress me in the best Suit of Cloaths I had: It was a day or two after the three Suits were made, and brought home; I told him, if he pleas'd, I would rather dress me in that Suit which I knew he lik'd best; he ask'd me, how I could know which he would like best, before he had seen them? I told him, I would presume for once to guess at his Fancy by my own; so I went away, and dress'd me in the second Suit, brocaded with Silver, and return'd in full Dress, with a Suit of Lace upon my Head, which would have been worth in *England* 200 l. Sterling; and I was every Way set out as well as *Amy* could dress me, who was a very gentile Dresser too: In this Figure I came to him, out of my Dressing-Room, which open'd with Folding-Doors into his Bed-Chamber.

He sat as one astonish'd a good-while, looking at me,

without speaking a Word, till I came quite up to him, kneel'd on one Knee to him, and almoſt, whether he would or no, kiss'd his Hand; he took me up, and ſtood up himself, but was surpriz'd when, taking me in his Arms, he perceiv'd Tears to run down my Cheeks; My Dear, *says he*, aloud, what mean these Tears? My Lord, *said I*, after some little Check, for I could not speak presently, I beseech you to believe me, they are not Tears of Sorrow, but Tears of Joy; it is impossible for me to see myself snatch'd from the Misery I was fallen into, and at once to be in the Arms of a Prince of such Goodness, such immense Bounty, and be treated in such a Manner—'tis not possible, my Lord, *said I*, to contain the Satisfaction of it, and it will break out in an Excess in some measure proportion'd to your immense Bounty, and to the Affection which your Highness treats me with, who am so infinitely below you.

It wou'd look a little too much like a Romance here, to repeat all the kind things he said to me, on that Occasion, but I can't omit one Passage; as he saw the Tears drop down my Cheek; he pulls out a fine Cambric Handkerchief, and was going to wipe the Tears off, but check'd his Hand, as if he was afraid to deface something; I say he check'd his hand, and toss'd the Handkerchief to me to do it myself; I took the hint immediately, and with a kind of pleasant Disdain, *How! my Lord*, said I, *Have you kiss'd me so often, and don't you know whether I am painted or not? Pray let your Highness satisfie yourself, that you have no Cheats put upon you; for once let me be vain enough to say I have not deceiv'd you with false Colours*: With this, I put a Handkerchief into his Hand, and, taking his Hand into mine, I made him wipe my Face so hard, that he was unwilling to do it for fear of hurting me.

VOL. I   g

He appear'd surpriz'd, more than ever, and swore, which was the first time that I had heard him swear, from my first knowing him, that he cou'd not have believ'd there was any such Skin, without Paint in the World: *Well, my Lord*, said I, *Your Highness shall have a further Demonstration* than this; *as to that which you are pleas'd to accept for Beauty, that it is the mere work of Nature*; And with that I stept to the Door, and rang a little Bell, for my Woman, *Amy*, and bade her bring me a Cup-full of hot Water, which she did; and when it was come, I desir'd *his Higness* to feel if it was warm; which he did, and I immediately wash'd my face all over with it before him; this was, indeed, more than Satisfaction, that is to say, than Believing, for it was an undeniable Demonstration, and he kiss'd my Cheeks and Breasts a thousand times, with expressions of the greatest surprise imaginable.

Nor was I a very indifferent Figure as to Shape; tho' I had had two Children by my Gentleman, and six by my true Husband, I say I was no despisable Shape; and my Prince (I must be allow'd the vanity to call him so) was taking his View of me as I walk'd from one End of the Room to the other, at last he leads me to the darkest Part of the Room and, standing behind me, bade me hold up my Head, when putting both his Hands round my Neck, as if he was spanning my Neck, to see how small it was, for it was long and small; he held my Neck so long and so hard in his Hand, that I complain'd he hurt me a little; what he did it for, I knew not, nor had I the least Suspicion, but that he was spanning my Neck; but when I said he hurt me, he seem'd to let go, and in half a Minute more led me to a Pier-Glass, and behold, I saw my Neck clasped with a fine Necklace of Diamonds; whereas I felt no more what he was doing, than if he had really done nothing at-all, nor did I suspect it, in the least: If I had an Ounce of Blood in me that did not fly up into my Face, Neck, and Breasts, it must be from some Interruption in the Vessels; I was all on fire with the Sight, and began to wonder what it was that was coming to me.

However, to let him see that I was not unqualified to receive benefits; I turned about, My Lord, *says I*, Your Highness is resolv'd to conquer by your Bounty, the very Gratitude of your Servants; you will leave no room for anything but Thanks, and make those Thanks useless too, by their bearing no Proportion to the Occasion.

I love, Child, *says he*, to see everything suitable; a fine Gown and Petticoat; a fine lac'd Head; A fine Face and Neck, and no Necklace, would not have made the Object perfect: But why that Blush, my dear, *says the Prince?* My Lord, *said I*, all your Gifts call for Blushes; but above all, I blush to receive what I am so ill able to merit, and may become so ill also.

Thus far I am a standing Mark of the Weakness of Great Men, in their Vice; that value not squandering away immense Wealth, upon the most worthless Creatures; or, to sum it up in a Word, they raise the Value of the Object which they pretend to pitch upon by their Fancy; I say, raise the Value of it, at their own Expence, give vast Presents for a ruinous Favour, which is so far from being equal to the Price, that nothing will, at last, prove more absurd, than the Cost Men are at to purchase their own Destruction.

I cou'd not, in the height of all this fine doings, I say I could not be without some just Reflection, tho' Conscience was, as I said, dumb as to any Disturbance it gave me in my Wickedness; my Vanity was fed up to such a height, that I had no room to give Way to such Reflections.

But I could not but sometimes look back, with Aſton-
ishment, at the Folly of Men of Quality, who, immense in
their Bounty, as in their Wealth, give, to a Profusion, and
without Bounds, to the moſt scandalous of our Sex, for
granting them the Liberty of abusing themselves, and
ruining both.

I, that knew what this Carcass of mine had been but a
few years before; how overwhelm'd with Grief, drown'd
in Tears, frighted with the Prospeɕt of Beggary, and sur-
rounded with Rags and Fatherless Children; that was
pawning and selling the Rags that cover'd me, for a Dinner, and sat on the Ground, despairing of Help, and ex-
peɕting to be ſtarv'd, till my children were snatch'd from
me to be kept by the Parish; I that was after this, a Whore
for Bread and, abandoning Conscience and Virtue, liv'd
with another Woman's Husband; I, that was despis'd by
all my Relations, and my Husband's too; I that was left
so entirely desolate, friendless, and helpless that I knew
not how to get the leaſt Help to keep me from ſtarving;
that I should be caress'd by a Prince, for the Honour of
having the scandalous Use of my Proſtituted Body, common before to his Inferiors; and perhaps wou'd not have
denied one of his Footmen but a little while before, if I
could have got my Bread by it.

I say I cou'd not but refleɕt upon the Brutality and
Blindness of Mankind; that, because Nature had given
me a good Skin, and some agreeable Features, should
suffer that Beauty to be such a Bait to Appetite as to do
such sordid, unaccountable things, to obtain the Possession of it.

It is for this Reason, that I have so largely set down the
Particulars of the Caresses I was treated with by the Jeweller, and also by this Prince; not to make the Story an In-

centive to the Vice, which I am now such a sorrowful
Penitent for being guilty of, *God forbid any shou'd make so
vile a use of so good a Design*, but to draw the juſt Picture
of a Man enslav'd to the Rage of his vicious Appetite;
how he defaces the Image of God in his Soul, dethrones
his Reason; causes Conscience to abdicate the Possession
and exalts Sence into the vacant Throne; how he deposes
the Man, and exalts the Brute.

Oh! could we hear now, the Reproaches this Great
Man afterwards loaded himself with, when he grew
weary of this admir'd Creature and became sick of his
Vice! how profitable would the Report of them be to the
Reader of this Story; but had he himself also known the
dirty Hiſtory of my Actings upon the Stage of Life, that
little time I had been in the World, how much more severe would those Reproaches have been upon himself;
But I shall come to this again.

I liv'd in this gay sort of Retirement almoſt three Years,
in which time no Amour of such a Kind, sure, was ever
carry'd up so high; the Prince knew no Bounds to his
Munificence; he cou'd give me nothing, either for my
wearing or using, or eating, or drinking, more than he
had done from the Beginning.

His Presents were, after that, in Gold, and very frequent, and large; often a hundred Piſtoles, never less
than fifty at a time; and I muſt do myself the Juſtice, that
I seem'd rather backward to receive than craving, and
encroaching; not that I had not an avaricious Temper,
nor was it, that I did not foresee that this was my Harveſt,
in which I was to gather up, and that it would not laſt
long; but it was, that really his Bounty always anticipated
my Expectations, and even my Wishes; and he gave me
Money so faſt that he rather pour'd it in upon me, than

left me room to ask it; so that before I could spend fifty Pistoles, I had always a hundred to make it up.

After I had been near a Year and a half in his Arms, as above, or thereabouts, I prov'd with Child; I did not take any Notice of it to him, till I was satisfied, that I was not deceiv'd; when one Morning early, when we were in Bed together, I said to him, My Lord, I doubt your Highness never gives yourself Leave to think what the Case should be, if I should have the honour to be with-Child by you: Why, my Dear, *says he*, we are able to keep it, if such a thing should happen; I hope you are not concerned about that: No, my Lord, *said I*, I should think myself very happy, if I could bring your Highness a Son, I should hope to see him a Lieutenant-General of the King's Armies, by the Interest of his Father and by his own Merit.

Assure yourself, Child, *says he*, if it should be so I will not refuse owning him for my Son, though it be, as they call it, a Natural Son, and shall never slight or neglect him, for the sake of his Mother: Then he began to importune me, to know if it was so; but I positively denied it so long, till at last I was able to give him the Satisfaction of knowing it himself by the Motion of the Child within me.

He profess'd himself overjoy'd at the Discovery, but told me, that now it was absolutely necessary for me to quit the Confinement, which *he said*, I had suffer'd for his sake, and to take a House somewhere in the Country, in order for Health as well as for Privacy, against my Lying-in: This was quite out of my way; but the Prince, who was a man of Pleasure, had, it seems, several Retreats of this kind which he made use of, I suppose, upon like Occasions; and so leaving it, as it were, to his Gentleman, he provided a very convenient House about four miles *South of Paris*, at the village of ——, where I had very agree-

able Lodgings, good Gardens, and all things very easie to
my Content; But one thing did not please me at all, *viz.*
that an Old Woman was provided, and put into the
House, to furnish everything necessary to my Lying-in
and to assist at my Travel.

I did not like this Old Woman at all; she looked so like
a Spy upon me, or, (as sometimes I was frighted to imagine) like one set privately to dispatch me out of the
World, as might best suit with the Circumstances of my
Lying-in; and when his Highness came the next time to
see me, which was not many Days, I expostulated a little
on the Subject of the Old Woman, and by the Management of my Tongue, as well as by the Strength of reasoning, I convinc'd him that it would not be at all convenient;
that it would be the greater Risque on his Side; and that
first, or last, it would certainly expose him and me also; I
assur'd him that my servant, being an *English* Woman,
never knew, to that Hour who his Highness was; that I
always call'd him the *Count de Clerac*; and that she knew
nothing else of him, nor ever should; that if he would
give me leave to choose proper Persons for my Use, it
should be so order'd that not one of them should know
who he was, or perhaps, ever see his Face; and that for
the reallity of the Child that should be born, his Highness
who had alone been at the first of it, should if he pleas'd be
present in the Room all the Time, so that he would need
no Witnesses on that Account.

This Discourse fully satisfied him, so that he order'd
his Gentleman to dismiss the Old Woman the same Day;
and without any Difficulty I sent my Maid *Amy* to *Callais*,
and thence to *Dover*, where she got an *English* Midwife,
and an *English* Nurse, to come over, on purpose to attend
an *English* Lady of Quality, as they styl'd me, for four

Months certain: The Midwife, *Amy* had agreed to pay a hundred Guineas to, and bear her Charges to *Paris*, and back again to *Dover*, the poor Woman that was to be my Nurse had twenty Pounds, and the same Terms for Charges, as the other.

I was very easie when *Amy* return'd, and the more because she brought with the Midwife, a good Motherly sort of Woman, who was to be her Assistant and would be very helpful on Occasion, and bespoke a Man-Midwife at *Paris* too, if there should be any Necessity for his Help: Having thus made Provision for everything, the *Count*, for so we all call'd him in publick, came as often to see me, as I could expect, and continued exceeding kind, as he had always been; one day, conversing together upon the subject of my being with Child, I told him how all things were in order; but that I had a strange Apprehension that I should die with that Child: He smil'd. *So all the Ladies say, my Dear*, says he, *when they are with Child.* Well, however, my Lord, *said I*, it is but just that Care should be taken, that what you have bestow'd in your Excess of Bounty upon me should not be lost; And upon this I pull'd a Paper out of my Bosom, folded up but not seal'd, and I read it to him; Wherein I had left Order, that all the Plate and Jewels, and fine Furniture, which his Highness had given me, should be restor'd to him by my Woman, and the Keys be immediately delivered to his Gentleman, in case of Disaster.

Then I recommended my Woman, *Amy*, to his Favour for a hundred Pistoles, on Condition she gave the keys up, as above, to his Gentleman, and his Gentleman's Receipt for them; when he saw this, *My Dear Child*, said he, and took me in his Arms, *What, have you been making your Will and disposing of your Effects? Pray who do you make*

your universal Heir? So far as to do juſtice to your Highness, in case of Mortality, I have, my Lord, *said I*; and
who should I dispose the valuable things to, which I have
had from your Hand, as Pledges of your Favour, and
Teſtimonies of your Bounty, but to the Giver of them? If
the child should live, your Highness will, I don't question,
act like yourself in that Part, and I shall have the utmoſt
satisfaction that it will be well us'd by your Direction.

I cou'd see he took this very well: *I have forsaken all the
Ladies in* Paris, says he, *for you; and I have liv'd every day
since I knew you, to see that you know how to merit all that a
Man of Honour can do for you; be easy,* Child, *I hope you
shall not die; and all you have is your own, to do with it what
you please.*

I was then within about two Months of my Time, and
that soon wore off. When I found my Time was come, it
fell out very happily, that he was in the House, and I entreated he would continue a few Hours in the House,
which he agreed to; they call'd his Highness to come into the Room if he pleas'd, as I had offer'd, and as I desir'd him, and I sent word, I would make as few Cries as
possible to prevent diſturbing him; he came into the
room once and call'd to me to be of good Courage; it
would soon be over, and then he withdrew again; and in
about half an Hour more *Amy* carried him the News that
I was Deliver'd and had brought him a charming Boy; he
gave her ten Piſtoles for her News, ſtay'd till they had ad-
juſted things about me, and then came into the Room
again, chear'd me and spoke kindly to me, and look'd on
the Child, then withdrew; and came again the next Day,
to visit me.

Since this, and when I have look'd back upon these
things with eyes unpossess'd with Crime, when the wick-

ed Part has appear'd in its clearer Light, and I have seen
it in its own natural Colours; when no more blinded with
the glittering Appearances, which at that time deluded
me, and, as *in like Cases, if I may guess at others by myself*,
too *much possess'd* the mind; I say, since this, I have often
wonder'd with what Pleasure or Satisfaction the Prince
cou'd look upon the poor innocent Infant, which, tho' his
own, and that he might that Way have some Attachment
in his Affections to it, yet muſt always afterwards be a
Remembrancer to him of his moſt early Crime; and,
which was worse, muſt bear upon itself, unmerited, an
eternal Mark of Infamy, which should be spoken of, upon all Occasions, to its reproach, from the Folly of its Father, and Wickedness of its Mother.

Great Men are, indeed deliver'd from the Burden of
their Natural Children, or Baſtards, as to their Maintenance: This is the main Affliction in other Cases, where
there is not Subſtance sufficient without breaking into
the Fortunes of the Family; in those Cases, either a Man's
legitimate Children suffer, which is very unnatural; or
the unfortunate Mother of that illegitimate Birth has a
dreadful Affliction either of being turn'd off with her
Child, and be left to ſtarve, &c., or of seeing the poor infant pack'd off with a Piece of Money to some of those
She-Butchers who take Children off of their Hands, as
'tis call'd; that is to say, ſtarve 'em and, in a Word, murther 'em.

Great Men, I say, are deliver'd from this Burthen, because they are always furnish'd to supply the Expence of
their Out-of-the-Way Off-spring by making little As-
signments upon the Bank of *Lyons*, or the Town-House
of *Paris*, and settling those Sums, to be receiv'd for the
Maintenance of such Expence as they see Cause.

Thus, in the Case of this Child of mine, while he and I convers'd there was no need to make any Appointment, as an Appanage, or Maintenance for the Child, or its Nurse; for he supplied me more than sufficiently for all those things; but afterward, when Time, and a particular Circumstance, put an End to our conversing together; as such things always meet with a Period, and generally break off abruptly; I say, after that, I found he appointed the Children a settled Allowance, by an Assignment of annual Rent upon the Bank of *Lyons*, which was sufficient for bringing them handsomely, tho' privately, up in the World; and that not in a Manner unworthy of their Father's Blood, tho' I came to be sunk and forgotten in the Case; nor did the Children ever know anything of their Mother, to this day, other than as you may have an Account hereafter.

But to look back to the particular Observation I was making, which I hope may be of Use to those who read my Story; I say it was something wonderful to me, to see this Person so exceedingly delighted at the Birth of this Child, and so pleas'd with it; for he would sit and look at it, and with an Air of Seriousness sometimes, a great while together; and particularly, I observ'd, he loved to look at it when it was asleep.

It was indeed a lovely, charming Child, and had a certain Vivacity in its Countenance that is, far from being common to all Children so young; and he would often say to me that he believ'd there was something extraordinary in the Child, and he did not doubt but he would come to be a Great Man.

I could never hear him say so, but tho' secretly it pleas'd me, yet it so closely touch'd me another Way, that I could not refrain Sighing, and sometimes Tears; and one time, in particular, it so affected me, that I could not conceal it from him; but when he saw Tears run down my Face, there was no concealing the Occasion from him; he was too importunate to be deny'd in a thing of that Moment; so I frankly answer'd, It sensibly affects me, My Lord, said I, that whatever the Merit of this little Creature may be, he must always have a Bend on his Arms; the Disaster of his Birth will be always, not a Blot only to his Honour, but a Bar to his Fortunes in the World; our Affection will be ever his Affliction, and his Mother's Crime be the Son's Reproach; the Blot can never be wip'd out by the most glorious Actions; nay, if it lives to raise a Family, *said I*, the infamy must descend even to its innocent Posterity.

He took the Thought, and sometimes told me afterwards, that it made a deeper impression on him, than he discovered to me at that time; but for the present, he put it off, with telling me these things cou'd not be help'd, that they serv'd for a Spur to the Spirits of brave Men, inspir'd them with the Principles of Gallantry; and prompted them to brave Actions; that tho' it might be true, that the mention of illegitimacy might attend the Name, yet that Personal Virtue plac'd a Man of Honour above the Reproach of his Birth; that as he had no Share in the Offence, he would have no Concern at the Blot; when having by his own Merit plac'd himself out of the reach of Scandal, his Fame shou'd drown the Memory of his Beginning.

That as it was usual for Men of Quality to make such little Escapes, so the Number of their Natural Children were so great, and they generally took such good Care of their Education, that some of the greatest Men in the World had a Bend in their Coats of Arms, and that it was of no Consequence to them, especially when their Fame began to rise upon the Basis of their acquir'd Merit; and upon this, he began to reckon up to me some of the greatest Families in *France*, and in *England* also.

This carry'd off our Discourse for a time; but I went farther with him once, removing the Discourse from the Part attending our Children to the Reproach which those Children would be apt to throw upon us, their Originals; and when speaking a little too feelingly on the Subject, he began to receive the Impression a little deeper than I wish'd he had done; at last he told me, I had almost acted the Confessor to him; that I might perhaps preach a more dangerous Doctrine to him, than we shou'd either of us like, or than I was aware of, *for, my Dear, says he,* if once we come to talk of Repentance, we must talk of parting.

If Tears were in my Eyes before, they flow'd too fast now to be restrain'd, and I gave him but too much Satisfaction by my Looks, that I had yet no Reflections upon my Mind, strong enough to go that Length, and that I could no more think of Parting, than he could.

He said a great many kind things, which were Great, like himself, and, extenuating our Crime, intimated to me, that he cou'd no more part with me, than I cou'd with him; so we both, as I may say, even against our Light, and against our Conviction, concluded to SIN ON; indeed, his Affection to the Child, was one great Tye to him, for he was extremely fond of it.

This Child liv'd to be a considerable Man: He was first, an Officer of the Guard *du Corps of France*; and afterwards Colonel of a Regiment of Dragoons, in *Italy*, and on many extraordinary Occasions shew'd that he was not unworthy of such a Father, but many ways deserving a legitimate Birth, and a better Mother: Of which hereafter.

I think I may say now, that I lived indeed like a Queen, or if you will have me confess, that my Condition had still the Reproach of a *Whore*, I may say, I was sure, the Queen of Whores; for no Woman was ever more valued, or more caress'd by a Person of such Quality, only in the Station of a Mistress; I had, indeed, one Deficiency, which Women in such Circumstances seldom are charge-able with; namely, I crav'd nothing of him; I never ask'd him for anything in my Life, nor suffer'd myself to be made use of, as is too much the Custom of Mistresses, to ask Favours for others; his bounty always prevented me in the first, and my strict concealing myself, in the last, which was no less to my Convenience than his.

The only Favour I ever ask'd of him was for his Gen-tleman, whom he had all along intrusted with the Secret of our Affair, and who had once so much offended him, by some Omissions in his duty, that he found it very hard to make his Peace; he came and laid his Case before my Woman, *Amy*, and begg'd her to speak to me, to intercede for him; which I did, and on my Account, he was re-ceiv'd again and pardon'd; for which, the grateful Dog requited me by getting-to-Bed to his Benefactress *Amy*; at which I was very angry; but *Amy* generously acknow-ledg'd that it was her Fault as much as his; that she lov'd the Fellow so much that she believ'd if he had not ask'd her, she should have ask'd him; I say this pacify'd me, and I only obtain'd of her, that she should not let him know, that I knew it.

I might have interspers'd this Part of my Story with a great many pleasant Parts, and Discourses which hap-pen'd between my Maid *Amy* and I; but I omit them, on account of my own Story, which has been so extraordin-ary: However, I must mention something as to *Amy*, and

her Gentleman; I enquir'd of *Amy*, upon what terms they
came to be so intimate; but *Amy* seemed backward to explain herself; I did not care to press her upon a Question
of that Nature, knowing that she might have answered
my Question with a Question and have said, Why, how
did I and the Prince come to be so intimate? so I left off
enquiring into it, till after some time she told it me all
freely of her own Accord; which, to cut it short, amounted
to no more than this, that *like* Mistress, *like* Maid; as they
had many leisure Hours together below, while they waited respectively, when his Lord and I were together above;
I say they could hardly avoid the usual Question one to
another, namely, Why might not they do the same thing
below, that we did above?

On that Account, indeed, as I said above, I could not
find in my Heart to be angry with *Amy*; I was indeed
afraid the Girl would have been with-Child too, but that
did not happen, and so there was no Hurt done; for *Amy*
had been hansell'd before as well as her Mistress, and by
the same Party too, *as you have heard.*

After I was up again, and my Child provided with a
good Nurse, and, withal, Winter coming on, it was proper to think of coming to *Paris* again, which I did; but as
I had now a Coach and Horses, and some Servants to attend me, by my Lord's Allowance, I took the Liberty to
have them come to *Paris* sometimes, and so to take a
Tour into the Garden of the Thuilleries and the other
pleasant Places of the City: It happen'd one day that my
Prince (if I may call him so) had a-Mind to give me some
Diversion and to take the Air with me, but that he might
do it, and not be publicly known, he comes to me in a
Coach of the Count de ——, a great Officer of the Court,
attended by his Liveries also; so that, in a word, it was im-

possible to guess by the Equipage who I was, or whom I belong'd; to also, that I might be the more effectually conceal'd, he ordered me to be taken up at a Mantua-Maker's House, where he sometimes came, whether upon other Amours or not was no Business of mine to enquire: I knew nothing whither he intended to carry me, but when he was in the Coach with me, he told me he had order'd his Servants to go to Court with me, and he would show me some of the *Beau Monde*; I told him, I car'd not where I went, while I had the Honour to have him with me; so he carried me to the fine Palace of *Meudon*, where the *Dauphine* then was, and where he had some particular Intimacy with one of the *Dauphine*'s Domesticks, who procur'd a Retreat for me in his Lodgings while we stay'd there, which was three or four Days.

While I was there, the King happen'd to come thither from *Versailles*, and, making but a short Stay, visited Madam the *Dauphiness*, who was then living: The Prince was here *Incognito*, only because of his being with me; and therefore when he heard that the KING was in the Gardens, he kept close within the Lodgings; but the Gentleman in whose Lodgings we were, with his Lady and several others, went out to see the KING, and I had the Honour to be ask'd to go with them.

After we had seen the KING, who did not stay long in the Gardens, we walk'd up the Broad Terrass, and, crossing the Hall, towards the Great Stair-Case, I had a Sight, which confounded me at once, as I doubt not it would have done to any Woman in the World: The Horse-Guards, or what they call there the *Gensd'arms*, had upon some Occasion been either upon Duty or been Review'd, or something, (I did not understand that Part) was the Matter, that occasion'd their being there, I know not what; but walking in the Guard-Chamber, and with his Jack-Boots on, and the whole Habit of the Troop, as it is worn when our Horse-Guards are upon Duty, as they call it, at St. *James*'s Park; I say, there, to my inexpressible Confusion, I saw Mr. ———, my firſt Husband, the Brewer.

I cou'd not be deceiv'd; I pass'd so near him that I al-moſt brush'd him with my Cloaths, and look'd him full in the Face, but having my Fan before my Face, so that he cou'd not know me; however, I knew him perfeᴄtly well, and I heard him speak, which was a second Way of knowing him; besides *being, you may be sure, aſtonish'd and surpriz'd at such a Sight*, I turn'd about after I had pass'd him some Steps, and pretending to ask the Lady that was with me, some Queſtions, I ſtood as if I had view'd the Great Hall, the outer Guard-Chamber, and some other things; but I did it, to take a full View of his Dress, that I might further inform myself.

While I ſtood thus amusing the Lady that was with me, with Queſtions, he walk'd, talking with another Man of the same Cloth, back again, juſt by me; and to my par-ticular Satisfaᴄtion, or dissatisfaᴄtion, take it which way you will, I heard him speak *English*, the other being, it seems, an *Englishman*.

I then ask'd the lady some other Queſtions. Pray, Madam, *says I*, what are these Troopers here? Are they the KING's Guards? No, *says she*, they are the *Gens-d'arms*; a small Detachment of them, I suppose, attended the KING to-Day, but they are not His Majeſty's ordin-ary Guard; another lady that was with her said, No, Ma-dam, it seems that is not the Case, for I heard them saying the *Gensd'arms* were here to-Day by special Order, some of them being to march towards the *Rhine*, and these attend for Orders, but they go back to-Morrow to *Orleans*, where they are expected.

This satisfied me in Part, but I found Means after this, to enquire, whose particular Troop it was that the Gentlemen that were here, belong'd to; and with that I heard they would all be at *Paris* the Week after.

Two Days after this we returned for *Paris*, when I took Occasion to speak to my Lord that I heard the *Gensd'arms* were to be in the City the next Week, and that I should be charm'd with seeing them March, if they came in a Body: He was so obliging in such things, that I need but just name a thing of that Kind, and it was done; so he ordered his Gentleman (I shou'd now call him *Amy*'s *Gentleman*) to get me a Place in a certain House, where I might see them March.

As he did not appear with me on this Occasion, so I had the Liberty of taking my Woman *Amy* with me, and stood where we were very well accommodated for the Observation which I was to make: I told *Amy* what I had seen, and she was as forward to make the Discovery as I was to have her, and almost as much surpriz'd at the thing itself; in a word, the *Gensd'arms* enter'd the City, as was expected, and made a most glorious Show indeed, being new-clothed and arm'd, and being to have their Standards bless'd by the Archbishop of *Paris*; on this occasion they indeed look'd very gay; and as they march'd very leisurely I had time to take as critical a View and make as nice a Search among them as I pleas'd: Here, in a particular Rank eminent for one monstrous-siz'd Man on the Right; here, I say, I saw my Gentleman again, and a very handsome jolly Fellow he was, as any in the Troop, tho' not so monstrous large as that great one I spoke of, who it seems was however, a Gentleman of a good Family in *Gascogne*, and was called the *Giant of Gascony*.

It was a kind of good Fortune to us, among the other Circumſtances of it, that something caus'd the Troops to Halt in their March, a little before that particular Rank came right-againſt that Window which I ſtood in, so that then we had Occasion to take our full View of him at a small Diſtance, and so as not to doubt of his being the same Person.

Amy, who thought she might on many accounts, venture with more Safety to be particular, than I cou'd, asked her Gentleman, how a particular Man who she saw there, among the *Gensd'arms* might be enquir'd after and found out; she having seen an *Englishman* riding there, which was suppos'd to be dead in *England* for several Years before she came out of *London*, and that his wife had marry'd again: It was a Queſtion the Gentleman did not well underſtand how to answer; but another Person that ſtood by, told her, if she wou'd tell him the Gentleman's Name, he wou'd endeavour to find him out for her, and ask'd jeſtingly if he was her Lover? *Amy* put that off with a Laugh, but ſtill continued her Enquiry, and, in such a Manner, as the Gentleman easily perceiv'd she was in earneſt; so he left bantering and ask'd her in what Part of the Troop he rode; she foolishly told him his Name, which she shou'd not have done; and pointing to the Cornet that Troop carried, which was not then quite out of Sight, she let him easily know whereabouts he rode, only she could not name the Captain; however, he gave her such Direƈtions afterwards that, in short, *Amy*, who was an indefatigable Girl, found him out; it seems he had not chang'd his Name, not supposing any Enquiry would be made after him here; but I say *Amy* found him out, and went boldly to his Quarters, ask'd for him, and he came out to her immediately.

I believe I was not more confounded at my first seeing him at *Meudon*, than he was at seeing *Amy*; he started, and turn'd pale as Death; *Amy* believ'd if he had seen her at first, in any convenient Place for so villainous a Purpose, he would have murther'd her.

But he started, as I say above, and ask'd in *English*, with an Admiration, What are you? *Sir*, says she, *don't you know me? Yes*, says he, *I knew you when you were alive, but what you are now*, whether Ghost or Substance, *I know not: Be not afraid, Sir, of that*, says Amy, *I am the same* Amy *that I was in your Service, and do not speak to you now for any Hurt, but that I saw you accidentally, Yesterday, ride among the Soldiers, I thought you might be glad to hear from your Friends at* London: Well, *Amy*, says he *then*, having a little recover'd himself, *How does every-body do? What, is your Mistress here?* Thus they began:—

Amy. My Mistress, Sir, alas! not the Mistress you mean; poor Gentlewoman, you left her in a sad Condition.

Gent. Why, that's true, *Amy*, but it cou'd not be help'd. I was in a sad Condition myself.

Amy. I believe so indeed, Sir, or else you had not gone away as you did; for it was a very terrible Condition you left them all in, that I must say.

Gent. What did they do, after I was gone?

Amy. Do, sir! very miserably, you may be sure. How could it be otherwise?

Gent. Well, that's true indeed, but you may tell me, *Amy*, what became of them if you please; for tho' I went so away, it was not because I did not love them all very well, but because I could not bear to see the Poverty that was coming upon them and which it was not in my power to help. *What could I do?*

Amy. Nay, I believe so indeed, and I have heard my Miſtress say, many timcs, shc did not doubt but your Affliction was as great as hers almoſt, *wherever you were.*

Gent. Why, did she believe I was alive, then?

Amy. Yes, Sir, she always said she believ'd you were alive; because she thought she should have heard something of you, if you had been dead.

Gent. Ay, ay, my Perplexity was very great indeed, or else I had never gone away.

Amy. It was very cruel, tho', to the poor Lady, Sir, *my Miſtress*; she almoſt broke her heart for you at firſt, for fear of what might befal you, and at laſt because she cou'd not hear from you.

Gent. Alas! *Amy*, what cou'd I do? things were driven to the laſt Extremity before I went; I cou'd have done nothing, but help ſtarve them all if I had ſtay'd, and besides, I cou'd not bear to see it.

Amy. You know, Sir, I can say little to what pass'd before, but I am a melancholy Witness to the sad Diſtresses of my poor Miſtress as long as I ſtay'd with her, and which would grieve your heart to hear them.

Here she tells my whole Story, to the Time that the Parish took off one of my Children, and which she perceiv'd very much affeā'd him; and he shook his Head, and said some things very bitter, when he heard of the Cruelty of his own Relations to me.

Gent. Well, *Amy*, I have heard enough so far; what did she do afterwards?

Amy. I can't give you any further Account, sir; my miſtress would not let me ſtay with her any longer; she said she could neither pay me, nor subsiſt me; I told her,

I wou'd serve her without any Wages; but I cou'd not
live without Victuals, you know; so I was forced to leave
her, *poor Lady*, sore against my Will, and I heard afterwards, that the Landlord seiz'd her Goods, so she was, I
suppose, turn'd out of Doors, for as I went by the Door
about a Month after, I saw the house shut up; and about
a Fortnight after that, I found there were Workmen at
work, fitting it up, as I suppose, for a new Tennant; but
none of the Neighbours could tell me what was become
of my poor Mistress, only that they said, she was so poor,
that it was next to begging; that some of the neighbour-
ing Gentlefolks had reliev'd her, or that else she must
have starv'd; then she went on, and told him that after
that they never heard any more of (*me*) her Mistress, but
that she had been seen once or twice in the City, very
shabby and poor in Cloaths, and it was thought she
work'd with her Needle, for her Bread: All this, the *Jade*
said with so much Cunning, and manag'd and humour'd
it so well, and wip'd her Eyes, and cry'd so artificially,
that he took it all as it was intended he should, and once
or twice she saw Tears in his Eyes too: He told her it was
a moving, melancholy Story, and it had almost broken
his Heart at first; but that he was driven to the last Extremity, and cou'd do nothing but stay and see 'em all
starve, which he cou'd not bear the Thoughts of, but
should have Pistol'd himself, if any such thing had happen'd while he was there; that he left (*me*) his Wife, all the
Money he had in the World but 2 5 l., which was as little
as he could take with him, to seek his Fortune in the
World; he cou'd not doubt but that his Relations, seeing
they were all Rich, wou'd have taken the poor Children
off, and not let them come to the Parish; and that his Wife
was young and handsome and, he thought, might Marry

again, perhaps to her Advantage; and for that very Reason, he never wrote to her, or let her know he was alive, that she might, in a reasonable Term of Years marry, and perhaps mend her Fortunes. That he resolv'd never to claim her, because he should rejoice to hear, that she had settled to her Mind; and that he wished there had been a Law made, to empower a Woman to marry, if her Husband was not heard of in so long time; which time, he thought, shou'd not be above four Year, which was long enough to send Word in, to a Wife or Family, from any Part of the World.

Amy said she could say nothing to that, but this, that she was satisfied, her Mistress would marry no-body unless she had certain Intelligence that he had been dead, from somebody that saw him buried; but, alas! *says Amy*, my Mistress was reduc'd to such dismal Circumstances that nobody would be so foolish to think of her, unless it had been somebody to go a-begging with her.

Amy then, seeing him so perfectly deluded, made a long and lamentable Outcry, how she had been deluded away to marry a poor Footman; for he is no worse or better, *says she*, tho' he calls himself a Lord's Gentleman; and here, says *Amy*, he has dragg'd me over into a strange Country to make a Begger of me; and then she falls a-howling again and sniveling; which, by the way, was all Hypocrisie, but acted so to the Life, as perfectly deceiv'd him, and he gave entire credit to every Word of it.

Why, *Amy*, *says he*, you are very well dress'd, you don't look as if you were in danger of being a Begger. *Ay*, hang him, *says Amy*, they love to have fine Cloaths here if they have never a Smock under them; but I love to have Money in Cash rather than a Chest full of fine Cloaths; besides, Sir, *says she*, most of the Cloaths I have were given me in the laſt Place I had, when I went away from my Miſtress.

Upon the whole of the Discourse, *Amy* got out of him, what Condition he was in and how he liv'd, upon her Promise to him, that if ever she came to *England*, and should see her old Miſtress, she should not let her know that he was alive: *Alas*,! sir *says Amy*, I may never come to see *England* again, as long as I live; and if I shou'd, it wou'd be ten Thousand to One, whether I shall see my old Miſtress; for how shou'd I know which Way to look for her? or what Part of *England* she may be in; not I, *says she*, I don't so much as know how to enquire for her; and if I shou'd, *says Amy*, ever be so happy as to see her, I would not do her so much Mischief as to tell her where you were, Sir, unless she was in a Condition to help herself and you too: This farther deluded him, and made him entirely open in his conversing with her: As to his own Circumſtances, he told her, she saw him in the higheſt Preferment he had arriv'd to, or was ever like to arrive to; for having no Friends or Acquaintances in *France*, and which was worse, *no Money*, he never expeĉted to rise; that he could have been made a Lieutenant to a Troop of Light-Horse but the Week before, by the Favour of an Officer in the *Gensd'arms* who was his Friend, but that he muſt have found 8000 Livres to have paid for it, to the Gentleman who possess'd it, and had Leave given him to sell: *But where could I get* 8000 *Livres*, says he, *that have never been Maſter of* 500 *Livres Ready-Money*, at a time, *since I came into* France?

O dear! Sir, *says Amy*, I am very sorry to hear you say so; I fancy if you once got up to some Preferment, you would think of my old Miſtress again, and do something for her; poor lady, *says Amy*, she wants it, to be sure, and then she falls a-crying again; 'tis a sad thing indeed, *says she*, that you should be so hard put to it for Money, when you had got a Friend to recommend you, and shou'd lose it for want of Money; ay, so it was, *Amy*, indeed, *says he*; but what can a Stranger do, that has neither Money nor Friends! Here *Amy* puts in again on my Account; well, *says she*, my poor Mistress has had the Loss, though she knows nothing of it; O dear! how happy it would have been, to be sure, Sir, you wou'd have helped her all you cou'd; *Ay*, says he, *Amy, so I wou'd, with all my Heart*, and even as I am, *I wou'd send her some Relief, if I thought she wanted it; only, that then letting her know I was alive, might do her some Prejudice, in case of her settling, or marrying any-body*.

Alas! *says Amy*. Marry! who will marry her in the poor Condition she is in? And so their Discourse ended for that time.

All this was meer Talk on both Sides, and Words of Course; for on further Enquiry *Amy* found, that he had no such offer of a Lieutenant's Commission, or anything like it; and that he rambled in his Discourse from one thing to another: But of that in its Place.

You may be sure, that this Discourse as *Amy* at first related it, was moving, to the last Degree, upon me; and I was once going to have sent him the 8000 Livres, to purchase the Commission he had spoken of; but as I knew his Character better than any-body, I was willing to search a little further into it; and so I sent *Amy* to enquire of some other of the Troop, to see what Character he had, and whether there was any thing in the story of a Lieutenant's Commission or no.

But *Amy* soon came to a better Understanding of him; for she presently learnt that he had a most scoundrel Character; that there was nothing of Weight in anything he said; but that he was, in short, a meer Sharper; one that would ſtick at nothing to get Money, and that there was no depending on anything he said; and that, more especially, about the Lieutenant's Commission, she underſtood, that there was nothing at-all in it; but they told her, how he had often made use of *that Sham* to borrow Money, and move Gentlemen to pity him and lend him Money in hopes to get him Preferment; that he had reported that he had a Wife, and five Children, in *England*, whom he maintain'd out of his Pay; and by these Shifts had run into Debt in several Places; and upon several Complaints for such things, he had been threatened to be turned out of the *Gensd'arms*; and that, in short, he was not to be believ'd in any thing he said, or truſted on any Account.

Upon this Information *Amy* began to cool in her further meddling with him; and told me it was not safe for me to attempt doing him any Good, unless I resolv'd to put him upon Suspicions and Enquiries, which might be to my Ruin, in the Condition I was now in.

I was soon confirm'd in this Part of his Character; for the next time that *Amy* came to talk with him, he discover'd himself more effectually; for while she had put him in Hopes of procuring One to advance the Money for the Lieutenant's Commission for him, upon easie Conditions, he by Degrees, dropped the Discourse, then pretended it was too late, and that he could not get it; and then descended to ask poor *Amy* to lend him 500 Piſtoles.

Amy pretended Poverty; that her Circumſtances were but mean; and that she cou'd not raise such a Sum; and this she did, to try him to the utmoſt; he descended to 300, then to 100, then to 50, and then to a Piſtole, which

she lent him; and he, never intending to pay it, play'd out
of her Sight, as much as he cou'd; And thus being satisfied that he was the same worthless Thing he had ever
been, I threw off all Thoughts of him; whereas had he
been a Man of any Sence and of any Principle of Honour,
I had it in my Thoughts to retire to *England* again, send
for him over, and have liv'd honeſtly with him: But as a
Fool is the worſt of Husbands to do a Woman Good, so a
Fool is the worſt Husband a Woman can do Good to: I
wou'd willingly have done him Good, but he was not
qualified to receive it or make the beſt Use of it; Had I
sent him ten Thousand Crowns inſtead of eight Thousand
Livres, and sent it with the express Condition, that he
should immediately have bought himself the Commission he talk'd of, with Part of the Money, and have sent
some of it to relieve the Necessities of his poor miserable
Wife at *London*, and to prevent his Children to be kept by
the Parish, it was evident he wou'd have been ſtill but a
private Trooper, and his Wife and Children should ſtill
have ſtarv'd at *London* or been kept of meer Charity, as,
for aught he knew, they then were.

Seeing therefore no Remedy, I was oblig'd to withdraw my Hand from him, that had been my firſt Deſtroy-
er, and reserve the Assiſtance that I intended to have giv-
en him, for another more desirable Opportunity; all that
I had now to do was to keep myself out of his Sight, which
was not very difficult for me to do, considering in what
ſtation he liv'd.

Amy and I had several Consultations then, upon the
main Queſtion, namely, how to be sure never to chop upon him again, by Chance and so be surpriz'd into a Discovery; which would have been a fatal Discovery indeed:
Amy propos'd that we shou'd always take care to know

where the *Gensd'arms* were quarter'd, and thereby effectually avoid them; and this was one Way.

But this was not so as to be fully to my Satisfaction; no ordinary Way of enquiring where the *Gensd'arms* were quarter'd were sufficient to me; but I found out a Fellow, who was compleatly qualified for the Work of a Spy (for *France* has Plenty of Such People), this Man I employ'd to be a constant and particular Attendant upon his Person and Motions, and he was especially employ'd and ordered to haunt him *as a Ghost*, that he should scarce let him be ever out of his Sight; he performed this to a Nicety, and fail'd not to give me a perfect Journal of all his Motions, from Day to Day; and, whether for his Pleasures, or his Business, was always at his heels.

This was somewhat expensive, and such a Fellow merited to be well paid; but he did his Business so exquisitely punctual, that this poor Man scarce went out of the House, without my knowing the Way he went, the Company he kept, when he went Abroad, and when he stay'd at Home.

By this extraordinary Conduct I made myself safe, and so went out in publick or stay'd at-home, as I found he was, or was not in a Possibility of being at *Paris*, at *Versailles*, or any Place I had Occasion to be at: This, tho' it was very chargeable, yet as I found it absolutely necessary, so I took no Thought about the Expence of it; for I knew I could not purchase my Safety too dear.

By this Management I found an Opportunity to see what a most insignificant, unthinking Life, the poor indolent Wretch, who by his unactive Temper had at first been my Ruin, now liv'd; how he only rose in the Morning, to go to-bed at Night; that saving the necessary Motion of the Troops, which he was oblig'd to attend, he was a mere motionless Animal, of no Consequence in the World; that he seem'd to be one who, tho' he was indeed alive, had no manner of Business in Life, but to ſtay to be call'd out of it; he neither kept any Company, minded any Sport, play'd at any Game, or indeed, did any thing of moment; but, *in short*, saunter'd about, like one, that it was not two Livres' Value whether he was dead or alive; that when he was gone, would leave no Remembrance behind him that ever he was here; that if he ever did any-thing in the World to be talk'd of, it was, only to get five Beggers, and ſtarve his Wife: The Journal of his Life, which I had conſtantly sent me every Week, was the leaſt significant of anything of its Kind, that was ever seen; as it had really nothing of Earneſt in it, so it wou'd make no Jeſt, to relate it; of was not important enough, so much as to make the Reader merry withal; and for that Reason I omit it.

Yet this *Nothing-Doing Wretch* I was oblig'd to watch and guard againſt, as againſt the only thing that was cap-able of doing me Hurt in the World, I was to shun him, as we would shun a Speƈtre, or even the Devil, if he was aƈtually in our Way; and it coſt me after the Rate of 1 50 Livres a Month, and very cheap too, to have this Creature conſtantly kept in View; *that is to say*, my Spy undertook, never to let him be out of his Sight an Hour, but so as that he cou'd give an Account of him; which was much the easier to be done, considering his Way of Living; for he was sure, that for whole Weeks together, he wou'd be ten hours of the Day, half asleep on a Bench at the Tavern-Door where he quarter'd, or drunk within the House.

Tho' this wicked life he led, sometimes mov'd me to pity him, and to wonder how so well-bred, Gentlemanly a Man as he once was, could degenerate into such a useless thing, as he now appear'd; yet, at the same time, it gave me most contemptible Thoughts of him, and made me often say, I was a Warning for all the Ladies of *Europe*, against marrying of F o o l s; A Man of Sence falls in the World, and gets-up again, and a Woman has some Chance for herself; but with a F o o l ! once fall, and ever undone; once in the Ditch, and die in the Ditch; once poor, and sure to starve.

But 'tis time to have done with him; once I had nothing to hope for, but to see him again; now my only Felicity was, if possible, never to see him, and above all to keep him from seeing me; which, as above, I took effectual Care of.

I was now return'd to *Paris*. My little *Son of Honour*, as I call'd him, was left at ———, where my last Country Seat then was, and I came to *Paris* at the Prince's Request; thither he came to me as soon as I arriv'd, and told me, he came to give me Joy of my Return, and to make his Acknowledgments, for that I had given him a S o n : I thought indeed, he had been going to give me a Present, and so he did the next Day, but in what he said then, he only jested with me: He gave me his Company all the evening, Supp'd with me about Midnight, and did me the Honour, as I then call'd it, to lodge me in his Arms all the Night, telling me, in jest, that the best Thanks for a Son born was giving the Pledge for another.

But as I hinted, so it was. The next Morning he laid me down, on my Toilet, a purse with 300 Pistoles: I saw him lay it down, and understood what he meant, but I took no Notice of it, till I came to it (as it were) casually; then I gave a great Cry-out and fell a-scolding in my Way, for he gave me all possible Freedom of Speech on such Occasions: I told him, he was unkind; that he would never

give me an Opportunity to ask him for anything; and
that he forc'd me to Blush, by being too much oblig'd,
and the like; all which I knew was very agreeable to him;
for as he was Bountiful, bcyond Mcasurc, so he was infinitely oblig'd by my being so backward to ask any Favours; and I was even with him, for I never ask'd him for
a Farthing in my Life.

Upon this rallying him he told me I had either perfectly studied the Art of Humour, or else what was the greatest Difficulty to others, was Natural to me; adding, That
nothing cou'd be more obliging to a Man of Honour,
than not to be solliciting and craving.

I told him, nothing cou'd be craving upon him; that
he left no room for it; that I hop'd he did not give, meerly
to avoid the Trouble of being importuned; I told him, he
might depend upon it, that I should be reduc'd very low
indeed, before I offer'd to disturb him that Way.

He said, a Man of Honour ought always to know what
he ought to do; and as he did nothing but what he knew
was reasonable, he gave me Leave to be free with him, if I
wanted anything; that he had too much Value for me, to
deny me anything if I ask'd, but that it was infinitely
agreeable to him to hear me say, that what he did was to
my Satisfaction.

We strain'd Compliments thus a great while, and as
he had me in his Arms most part of the Time, so upon all
my Expressions of his Bounty to me, he put a Stop to me
with his Kisses, and wou'd admit me to go on no further.

I should in this Place mention that this Prince was not
a Subject of *France*, tho' at that time he resided at *Paris*,
and was much at Court, where, I suppose, he had or expected some considerable Employment: But I mention
it on this Account; that a few Days after this, he came to

me, and told me he was come to bring me not the most welcome News that ever I heard from him in his Life; I look'd at him, a little surpriz'd, but he return'd, Do not be uneasie; it is as unpleasant to me, as to you, but I came to consult with you about it, and see, if it cannot be made a little easie to us both.

I seem'd still more concern'd and surpriz'd; at last he said, it was, that he believed he should be oblig'd to go into *Italy*; which though otherwise it was very agreeable to him, yet his parting with me, made it a very dull thing but to think of.

I sat mute, as one Thunder-struck, for a good-while, and it presently occurr'd to me, that I was going to lose him, which indeed I cou'd but ill bear the Thoughts of; and as he told me, I turn'd pale: What's the matter? *said he, hastily*; I have surpriz'd you indeed; and stepping to the Side-board fills a Dram of Cordial-Water (which was of his own bringing) and comes to me, Be not surpriz'd, said he, I'll go nowhere without you; adding several other things so kind as nothing could exceed it.

I might, indeeed, turn pale, for I was very much surpriz'd at first, believing that this was, as it often happens in such Cases, only a Project to drop me, and break off an Amour, which he had now carried on so long; and a thousand Thoughts whirl'd about my Head in the few Moments while I was kept in suspence (for they were but a few)—I say, I was indeed surpriz'd, and might, perhaps, look pale, but I was not in any Danger of Fainting that I knew of.

However, it not a little pleas'd me to see him so concern'd and anxious about me; but I stopp'd a little, when he put the Cordial to my Mouth, and taking the Glass in my Hand, *I said*, My Lord, your Words are infinitely

more of a Cordial to me, than this Citron; for as nothing
can be a greater Affliction, than to lose you, so nothing
can be a greater Satisfaction than the Assurance, that I
shall not have that Misfortune.

He made me sit down and sat down by me, and after
saying a thousand kind things to me, he turns upon me,
with a Smile, Why, will you venture yourself to *Italy* with
me? *says he*. I stopp'd a-while and then answer'd that I
wonder'd he would ask me that Question; for I would go
any-where in the World, or all over the World, wherever
he shou'd desire me, and give me the Felicity of his Company.

Then he enter'd into a long Account of the Occasion of
his Journey, and how the King had Engaged him to go,
and some other Circumstances, which are not proper to
enter into here, it being by no means proper to say anything, that might lead the reader into the least Guess at
the Person.

But to cut short this Part of the Story, and the History
of our Journey, and stay Abroad, which would almost fill
up a Volume of itself, I say, we spent all that Evening in
cheerful Consultations about the Manner of our Travelling; the Equipage and Figure he should go in, and in
what Manner I should go: Several ways were propos'd,
but none seem'd feasible; till at last, I told him, I thought
it would be so troublesome, so expensive, and so public,
that it would be many Ways inconvenient to him; and
tho' it was a kind of Death to me, to lose him, yet that rather than so very much perplex his Affairs, I would submit to any-thing.

At the next Visit I fill'd his Head with the same Difficulties, and then at last, came over him with a Proposal,
that I would stay in *Paris*, or where else he shou'd direct,

and when I heard of his safe Arrival would come away by myself, and place myself as near him as I cou'd.

This gave him no Satisfaction at-all, nor wou'd he hear any more of it, but if I durst venture myself, as he call'd it, such a Journey, he wou'd not lose the Satisfaction of my Company; and as for the Expence, that was not to be nam'd, neither indeed was there room to name it; for I found that he travell'd at the KING's Expense, as well for himself as for all his Equipage, being upon a Piece of Secret Service of the last Importance.

But after several Debates between ourselves he came to this Resolution, *viz.* that he wou'd travel *Incognito*, and so he shou'd avoid all publick notice, either of himself, or of who went with him; and that then he shou'd not only carry me with him, but have a perfect Leisure of enjoying my agreeable Company (*as he was pleas'd to call it*) all the Way.

This was so obliging, that nothing cou'd be more; so upon this Foot, he immediately set to work to prepare things for his Journey; and by his Directions, so did I too: But now I had a terrible Difficulty upon me, and which way to get over it, I knew not; and that was, in what Manner to take care of what I had to leave behind me; I was Rich, as I have said, very Rich, and what to do with it, I knew not, nor who to leave in trust, I knew not; I had no-body but *Amy*, in the World, and to travel without *Amy*, was very uncomfortable; or to leave all I had in the World with her, and if she miscarried, be ruined at once, was still a frightful Thought; for *Amy* might die, and whose Hands things might fall into, I knew not: This gave me great Uneasiness, and I knew not what to do; for I could not mention it to the Prince, lest he should see that I was richer than he thought I was.

But the Prince made all this easie to me, for in concert-
ing Measures for our Journey, he started the thing himself, and ask'd me merrily one Evening, who I would
trust with all my Wealth in my Absence.

My Wealth, my Lord, said I, except what I owe to your
Goodness, is but small; but yet that little I have, I confess, causes some Thoughtfulness, because I have no Acquaintance in *Paris*, that I dare trust with it, nor any-
body but my Woman, to leave in the House, and how to
do without her upon the Road, I do not well know.

As to the Road, be not concerned, *says the Prince*, I'll
provide you Servants to your Mind, and as for your Woman, if you can trust her, leave her here, and I'll put you
in a Way how to secure things as well as if you were at
Home: I bow'd and told him I coul'd not be put into better hands than his own, and that therefore I would govern
all my Measures by his Directions; so we talked no more
of it that Night.

The next Day he sent me in a great iron Chest, so large,
that it was as much as six lusty Fellows could get up the
Steps into the House; and in this I put, indeed, all my
Wealth. And for *Amy's* safety he ordered a good, honest
ancient Man and his Wife to be in the House with her to
keep her Company, and a Maid-Servant and Boy, so that
there was a good Family, and *Amy* was Madam the Mistress of the House.

Things being thus secur'd, we set out *Incog.* as he
call'd it; but we had two Coaches and Six Horses; two
Chaises; and about eight Men-Servants on Horse-back
all very well Arm'd.

Never was Woman better us'd in this World, that
went upon no other Account than I did; I had three Women Servants to wait on me, one whereof was an old Ma-

dam ———, who, thoroughly underßtood her Business and manag'd everything as if she had been *Major-Domo*, so I had no Trouble; they had one Coach to themselves, and the Prince and I in the other; only that sometimes, where he knew it necessary, I went into their Coach, and one particular Gentleman of the Retinue rode with him.

I shall say no more of the Journey, than that when we came to those frightful Mountains, the *Alps*, there was no travelling in our Coaches, so he ordered a Horse-Litter, but carried by Mules, to be provided for me, and himself went on Horse-back; the Coaches went some other way back to *Lyons*; then we had Coaches hir'd at *Turin*, which met us at *Susa*, so that we were accommodated again, and went by easie Journeys afterwards, to *Rome*, where his Business, *whatever it was*, call'd him to ßtay some time; and from thence to Venice.

He was as good as his Word, indeed, for I had the Pleasure of his Company, and, in a word, engross'd his Conversation almoßt all the Way: he took Delight in showing me everything that was to be seen, and particularly, in telling me something of the Hißtory of everything he show'd me.

What valuable Pains were here thrown away upon One, whom he was sure, at laßt to abandon with Regret! How below himself, did a Man of Quality and of a thousand Accomplishments, behave in all this! 'Tis one of my Reasons for entering into this Part, which otherwise wou'd not be worth relating: Had I been a Daughter, or a Wife, of whom it might be said, that he had a jußt Concern in their Inßtruction, or Improvement, it had been an admirable Step, but all this to a Whore!—to one who he carried with him upon no Account, that could be rationally agree-

able; and none but to gratify the meanest of human Frail-
ties: This was the Wonder of it.

But such is the Power of a vicious Inclination; Whoring was, in a Word, his Darling Crime, the worst Excursion he made; for he was otherwise one of the most excel-
lent Persons in the World; no Passions, no furious Excursions, no ostentatious Pride, the most humble, courteous, affable Person in the World; not an Oath, not an
indecent Word or the least Blemish in Behaviour, was to
be seen in all his Conversation, except as before excepted;
and it has given me Occasion for many dark Reflections
since, to look back and think, that I should be the Snare
of such a Person's Life, that I should influence him to so
much Wickedness; and that I should be the instrument
in the Hand of the Devil to do him so much Prejudice.

We were near two years upon this *Grand Tour*, as it
may be call'd, during most of which I resided at *Rome*,
or at *Venice*, having only been twice at *Florence*, and once
at *Naples*: I made some very diverting and useful Obser-
vations in all these Places, and particularly of the Conduct of the Ladies; for I had Opportunity to converse
very much among them, by the help of the old Witch,
that travell'd with us; she had been at *Naples*, and at *Venice*, and had lived in the former, several Years, where, as I
found, she had liv'd but a loose Life, as indeed the Women of *Naples* generally do; and, in short, I found she
was fully acquainted with all the intriguing Arts of that
Part of the World.

Here my lord bought me a little Female *Turkish* Slave,
who, being Taken at Sea by a *Malthese* Man of War, was
brought in there; and of her I learnt the *Turkish* Language, their Way of Dressing, and Dancing, and some
Turkish, or rather *Moorish*, Songs, of which I made Use,

to my Advantage on an extraordinary Occasion, some Years after, as you shall hear in its Place. I need not say I learnt *Italian* too, for I got pretty well Miſtress of that, before I had been there a Year, and as I had Leisure enough, and lov'd the Language, I read all the *Italian* Books I cou'd come at.

I began to be so in Love with *Italy*, especially with *Naples* and *Venice*, that I cou'd have been very well satisfied to have sent for *Amy*, and have taken up my residence there for Life.

As to *Rome*, I did not like it at-all : The Swarms of Ecclesiaſtics of all Kinds, on one side, and the scoundrelly Rabbles of the Common People, on the other, make *Rome* the unpleasanteſt Place in the World, to live in ; the innumerable Number of Valets, Lackeys, and other Servants, is such, that they us'd to say that there are very few of the Common People in *Rome*, but what have been Footmen, or Porters or Grooms to Cardinals, or Foreign Ambassadors : in a Word, they have an Air of sharping, and cozening, quarrelling and scolding, upon their general Behaviour ; and when I was there, the footmen made such a Broil between two Great Families in *Rome*, about which of their Coaches (the Ladies being in the Coaches on either side) shou'd give way to t'other ; that there was above thirty People wounded on both Sides, five or six kill'd outright ; and both the Ladies frighted almoſt to Death.

But I have no Mind to write the Hiſtory of my Travels on this side of the World, at leaſt, not now ; it would be too full of Variety.

I muſt not, however, omit that the Prince continued in all this journey, the moſt kind, obliging Person to me in the World, and so conſtant, that tho' we were in a Country, where 'tis well known all manner of Liberties are

taken, I am yet well assur'd, he neither took the Liberty
he knew he might have, nor so much as desir'd it.

I have often thought of this Noble Person on that Account; had he been but half so true, so faithful and conſtant to the Beſt Lady in the World, I mean his Princess;
how glorious a virtue had it been in him? and how free
had he been from those juſt Reflections which touch'd
him, in her behalf, when it was too late.

We had some very agreeable Conversations upon this
Subject, and once he told me, with a kind of more than
ordinary Concern upon his thoughts, that he was greatly
beholden to me for taking this hazardous and difficult
journey; for that I had kept him Honeſt; I look'd up in
his Face, and colour'd as red as Fire: Well, well, *says he*,
do not let that surprize you; I do say, you have kept me
Honeſt: My Lord, *said I*, 'tis not for me to explain your
Words, but I wish I cou'd turn 'em my own way; I hope,
says I, and believe we are both as Honeſt as we can be, in
our Circumſtances; ay, ay, *says he*, and honeſter than I
doubt I shou'd have been, if you had not been with me; I
cannot say but if you had not been here, I should have
wander'd among the gay World here, in *Naples*, and in
Venice too, for 'tis not such a Crime here, as 'tis in other
Places; but I proteſt, *says he*, I have not touch'd a Woman
in *Italy*, but yourself; and more than that, I have not so
much as had any Desire to it; so that, I say, you have kept
me Honeſt.

I was silent, and was glad that he interrupted me, or
kept me from speaking, with kissing me, for really I knew
not what to say: I was once going to say that if his Lady,
the Princess, had been with him, she wou'd, doubtless,
have had the same Influence upon his Virtue, with infinitely more Advantage to him; but I consider'd this might

give him Offence; and, besides, such things might have been dangerous to the Circumstances I stood in, so it passed off: But I must confess, I saw that he was quite another Man, as to Women, than I understood he had always been before; and it was a particular Satisfaction to me, that I was thereby convinc'd that what he said was true, and that he was, as I may say, *all my Own*.

I was with-Child again in this Journey, and Lay-in at *Venice*, but was not so happy as before; I brought him another Son, and a very fine Boy it was, but it liv'd not above two Months; nor, after the first Touches of Affection (which are usual, I believe, to all Mothers) were over, was I sorry the Child did not live, the necessary Difficulties attending it in our travelling being consider'd.

After these several Perambulations, my Lord told me, his Business began to close, and we would think of returning to *France*, which I was very glad of, but principally on Account of my Treasure I had there, which, as you have heard, was very considerable: It is true, I had Letters very frequently from my Maid *Amy*, with Accounts, that everything was very safe, and that was very much to my Satisfaction: However, as the Prince's Negotiations were at an End, and he was oblig'd to return, I was very glad to go; so we return'd from *Venice* to *Turin*; and on the Way, I saw the famous City of *Milan*; from *Turin*, we went over the Mountains again, as before, and our Coaches met us at *Pont-à-Voisin*, between *Chamberry* and *Lyons*; and so, by easie Journeys, we arriv'd safely at *Paris*, having been absent about two Years, wanting about eleven Days, as above.

I found the little Family we left, just as we left them; and *Amy* cry'd for Joy, when she saw me, and I almost did the same.

The Prince took his Leave of me the Night before; for as he told me, he knew he shou'd be met upon the Road by several Persons of Quality, and perhaps, by the Princess herself; so we lay at two different inns that Night, left some shou'd come quite to the Place, as indeed it happen'd.

After this, I saw him not, for above twenty Days, being taken-up in his Family, and also with Business; but he sent me his Gentleman, to tell me the Reason of it, and bid me not be uneasie; and that satisfied me effectually.

In all this Affluence of my good Fortune, I did not forget that I had been Rich and Poor once already, alternately; and that I ought to know, that the Circumstances I was now in, were not to be expected to last always; that I had one Child, and expected another; and if I bred often, wou'd something impair me in the Great Article that supported my Interest, I mean, what he call'd Beauty; that as that declin'd I might expect the Fire wou'd abate, and the warmth with which I was now caress'd, would cool, and in time, like the other Mistresses of Great Men, I might be dropt again; and that, therefore, it was my Business to take Care that I shou'd fall as softly as I cou'd.

I say, I did not forget, therefore, to make as good Provision for myself, as if I had had nothing to have subsisted on, but what I now gain'd, whereas I had not less than ten Thousand Pounds, as I said above, which I had amass'd, or secur'd rather, out of the Ruins of my faithful Friend, the Jeweller; and which, he little thinking of what was so near him when he went out, told me, tho' in a kind of a Jest, was all my own, if he was knock'd o' th' Head, and which, upon that Title, I took Care to preserve.

My greatest Difficulty now, was how to secure my Wealth, and to keep what I had got; for I had greatly added to this Wealth, by the generous Bounty of the Prince ———, and the more, by the private retir'd Manner of Living, which he rather desir'd for Privacy, than Parsimony; for he supply'd me for a more magnificent Way of Life than I desir'd, if it had been proper.

I shall cut short the History of this prosperous Wickedness, with telling you I brought him a third Son, within little more than eleven Months after our Return from *Italy*; that now I liv'd a little more openly, and went by a particular Name which he gave me Abroad, but which I must omit, *viz.* the Countess de ———, and had Coaches, and Servants, suitable to the Quality he had given me the Appearance of; and which is more than usually happens in such Cases, this held eight Years from the Beginning, during which Time, as I had been very faithful to him, so, I must say, as above, that I believe he was so separated to me, that whereas he usually had two or three Women, which he kept privately, he had not in all that Time meddled with any of them, but that I had so perfectly engross'd him, that he dropt them all; not perhaps that he sav'd much by it, for I was a very chargeable Mistress to him, that I must acknowledge; but it was all owing to his particular Affection to me, not to my Extravagance; for, as I said, he never gave me leave to ask him for any thing, but pour'd in his Favours and Presents faster than I expected, and so fast as I could not have the Assurance to make the least Mention of desiring more.

Nor do I speak this of my own Guess, I mean about his Constancy to me and his quitting all other Women, but the old *Harradan*, as I may call her, who he made the Guide of our Travelling, and who was a strange old Creature, told me a Thousand Stories of his gallantry, as she call'd it, and how, as he had no less than three Miſtresses at one time, and, as I found, all of her procuring, he had of a sudden, dropt them all, and that he was entirely loſt to both her and them; that they did believe he had fallen into some new Hands, but she could never hear who, or where, till he sent for her to go this Journey; and then the old Hag complimented me upon his Choice, That she did not wonder I had so engross'd him; so much Beauty, *&c.* and there she ſtopt.

Upon the whole, I found by her, what was, you may be sure, to my particular Satisfaction, *viz.* that, as above, I had him all my own.

But the higheſt Tide has its Ebb; and in all things of this Kind, there is a Reflux which sometimes also is more impetuously violent than the firſt Aggression: My Prince was a Man of vaſt Fortune, tho' no Sovereign, and therefore there was no Probability that the Expence of keeping a Miſtress could be injurious to him, as to his Eſtate; he had also several Employments, both out of *France*, as well as in it; for, as above, I say, he was not a Subject of *France*, tho' he liv'd in that Court: He had a Princess, a Wife, with whom he had liv'd several Years, and a Woman (*so the Voice of Fame reported*) the moſt valuable of her Sex; of Birth equal to him, if not superior, and of Fortune proportionable; but in Beauty, Wit, and a thousand good Qualities, superior not to moſt Women, but even to all her Sex; and as to her Virtue, the Character, which was moſt juſtly her due, was that of, not only the beſt of Princesses, but even the beſt of Women.

They liv'd in the utmoſt Harmony, as with such a Princess it was impossible to be otherwise; but yet the Princess was not insensible that her Lord had his *Foibles*; that he did make some Excursions; and particularly, that

he had one Favourite Miſtress which sometimes engross'd him more than she (the Princess) cou'd wish, or
be easily satisfied with: However, she was so good, so
generous, so truly kind a Wife, that she never gave him
any Uneasiness on this Account; except so much as muſt
arise from his Sence of her bearing the Affront of it with
such Patience, and such a profound Reſpect for him, as
was in itself enough to have reform'd him, and did sometimes shock his generous Mind, so as to keep him at
Home, as I may call it, a great-while together; and it was
not long before I not only perceiv'd it by his Absence, but
really got a Knowledge of the Reason of it, and once or
twice he even acknowledg'd it to me.

It was a Point that lay not in me to manage; I made a
kind of Motion, once or twice, to him to leave me and
keep himself to her, as he ought by the Laws and Rites of
Matrimony to do, and argued the Generosity of the Princess to him, to persuade him; but I was a Hypocrite, for
had I prevailed with him really to be honeſt, I had loſt
him, which I could not bear the Thoughts of; and he
might easily see I was not in earneſt; one time in particular, when I took upon me to talk at this rate, I found when
I argued so much for the Virtue and Honour, the Birth,
and above all the generous Usage he found in the Person
of the Princess, with reſpect to his private Amours, and
how it should prevail upon him, *&c.*—I found it began
to affect him, and he return'd, *And do you indeed,* says he,
*persuade me to leave you? Would you have me think you sin-
cere?* I look'd up in his Face, smiling, *Not for any other
Favourite,* my Lord, *said I, that wou'd break my Heart; but
for Madam, the Princess!* said I, and then I could say no
more, Tears follow'd, and I sat silent a-while: Well, *said
he,* if ever I do leave you it shall be on the Virtuous Ac-

count; it shall be for the Princess, I assure you it shall be for no other Woman; *That's enough, my Lord*, said I, *There I ought to submit; and while I am assur'd it shall be for no other Mistress, I promise your Highness, I will not repine; or that, if I do, it shall be a silent Grief, it shall not interrupt your Felicity.*

All this while I said I knew not what, and said what I was no more able to do, than he was able to leave me; which, at that time, he own'd he could not do, no, not for the Princess herself.

But another Turn of Affairs determin'd this Matter; for the Princess was taken very ill, and in the Opinion of all her Physicians, very dangerously so; in her Sickness she desir'd to speak with her Lord and to take her Leave of him: At this grievous Parting, she said so many passionate kind Things to him; lamented that she had left him no Children (she had had three, but they were dead); hinted to him, that it was one of the chief things which gave her Satisfaction in Death, as to this World, that she should leave him room to have Heirs to his Family, by some Princess that should supply her Place; with all Humility, but with a Christian Earnestness, recommended to him to do Justice to such Princess, whoever it should be, from whom, *to be sure*, he would expect Justice; that is to say, to keep to her singly, according to the solemnest Part of the Marriage-Covenant ; humbly ask'd His Highness's Pardon, if she had any way offended him; and appealing to Heaven before whose Tribunal she was to appear, that she had never violated her Honour, or her Duty to him; and praying to Jesus, and the Blessed Virgin, for his Highness; and thus, with the most moving and most passionate Expressions of her Affection to him, took her last Leave of him, and died the next Day.

This Discourse from a Princess so valuable in herself, and so dear to him, and the Loss of her following so immediately after, made such deep impressions on him, that he look'd back with Detestation upon the former Part of his Life; grew melancholly and reserv'd; chang'd his Society, and much of the general Conduct of his Life; resolved on a Life regulated most strictly by the Rules of Virtue and Piety; and, in a word, was quite another Man.

The first Part of his Reformation, was a Storm upon me; for about ten Days after the Princess's Funeral, he sent a Message to me by his Gentleman, intimating, tho' in very civil Terms, and with a short Preamble or Introduction, that he desir'd I would not take it ill that he was oblig'd to let me know, that *he could see me no more*: His Gentleman told me a long Story of the new Regulation of Life his Lord had taken up, and that he had been so afflicted for the Loss of his Princess, that he thought it would either shorten his Life, or he would retire into some Religious House, to end his Days in Solitude.

I need not direct any body to suppose how I receiv'd this News; I was indeed exceedingly surpriz'd at it, and had much a-do to support myself, when the first Part of it was deliver'd; tho' the Gentleman deliver'd his Errand with great Respect, and with all the Regard to me, that he was able, and with a great deal of Ceremony, also telling me how much he was concern'd to bring me such a Message.

But when I heard the Particulars of the Story at large, and especially, that of the Lady's Discourse to the Prince a little before her Death, I was fully satisfied; I knew very well he had done nothing but what any Man must do that had a true Sence upon him of the Justice of the Princess's Discourse to him, and of the Necessity there was of his

altering his Course of Life, if he intended to be either a
Chriſtian, or an honeſt Man: I say, when I heard this, I
was perfeƈtly easie. I confess it was a Circumſtance that it
might be reasonably expeƈted shou'd have wrought something also upon me: I that had so much to refleƈt upon
more than the Prince; that had now no more Temptation
of Poverty, or of the powerful Motive, which *Amy* us'd
with me, namely, *Comply and Live; deny and ſtarve*; I say,
I that had no Poverty to introduce Vice, but was grown
not only well supply'd but Rich, and not only Rich, but
was very Rich; in a word, richer than I knew how to think
of; for the Truth of it was, that thinking of it sometimes,
almoſt distraƈted me, for want of knowing how to dispose of it, and for fear of losing it all again by some Cheat
or Trick, not knowing any body that I could commit the
Truſt of it to.

Besides, I should add at the Close of this Affair, that
the Prince did not, as I may say, turn me off rudely, and
with Disguſt, but with all the Decency and Goodness pe-
culiar to himself, and that could consiſt with a Man reform'd and ſtruck with the Sence of his having abus'd so
good a Lady as his late Princess had been; nor did he send
me away empty, but did every thing like himself; and in
particular order'd his Gentleman to pay the Rent of the
House, and all the Expence of his two Sons; and to tell me
how they were taken Care of, and where; and also, that I
might, at all times, inspeƈt the Usage they had, and if I
dislik'd anything it should be reƈtified. And having thus
finish'd every thing, he retired into *Lorrain*, or somewhere
that Way, where he had an Eſtate, and I never heard of
him more, I mean, not as a Miſtress.

Now I was at Liberty to go to any Part of the World,
and take Care of my Money myself; The firſt thing

that I resolv'd to do was to go directly to *England,* for there I thought, being among my Countryfolks, (for I esteemed myself an *English-Woman,* tho' I was born in *France,*) but there, I say, I thought I cou'd better manage things, than in *France,* at least, that I would be in less Danger of being circumvented and deceiv'd; but how to get away with such a Treasure as I had with me, was a difficult Point, and what I was greatly at a Loss about.

There was a *Dutch* Merchant in *Paris,* that was a Person of great Reputation for a Man of Substance, and of Honesty, but I had no manner of Acquaintance with him, nor did I know how to get acquainted with him, so as to discover my Circumstances to him; but at last I employ'd my Maid *Amy* such I must be allow'd to call her, (notwithstanding what has been said of her) because she was in the Place of a Maid Servant; I say, I employ'd my Maid *Amy* to go to him, and she got a Recommendation to him from somebody else, I knew not who; so that she got access to him well enough.

But now was my Case as bad as before; for when I came to him what cou'd I do? I had Money and Jewels, to a vast Value, and I might leave all those with him; that I might indeed, do, and so I might with several other Merchants in *Paris,* who wou'd give me Bills for it payable at *London,* but then I ran a Hazard of my Money; and I had no-body at *London* to send the Bills to, and so to stay till I had an Account that they were accepted; for I had not one Friend in *London,* that I could have recourse to, so that indeed I knew not what to do.

In this Case I had no Remedy, but that I must trust somebody; so I sent *Amy* to this *Dutch* Merchant, as I said above; he was a little surpriz'd when *Amy* came to him, and talk'd to him of remitting a Sum of about 12,000

Pistoles to *England*, and began to think she came to put some Cheat upon him; but when he found that *Amy* was but a Servant, and that I came to him myself, the case was alter'd presently.

When I came to him myself, I presently saw such a plainness in his Dealing, and such Honesty in his Countenance, that I made no Scruple to tell him my whole Story, *viz.* That I was a Widow; that I had some Jewels to dispose of, and also some Money which I had a-mind to send to *England*, and to follow there myself; but being but a Woman, and having no Correspondence in *London*, or anywhere else, I knew not what to do, or how to secure my Effects.

He dealt very candidly with me, but advis'd me, when he knew my Case, so particularly, to take Bills upon *Amsterdam*, and to go that Way to *England*; for that I might lodge my Treasure in the Bank there, in the most secure Manner in the World; and that there he cou'd recommend me to a Man who perfectly understood Jewels, and would deal faithfully with me in the disposing them.

I thank'd him; but scrupled very much the travelling so far in a strange Country, and especially with such a Treasure about me; that whether known or conceal'd, I did not know how to venture with it: Then he told me, he wou'd try to dispose of them there, that is, at *Paris*, and convert them into Money, and so get me Bills for the whole; and in a few Days he brought a *Jew* to me, who pretended to buy the Jewels.

As soon as the *Jew* saw the Jewels, I saw my Folly; and it was ten Thousand to one but I had been ruin'd and perhaps, put to Death in as cruel a Manner as possible; and I was put in such a Fright by it, that I was once upon the point of flying for my Life, and leaving the Jewels and

Money too, in the Hands of the *Dutchman*, without any Bills, or any thing else; The Case was thus :

As soon as the *Jew* saw the Jewels, he falls a-jabbering in *Dutch*, or *Portugeuse*, to the Merchant, and I could presently perceive that they were in some great Surprize, both of them; the *Jew* held up his Hands, look'd at me with some Horror, then talk'd *Dutch* again, and put himself into a thousand Shapes, twisting his Body, and wringing up his Face this way, and that Way, in his Discourse, stamping with his Feet, and throwing abroad his Hands, as if he was not in a Rage only, but in a meer Fury; then he wou'd turn, and give a Look at me, like the Devil; I thought I never saw anything so frightful in my Life.

At length I put in a Word; Sir, *says I*, to the *Dutch* Merchant, What is all this Discourse to my Business? What is this Gentleman in all these Passions about? I wish, if he is to treat with me, he would speak, that I may understand him; or if you have Business of your own between you, that is to be done first, let me withdraw and I'll come again when you are at leisure.

No, no, madam, *says the Dutchman*, very kindly, you must not go, all our Discourse is about you, and your Jewels, and you shall hear it presently, it concerns you very much, I assure you: Concerns me, *says I*, what can it concern me so much as to put this Gentleman into such Agonies? And what makes him give me such Devil's Looks as he does? Why, he looks as if he would devour me.

The *Jew* understood me presently, continuing in a kind of Rage and speaking in *French*, Yes, madam, it does concern you much, very much, very much, repeating the Words, shaking his Head, and then turning to the *Dutchman*, Sir, *says he*, pray tell her what is the Case; no, *says the Merchant*, not yet, let us talk a little further of it by ourselves; upon which, they withdrew into another Room, where still they talk'd very high, but in a Language I did not understand: I began to be a little surpriz'd at what the *Jew* had said, you may be sure, and eager to know what he meant, and was very impatient till the *Dutch* Merchant came back, and that so impatient, that I call'd one of his Servants to let him know, I desir'd to speak with him; when he came in, I ask'd his Pardon for being so impatient, but told him I cou'd not be easie, till he had told me what the Meaning of all this was: Why Madam, *says the Dutch merchant*, in short, the meaning is, what I am surprised at too: This Man is a *Jew*, and understands Jewels perfectly well, and that was the Reason I sent for him, to dispose of them to him, for you; but as soon as he saw them he knew the Jewels very distinctly, and flying out in a Passion, as you see he did; told me in short that they were the very Parcel of Jewels which the *English* Jeweller had about him, who was robb'd going to *Versailles*, (about eight Years ago), to show them to the Prince de ———, and that it was for these very Jewels that the poor Gentleman was murther'd; and he is in all this Agony to make me ask you, how you came by them; and he says you ought to be charg'd with the Robbery and Murther, and put to the Question, to discover who were the Persons that did it, that they might be brought to Justice: While he said this the *Jew* came impudently back, into the Room, without calling, which a little surpriz'd me again.

The *Dutch* Merchant spoke pretty good *English*, and he knew that the *Jew* did not understand *English* at-all, so he told me the latter Part, when the *Jew* came into the Room, in *English*; at which I smil'd, which put the *Jew* into his mad Fit again, and shaking his Head, and making his Devil's Faces again, he seem'd to threaten me for Laughing; saying in *French*, This was an Affair I shou'd have little Reason to laugh at, and the like; at this I laugh'd again and flouted him, letting him see that I scorn'd him, and turning to the *Dutch* Merchant, *Sir,* says I, *That those Jewels were belonging to Mr. —— the English Jeweller,*naming his Name readily,*in that,* says I, *this Person is right, but that I should be question'd* how I came to have them, *is a Token of his Ignorance; which, however, he might have manag'd with a little more good Manners, till I had told him who I am; and both he, and you too, will be more easie in that Part, when I should tell you, that I am the unhappy Widow of that Mr. —— who was so barbarously murthered going to* Versailles; *and that he was not robb'd of those Jewels, but of others, Mr. —— having left those behind him, with me, lest he should be robb'd; had I, Sir, come otherwise by them, I should not have been weak enough to have expos'd them to Sale here, where the Thing was done, but have carried them further off.*

This was an agreeable Surprize to the *Dutch* Merchant, who, being an honest Man himself, believ'd everything I said, which indeed, being all really and literally true, except the Deficiency of my Marriage, I spoke with such an unconcerned Easiness, that it might plainly be seen, that I had no Guilt upon me, as the *Jew* suggested.

The *Jew* was confounded when he heard, that I was the *Jeweller's Wife*; but as I had rais'd his Passion with saying he look'd at me with a Devil's Face, he studied Mischief in his Heart, and answer'd *That should not serve my Turn;* so call'd the *Dutchman* out again, when he told him, that he resolv'd to prosecute this matter further.

There was one kind Chance in this Affair, which indeed, was my Deliverance, and that was, that the fool cou'd not reſtrain his Passion, but muſt let it fly to the *Dutch* Merchant; to whom, when they withdrew a second time, as above, he told, that he would bring a process againſt me for the Murther, and that it should coſt me dear, for using him at that rate; and *away he went*, desiring the *Dutch* Merchant to tell him when I wou'd be there again: Had he suspeᶜted, that the *Dutchman* wou'd have communicated the Particulars to me, he wou'd never have been so foolish as to have mention'd that Part to him.

But the Malice of his Thoughts anticipated him, and the *Dutch* Merchant was so good, as to give me an Account of his Design, which indeed, was wicked enough in its Nature; but to me it would have been worse, than otherwise it wou'd to another; for upon Examination I cou'd not have prov'd myself to be the Wife of the Jeweller, so the Suspicion might have been carried on with the better Face; and then I shou'd also have brought all his Relations in *England* upon me; who, finding by the Proceedings that I was not his Wife, but a Miſtress, or in *English* a *Whore*, would immediately have laid Claim to the Jewels, as I had owned them to be his.

This Thought immediately rush'd into my Head, as soon as the *Dutch* Merchant had told me, what wicked things were in the Head of that cursed *Jew*; and the Villain *(for so I muſt call him)* convinc'd the *Dutch* Merchant that he was in earneſt, by an Expression which shew'd the reſt of his Design, and that was a Plot to get the reſt of the Jewels into his Hand.

When firſt he hinted to the *Dutchman*, that the Jewels were such a Man's, meaning my Husband's, he made wonderful Explanations on account of their having been conceal'd so long; where muſt they have lain? and what was the Woman that brought them? and that she, meaning me, ought to be immediately apprehended, and put into the Hands of Juſtice; and this was the time that as I said, he made such horrid Geſtures, and look'd at me so like a Devil.

The Merchant hearing him talk at that rate, and seeing him in earneſt, said to him, Hold your Tongue a little, this is a thing of Consequence; if it be so, let you and I go into the next Room and consider of it there; and so they withdrew and left me.

Here, as before, I was uneasie and call'd him out, and having heard how it was, gave him that Answer, *that I was his Wife,* or Widow, which the malicious *Jew* said *shou'd not serve my turn*; and then it was, that the Dutchman call'd him out again; and in this time of his withdrawing, the Merchant, finding as above, that he was really in earneſt, counterfeited a little to be of his Mind, and enter'd into proposals with him for the thing itself.

In this they agreed to go to an Advocate, or Council, for Directions how to proceed, and to meet again the next Day, againſt which time the Merchant was to appoint me to come again with the Jewels, in order to sell them: *No,* says the merchant, *I will go further with her than so; I will desire her to leave the Jewels with me, to show to another Person, in order to get the better Price for them: That's right,* says the Jew, *and I'll engage she shall never be Miſtress of them again; they shall either be seiz'd by us,* says he, *in the King's Name, or she shall be glad to give them up to us, to prevent her being put to the Torture.*

The merchant said Yes to everything he offer'd, and they agreed to meet the next Morning about it, and I was to be persuaded to leave the Jewels with him, and come to them the next Day, at four o'Clock in order to make a good Bargain for them; and on these Conditions they parted; but the honest *Dutchman*, filled with Indignation at the barbarous Design, came directly to me and told me the whole Story; *And now*, Madam, says he, *you are to consider immediately what you have to do.*

I told him, if I was sure to have Justice, I would not fear all that such a Rogue cou'd do to me; but how such things were carried on in *France* I knew not, I told him the greatest Difficulty would be to prove our Marriage, for that it was done in *England*, and in a remote Part of *England* too, and which was worse, it would be hard to produce authentick Vouchers of it, because we were Married in Private: *But as to the Death of your Husband*, Madam, *what can be said to that?* said he; *nay*, said I, *what can they say to it?* In *England*, added I, if they wou'd offer such an Injury to any one, they must prove the Fact, or give just Reason for their Suspicions; that my Husband was Murther'd, that every one knows; but that he was robb'd, or of what, or how much, that none knows, no, not myself; and why was I not question'd for it then? I have liv'd in *Paris* ever since, liv'd publicly, and no Man has had yet the Impudence to suggest such a thing of me.

I am fully satisfied of that, *says the Merchant*, but as this is a Rogue, who will stick at nothing, what can we say? and who knows what he may swear? Suppose he should swear, that he knows your Husband had those particular Jewels with him the Morning when he went out, and that he shew'd them to him, to consider their Value and what Price he should ask the Prince de —— for them.

Nay, by the same Rule, *said I*, he may swear that I murther'd my Husband, if he finds it for his Turn: That's true, *said he*, and if he shou'd, I do not see what cou'd save you; but, added, I have found out his more immediate Design; his Design is to have you carried to the *Châtelette*, that the Suspicion may appear juſt; and then to get the Jewels out of your Hands, if possible, then, at laſt, to drop the Prosecution, on your consenting to quit the Jewels to him; and how you will do to avoid this, is the Queſtion which I would have you consider of.

My Misfortune, sir, *said I*, is that I have no Time to consider, and I have no Person to consider with or advise about it; I find that Innocence may be oppress'd by such an impudent Fellow as this; he that does not value a Perjury, has any Man's Life at his Mercy; but, Sir, *said I*, is the Juſtice such here, that while I may be in the Hands of the Publick, and under Prosecution, he may get hold of my Effeƈts and get my Jewels into his Hands?

I don't know, *says he*, what may be done in that Case; but if not he, if the Court of Juſtice shou'd get hold of them, I do not know but you may find it as difficult to get them out of their Hands again, and, at leaſt, it may coſt you half as much as they are worth; so I think it would be a much better Way, to prevent their coming at them at all.

But what Course can I take to do that, *says I*, now they have got Notice, that I have them? If they get me into their Hands, they will oblige me to produce them, or perhaps, sentence me to Prison till I do.

Nay, *says he*, as this Brute says too, put you to the Queſtion, that is, to the Torture, on Pretence of making you confess who were the Murtherers of your Husband.

Confess! *said I*; how can I confess what I know nothing of?

If they come to have you to the Rack, *said he*, they will make you confess you did it yourself, whether you did it or no, and then you are caſt.

The very word Rack frighted me to Death almoſt, and I had no Spirit left in me: Did it myself! *said I*; that's impossible!

No, Madam, *says he*, 'tis far from impossible; the moſt innocent People in the World have been forc'd to confess themselves Guilty of what they never heard of, much less, had any Hand in.

What then muſt I do? *said I*; what wou'd you advise me to?

Why, *says he*, I wou'd advise you to be gone; you intended to go away in four or five Days; and you may as well go in two Days; and if you can do so, I shall manage it so that he shall not suspeƈt your being gone, for several Days after. Then he told me, how the Rogue wou'd have me order'd to bring the Jewels the next Day for Sale; and that then he wou'd have me apprehended; how he had made the *Jew* believe he wou'd join with him in his Design; and that he (the Merchant) wou'd get the Jewels into his Hands: Now, *says the Merchant*, I shall give you Bills for the Money you desir'd, immediately, and such as shall not fail of being paid; take your jewels with you, and go this very evening to *St. Germain-en-Lay*; I'll send a Man thither with you, and from thence, he shall guide you to-morrow to *Roan*, where there lies a Ship of mine, juſt ready to sail for *Rotterdam*; you shall have your Passage in that Ship, on my Account, and I will send Orders for him to sail as soon as you are on Board, and a Letter to my Friend at *Rotterdam*, to Entertain and take Care of you.

This was too kind an Offer for me, as things ſtood, not to be accepted and be thankful for; and as to going away, I had prepar'd every thing for parting; so that I had little to do, but to go back, take two or three Boxes and Bundles, and such things, and my Maid *Amy*, and be gone.

Then the Merchant told me the Measures he had resolv'd to take to delude the *Jew,* while I made my Escape, which were very well contriv'd indeed: FIRST, *said he,* when he comes to-Morrow, I shall tell him that I propos'd to you to leave the Jewels with me, as we agreed; but that you said, you would come and bring them in the Afternoon, so that we must stay for you till four a-Clock; but then, at that time I will show a Letter from you, as if just come in, wherein you shall excuse your not coming; for that some Company came to visit you, and prevented you; but that you desire me to take Care that the Gentleman be ready to buy your Jewels; and that you will come to Morrow at the same Hour, without fail.

When to-Morrow is come, we shall wait at the Time, but you not appearing, I shall seem most dissatisfied, and wonder what can be the Reason; and so we shall agree to go the next Day to get out a Process against you; but the next Day, in the Morning, I'll send to give him Notice, that you have been at my House, but he not being there, have made another Appointment, and that I desire to speak with him; when he comes I'll tell him you appear perfectly blind, as to your Danger; and that you appear'd much disappointed that he did not come, tho' you could not meet the Night before, and oblig'd me to have him here to-Morrow at three a-Clock; *when to-Morrow comes,* says he, *you shall send word, that you are taken so ill, that you cannot come out for that Day; but that you will not fail the next Day; and the next Day you shall neither come nor send, nor let us ever hear any more of you, for by that time you shall be in* Holland, *if you please.*

I cou'd not but approve all his Measures, seeing they were so well contriv'd and in so friendly a Manner, for my Benefit; and as he seem'd to be so very sincere, I re-

solv'd to put my Life in his Hands: Immediately I went
to my Lodgings and sent away *Amy* with such Bundles as
I had prepared for my Travelling; I also sent several Parcels of my fine Furniture to the Merchant's House, to be
laid up for me, and bringing the Key of the Lodgings
with me, I came back to his house: Here we finish'd our
Matters of Money, and I deliver'd into his Hands seven
Thousand eight Hundred Pistoles in Bills and Money; a
Copy of an Assignment on the Town-House of *Paris* for
4000 Pistoles at 3 *per Cent.* Interest, attested, and a Pro-
curation for receiving the interest half-yearly, but the
Original I kept myself.

I cou'd have trusted all I had with him, for he was perfectly honest, and had not the least View of doing me any
Wrong; indeed, after it was so apparent that he had, as it
were, sav'd my Life, or at least saved me from being expos'd and ruin'd; I say, after this, how could I doubt him
in anything?

When I came to him he had every-thing ready as I
wanted, and as he had propos'd; as to my Money, he gave
me first of all an accepted Bill, payable at *Rotterdam*, for
4000 Pistoles, and drawn from *Genoa* upon a merchant
at *Rotterdam*, payable to a Merchant at *Paris* and en-
dors'd by him to my Merchant; this he assur'd me wou'd
be punctually paid, and so it was, to a Day; the rest I had
in other Bills of Exchange drawn by himself upon other
Merchants in *Holland*: Having secured my Jewels too,
as well as I cou'd, he sent me away the same Evening in a
Friend's Coach, which he had procur'd for me, to *St.
Germains*, and the next Morning to *Roan*; he also sent a
Servant of his own, on Horseback, with me, who provided everything for me, and who carried his Orders to
the Captain of the Ship, which lay about three Miles be-

low *Roan*, in the River, and by his Directions I went immediately on Board: The third Day after I was on Board, the Ship went away, and we were out at Sea the next Day after that; And thus I took my Leave of *France*, and got clear of an ugly Business, which, had it gone on, might have ruin'd me, and sent me back as Naked to *England*, as I was a little before I left it.

And now *Amy* and I were at Leisure to look upon the Mischiefs that we had escap'd; and had I had any Religion, or any Sence of a Supreme Power managing, directing, and governing in both Causes and Events in this World, such a Case as this wou'd have given any-body room to have been very thankful to the Power who had not only put such a Treasure into my Hand, but given me such an Escape from the Ruin that threaten'd me; but I had none of those things about me; I had indeed a grateful Sence upon my Mind of the generous Friendship of my Deliverer, the *Dutch* Merchant; by whom I was so faithfully serv'd, and by whom, as far as relates to second Causes, I was preserved from Destruction.

I say, I had a grateful Sence upon my Mind of his Kindness and Faithfulness to me, and I resolv'd to show him some Testimony of it, as soon as I came to the End of my Rambles, for I was yet but in a State of Uncertainty, and sometimes that gave me a little Uneasiness too; I had Paper indeed, for my Money, and he had shew'd himself very good to me, in conveying me away, as above: But I had not seen the End of things yet; for unless the Bills were paid, I might still be a great Loser by my *Dutchman*, and he might, perhaps have contriv'd all that Affair of the *Jew*, to put me into a Fright, and get me to run away, and that as if it were to save my Life; that if the Bills should be refus'd I was cheated, with a

Witness, and the Like; but these were but Surmises, and indeed, were perfectly without Cause; for the honest Man acted as honest Men always do, with an upright and dis-interested Principle; and with a Sincerity not often to be found in the World; what Gain he made by the Exchange, was just, and was nothing but what was his Due and was in the Way of his Business; but otherwise he made no Advantage of me at-all.

When I pass'd in the ship between *Dover* and *Calais,* and saw beloved *England* once more under my View, *England*, which I counted my Native Country, being the Place I was bred up in, though not born there; a strange kind of Joy possess'd my Mind, and I had such a longing Desire to be there, that I would have given the Master of the Ship twenty Pistoles to have stood-over and set me on shore in the *Downs*; and when he told me, he could not do it, that is, that he durst not do it, if I would have given him a hundred Pistoles, I secretly wished that a Storm wou'd rise that might drive the Ship over to the Coast of *England*, whether they wou'd or not, that I might be set on Shore any-where upon *English* Ground.

This wicked Wish had not been out of my Thoughts above two or three Hours, but the Master steering away to the *North*, as was his Course to do, we lost Sight of Land on that Side and only had the *Flemish* Shore in View on our Right-hand, or, as the Seamen call it, the Star-board-Side; and then with the Loss of the Sight the wish for Landing in *England* abated; and I consider'd how foolish it was to wish myself out of the Way of my Busi-ness; that if I had been on Shore in *England*, I must go back to *Holland* on account of my Bills, which were so considerable, and I having no Correspondence there, that I cou'd not have manag'd it without going myself; But we had not been out of Sight of *England* many Hours before the Weather began to change, the Winds whistl'd and made a Noise, and the Seamen said to one-another that it wou'd blow hard at Night: It was then about two Hours before Sun-set, and we were pass'd by *Dunkirk* and I think they said we were in Sight of *Ostend*; but then the Wind grew high, and the Sea swell'd, and all things look'd terrible, especially to us, that understood nothing but just what we saw before us; in short, Night came on, and very dark it was, the Wind freshen'd and blew harder and harder, and about two hours within night it blew a terrible Storm.

I was not quite a Stranger to the Sea, having come from *Rochelle* to *England* when I was a Child, and gone from *London* by the River *Thames* to *France* afterward, as I have said: But I began to be alarm'd a little with the terrible Clamour of the Men over my Head, for I had never been in a Storm, and so had never seen the like, or heard it; and once, offering to look out at the Door of the Steerage, as they call'd it, it struck me with such Horrour, the darkness, the fierceness of the Wind, the dreadful height of the Waves, and the Hurry the *Dutch* Sailors were in, whose Language I did not understand one Word of; neither when they cursed nor when they pray'd; I say, all these things together, fill'd me with Terror; and, in short, I began to be very much frighted.

When I was come back into the Great Cabbin, there sat *Amy*, who was very Sea-sick, and I had a little before given her a Sup of Cordial-waters, to help her stomach: When *Amy* saw me come back, and sit down without speaking, for so I did, she look'd two or three times up at me, at last she came running to me, Dear Madam! *says she*, what is the Matter? What makes you look so pale?

why, you ain't well; what is the Matter? I said nothing
still, but held up my Hands two or three times. *Amy* doubled her Importunities; upon that I said no more but,
Step to the Steerage-Door, and look out, as I did; so she went
away immediately and looked too, as I had bidden her;
but the poor girl came back again in the greatest Amaze-
ment and Horrour, that ever I saw any poor Creature in,
wringing her Hands, and crying out she was undone! she
was undone! she shou'd be drown'd! they were all lost!
Thus she ran about the Cabbin like a mad thing, and as
perfectly out of her Senses, as any one in such a Case could
be suppos'd to be.

I was frighted, my self, but when I saw the Girl in such
a terrible Agony, it brought me a little to myself, and I
began to talk to her, and put her in a little Hope; I told
her, there was many a Ship in a Storm, that was not cast-
away; and I hop'd we shou'd not be drown'd; that it was
true, the Storm was very dreadful, but I did not see that
the Seamen were so much concern'd as we were; and so I
talk'd to her as well as I cou'd, tho' my heart was full
enough of it, as well as *Amy*'s, and Death began to stare
in my Face, ay, and, something else too, that is to say,
Conscience, and my Mind was very much Disturbed, but
I had nobody to comfort me.

But *Amy* being in so much worse a Condition, that is to
say, so much more terrify'd at the Storm, than I was, I had
something to do to comfort her; she was, as I have said,
like one distracted, and went raving about the Cabbin,
crying out, she was undone! undone! she shou'd be
drown'd! *and the like;* and at last, the Ship giving a Jerk,
by the Force, I suppose, of some violent Wave, it threw
poor *Amy* quite down, for she was weak enough before,
with being Sea-sick; and as it threw her forward, the poor

Girl struck her Head against the Bulk-head, as the Sea-men call it, of the Cabbin, and laid her as dead as a stone, upon the Floor, or Deck, that is to say, she was so to all Appearance.

I cry'd out for Help, but it had been all one, to have cry'd out on the top of a Mountain, where no-body had been within five Miles of me; for the Seamen were so en-gag'd and made so much Noise, that no-body heard me, or came near me; I open'd the Great-Cabbin Door and look'd into the Steerage, to cry for Help, but there, to in-crease my Fright, were two Seamen on their Knees, at Prayers, and only one Man who steer'd, and he made a groaning Noise too, which I took to be saying his Prayers, but it seems it was answering to those above, when they call'd to him to tell him which Way to steer.

Here was no Help for me, or for poor *Amy*, and there she lay so still, and in such a Condition, that I did not know whether she was dead or alive; In this Fright I went to her, and lifted her a little way up, setting her on the Deck, with her Back to the Boards of the Bulk-head, and got a little Bottle out of my Pocket, and held it to her Nose, and rubb'd her Temples, and what else I could do, but still *Amy* show'd no Signs of Life, till I felt for her Pulse, but could hardly distinguish her to be alive; how-ever, after a great while, she began to revive, and in about half an Hour she came to herself, but remember'd no-thing at first of what had happen'd to her, for a good-while more.

When she recover'd more fully, she ask'd me where she was? I told her she was in the Ship yet, but God knows how long it might be; Why, Madam, *says she*, is not the Storm over? *No, no*, says I, *Amy*; *why, Madam*, says she, *it was calm just now* (meaning when she was in the swooning Fit occasion'd by her fall). *Calm* Amy, *says I, 'tis far from calm; it may be it will be calm by-and-by, when we are all drown'd and gone to* HEAVEN.

HEAVEN! Madam, *says she,* what makes you talk so? HEAVEN! I go to HEAVEN! *No, no,* If I am drown'd, I am damn'd! *Don't you know what a wicked Creature I have been?* I have been a Whore to two Men, and have liv'd a wretched abominable Life of Vice and Wickedness for fourteen Years. O, Madam, *you know it, and* God *knows it;* and now *I am to die; to be drown'd.* O! what will become of me? I *am undone for Ever!* Ay, Madam, *for Ever! to all Eternity! O, I am loſt! I am loſt! If I am drown'd I am loſt for Ever!*

All these, you will easily suppose, muſt be so many Stabs into the very Soul of one in my own Case; it immediately occurr'd to me, *Poor* Amy! *what art thou, that I am not?* what haſt thou been that I have not been? Nay, I am guilty of my own Sin, and thine too. Then it came to my Remembrance that I had not only been the same with *Amy,* but that I had been the Devil's inſtrument to make her wicked; that I had ſtripp'd her, and proſtituted her to the very Man that I had been Naught with myself; that she had but followed me; I had been her wicked Example; and I had led her into all; and that as we had sinn'd together, now we were likely to sink together.

All this repeated itself to my Thoughts at that very Moment; and every one of *Amy*'s Cries sounded thus in my Ears: I am the wicked Cause of it all; I have been thy Ruin, *Amy;* I have brought thee to this, and now thou art to suffer for the Sin I have entic'd thee to; and if thou art loſt for ever, *what muſt I be?* what muſt be my Portion ?

It is true, this Difference was between us, that I said all these things within myself, and sigh'd and mourn'd inwardly; but *Amy*, as her Temper was more violent, spoke aloud, and cry'd and call'd out aloud like one in an Agony.

I had but small Encouragement to give her, and indeed cou'd say but very little; but I got her to compose herself a little, and not let any of the People of the Ship understand what she meant, or what she said; but even in her greatest Composure, she continued to express herself with the utmost Dread and Terror, on account of the wicked Life she had liv'd, and crying out, she should be damn'd and the like; which was very terrible to me who knew what Condition I was in myself.

Upon these serious Considerations, I was very penitent too, for my former sins, and cry'd out, *tho' softly*, two or three times, *Lord, have Mercy upon me*, to this, I added abundance of Resolutions, of what a Life I wou'd live, if it should please God to but spare my Life but this one time; how I would live but a single and a virtuous Life, and spend a great deal of what I had thus wickedly got, in Acts of Charity and doing Good.

Under these dreadful Apprehensions, I look'd back on the Life I had led, with the utmost Contempt and Abhorrence; I blush'd, and wonder'd at myself, how I cou'd act thus, how I could divest myself of Modesty and Honour, and prostitute myself for Gain; and I thought, if ever it shou'd please God to spare me this one time from Death, it would not be possible that I shou'd be the same Creature again.

Amy went further; she pray'd, she resolv'd, she vow'd to lead a new Life, if God would spare her but this time; It now began to be Day-light, for the Storm held all Night-long, and it was some Comfort to see the Light of another Day, which indeed, none of us expected; but the Sea went Mountains high, and the Noise of the Water was as frightful to us, as the Sight of the Waves; nor was any Land to be seen; nor did the Seamen know whereabout they were; at laſt, to our great Joy, they made Land, which was in *England*, and on the Coaſt of *Suffolk*; and the Ship being in the utmoſt Diſtress, they ran for the Shore, at all Hazards, and with great Difficulty, got into *Harwich*, where they were safe as to the Danger of Death; but the ship was so full of Water and so much damag'd, that if they had not laid her on Shore the same Day she wou'd have sunk before Night, according to the Opinion of the Seamen, and of the Workmen on Shore too, who were hir'd to as-siſt them in ſtopping their Leaks.

Amy was reviv'd as soon as she heard they had espy'd Land, and went out upon the Deck, but she soon came in again to me, O, *Madam*, says she, *there's the Land indeed, to be seen; it looks like a Ridge of Clouds, and may be all a Cloud, for aught I know, but if it be Land, 'tis a great Way off; and the Sea is in such a Combuſtion, we shall all perish before we can reach it; 'tis the dreadfulleſt Sight, to look at the Waves, that ever was seen; why, they are as high as Mountains, we shall certainly be all swallow'd up, for-all the Land is so near.*

I had conceiv'd some Hope, that if they saw Land we should be deliver'd; and I told her, she did not under-ſtand things of that Nature; that she might be sure, if they saw Land, they would go directly toward it, and wou'd make into some Harbour; but it was, as *Amy* said, a frightful Diſtance to it: The Land look'd like Clouds, and the Sea, went as high as Mountains so that no Hope appear'd in the seeing the Land; but we were in fear of foundring, before we cou'd reach it; this made *Amy* so desponding ſtill; but as the Wind, which blew from the *Eaſt*, or that Way, drove us furiously towards the Land;

so when about half an Hour after, I ſtept to the Steerage-Door and look'd out, I saw the Land much nearer than *Amy* represented it; so I went in and encourag'd *Amy* again, and indeed, was encourag'd myself.

In about an Hour, or something more, we see, to our infinite Satisfaction, the open Harbour of *Harwich*, and the Vessel ſtanding directly towards it, and in a few Minutes more, the Ship was in smooth Water, to our inexpressible Comfort; and thus I had, tho' againſt my Will, and contrary to my true intereſt, what I wish'd for, to be driven away to *England*, tho' it was by a ſtorm.

Nor did this Incident do either *Amy* or me much Service; for, the Danger being over, the Fears of Death vanish'd with it; ay, and our Fear of what was beyond Death also; Our Sence of the Life we had liv'd, went off, and with our return to Life our wicked Taſte of Life return'd, and we were both the same as before, if not worse: So certain is it, that the Repentance which is brought about by the meer Apprehensions of Death, wears off as those Apprehensions wear off; and Death-Bed Repentance, or Storm-Repentance, which is much the same, is seldom true.

However, I do not tell you, that this was all at once, neither; the fright we had at Sea laſted a little while afterwards, at leaſt, the Impression was not quite blown off, as soon as the Storm; especially poor *Amy*, as soon as she set her Foot on Shore, she fell flat upon the Ground, and kiss'd it, and gave God thanks for her Deliverance from the Sea; and turning to me when she got up, I hope, Madam, *says she*, you will never go upon the Sea again.

I know not what ail'd me, not I; but *Amy* was much more penitent at Sea, and much more sensible of her Deliverance when she Landed, and was safe, than I was; I was in a kind of Stupidity, I know not well what to call it; I had a mind full of Horrour in the time of the Storm, and saw Death before me, as plainly as *Amy*, but my Thoughts got no Vent as *Amy*'s did; I had a silent sullen kind of Grief, which cou'd not break out either in Words or Tears, and which was, therefore, much the worse to bear.

I had a Terror upon me for my wicked Life paſt, and firmly believ'd I was going to the Bottom, launching into Death, where I was to give an Account of all my paſt Actions; and in this State, and on that Account, I look'd back upon my Wickedness with Abhorrence, as I have said above; but I had no Sence of Repentance, from the true Motive of Repentance; I saw nothing of the Corruption of Nature, the Sin of my Life as an Offence againſt God; as a thing odious to the Holiness of His Being; as abusing his Mercy, and despising His Goodness; in short, I had no thorow effeftual Repentance; no Sight of my Sins in their proper Shape; no View of a Redeemer, or Hope in him: I had only such a Repentance as a Criminal has at the Place of Execution, who is sorry, not that he has committed the Crime, as it is a Crime, but sorry *that he is to be Hanged for it.*

It is true, *Amy*'s Repentance wore off too, as well as mine, but not so soon; however, we were both very grave for a time.

As soon as we could get a Boat from the Town, we went on Shore, and immediately went to a Public-House in the Town of *Harwich*, where we were to consider seriously, what was to be done, and whether we should go up to *London*, or ſtay till the Ship was refitted, which they said, would be Fortnight, and then go for *Holland*, as we intended, and as Business requir'd.

Reason directed that I shou'd go to *Holland*, for there I had all my Money to receive, and there I had Persons of good Reputation and Character to apply to, having Letters to them from the honest *Dutch* Merchant at *Paris*, and they might, perhaps give me a Recommendation again, to Merchants in *London*, and so I should get Acquaintance with some People of Figure, which was what I lov'd; whereas now I knew not one Creature in the whole City of *London* or any-where else, that I cou'd go and make myself known to: Upon these Considerations I resolv'd to go to *Holland*, whatever came of it.

But *Amy* cry'd and trembled and was ready to fall into Fits, when I did but mention going upon the Sea again, and begg'd of me, not to go, or, if I wou'd go, that I wou'd leave her behind, tho' I was to send her a-begging; The People in the Inn laugh'd at her, and jested with her; ask'd her if she had any Sins to confess, that she was asham'd shou'd be heard of? and that she was troubled with an evil Conscience; told her, if she came to Sea, and to be in a Storm, if she had lain with her Master, she would certainly tell her Mistress of it; and that it was a common thing, for poor Maids to confess all the Young-Men they had lain with; that there was one poor Girl that went over with her Mistress, whose Husband was a ——r in —— in the city of *London*, who confess'd in the Terror of a Storm, that she had lain with her Master, and all the Apprentices so often, and in such and such Places, and made the poor Mistress, when she return'd to *London*, fly at her Husband, and make such a Stir, as was indeed, the Ruin of the whole Family: *Amy* could bear all that well enough; for tho' she had indeed lain with her Master, it was with her Mistress's Knowledge and Consent, and, which was worse, was her Mistress's own doing; *I record it to the Reproach of my own Vice,* and to expose the Excesses of such Wickedness as they deserve to be expos'd.

I thought *Amy*'s Fear would have been over by that time the Ship would be gotten ready, but I found the Girl was rather worse and worse; and when I came to the Point, that we must go on Board, or lose the Passage, *Amy* was so terrified, that she fell into Fits, so the Ship went away without us.

But my going being absolutely necessary, as above, I was oblig'd to go in the Packet-Boat some time after, and leave *Amy* behind at *Harwich,* but with Directions to go to *London* and stay there, to receive Letters and Orders from me what to do: Now I was become, from a Lady of Pleasure, a Woman of Business, and of great Business, too, I assure you.

I got me a Servant at *Harwich,* to go over with me, who had been at *Rotterdam,* knew the Place and spoke the Language, which was a great help to me, and away I went; I had a very quick Passage and pleasant Weather, and, coming to *Rotterdam,* soon found out the Merchant to whom I was recommended, who receiv'd me with extraordinary Respect; and first he acknowledged the accepted bill for 4000 Pistoles, which he afterwards paid punctually; other Bills that I had also payable at *Amsterdam,* he procur'd to be receiv'd for me; and whereas one of the Bills for a Thousand two Hundred Crowns, was protested at *Amsterdam,* he paid it me himself, for the Honour of the Endorser, as he call'd it, which was my Friend the Merchant at *Paris.*

There I enter'd into a Negotiation, by his Means, for my Jewels, and he brought me several Jewellers, to look on them, and particularly, one to Value them, and to tell me what every Particular was worth: This was a Man who had great Skill in Jewels, but did not Trade at that time; and he was desir'd by the Gentleman that I was with, to see that I might not be impos'd upon.

All this Work took me up near half a Year, and by managing my Business thus myself, and having large Sums to do with, became as expert in it, as any She-Merchant of them all; I had credit in the Bank for a large Sum of Money, and Bills and Notes for much more.

After I had been here about three Months, my maid *Amy* writes me word, that she had receiv'd a Letter from her Friend, as she call'd him, that, *by the way*, was the Prince's Gentleman, that had been *Amy*'s extraordinary Friend indeed; for *Amy* own'd to me, he had lain with her a hundred times; that is to say, as often as he pleas'd; and perhaps, in the eight Year which that Affair lasted, it might be a great deal oftener: This was what she call'd her Friend, whom she corresponded with upon this particular Subject, and among other things sent her this particular News that my extraordinary Friend, my real Husband who rode in the *Gensd'arms*, was dead; that he was killed in a Rencounter, as they call it, or accidental Scuffle among the Troopers; and so the Jade congratulated me upon my being now a real Free-Woman; and now, Madam, *says she, at the End of her Letter*, you have nothing to do but to come hither, and set up a Coach, and a good Equipage; and if Beauty and a good Fortune won't make you a Duchess, nothing will; *but I had not fixed my Measures yet;* I had no Inclination to be a Wife again, I had had such bad Luck with my first Husband, I hated the Thoughts of it; I found that a Wife is treated with Indifference, a Mistress with a strong Passion; a Wife is look'd upon as but an Upper-Servant, a Mistress is a Sovereign; a Wife must give up all she has; have every Reserve she makes for herself, be thought hard of, and be upbraided with her very *Pin-Money*; whereas a Mistress makes the Saying true, *that what a Man has*, is hers, *and what she has*, is her own; the Wife bears a thousand Insults, and is forc'd to sit still and bear it, or part and be undone; a Mistress insulted, helps herself immediately, and takes another.

These were my wicked Arguments for Whoring, for I never set against them the Difference another way, I may say, every other way; *how that*, FIRST, A Wife appears boldly and honourably with her Husband; lives at Home and possesses his House, his Servants, his Equipages, and has a Right to them all, and to call them her own; entertains his Friends, owns his Children, and has the return of Duty and Affection from them, as they are here her own, and claims upon his Estate, by the Custom of *England*, if he dies, and leaves her a Widow.

The Whore skulks about in Lodgings; is visited in the dark, disown'd upon all Occasions, before God and Man, is maintain'd indeed, for a time, but is certainly condemn'd to be abandon'd at last, and left to the Miseries of Fate and her own just Disaster: If she has any Children, her Endeavour is to get rid of them, and not maintain them; and if she lives, she is certain to see them all hate her, and be asham'd of her; while the Vice rages, and the Man is in the Devil's Hand, *she has him*; and while she has him, she makes a *Prey of him*; but if he happen to fall Sick, if any Disaster befals him, the Cause of all lies upon her; he is sure to lay all his Misfortunes at her Door; and if once he comes to Repentance, or makes one step towards a Reformation, he begins with her; leaves her; uses her as she deserves; hates her; abhors her; *and sees her no more;* and that with this never-failing Addition, namely, That the more sincere and unfeign'd his Repentance is, the more earnestly he looks up; and the more effectually he looks in, the more his Aversion to her, increases; and he curses her from the Bottom of his Soul; nay; it must be from a kind of Excess of Charity, if he so much as wishes God may forgive her.

The opposite Circumstances of a *Wife* and *Whore*, are such, and so many, and I have since seen the Difference with such Eyes, as I could dwell upon the Subject a greatwhile, but my Business is History; I had a long Scene of Folly yet to run over; perhaps the Moral of all my Story may bring me back-again to this Part, and if it does, I shall speak of it fully.

While I continued in *Holland* I receiv'd several letters from my Friend (so I had good Reason to call him) the Merchant in *Paris*, in which he gave me a further Account of the Conduct of that Rogue the *Jew*, and how he acted after I was gone; how Impatient he was while the said Merchant kept him in suspence, expecting me to come again; and how he rag'd when he found I came no more.

It seems, after he found I did not come, he found out by his unweary'd Enquiry where I had liv'd, and that I had been kept as a Mistress, by some Great Person, but he cou'd never learn by who, except that he learnt the Colour of his Livery; in Pursuit of this Enquiry, he guess'd at the right Person, but cou'd not make it out, or offer any positive Proof of it; but he found out the Prince's Gentleman, and talk'd so saucily to him of it, that the Gentleman treated him, as the *French* call it, *au Coup de Bâton*; that is to say, Can'd him very severely, as he deserv'd; and that not satisfying him, or curing his Insolence, he was met late one Night upon the *Pont Neuf* in

Paris, by two Men, who, muffling him up in a great Cloak, carried him into a more private Place, and cut off both his Ears, telling him it was for talking impudently of his Superiors; adding that he shou'd takc Care to govern his Tongue better, and behave with more Manners, or the next time they would cut his Tongue out of his Head.

This put a Check to his Sauciness that Way; but he comes back to the Merchant, and threaten'd to begin a Process against him, for corresponding with me, and being accessory to the Murder of the Jeweller, etc.

The Merchant found by his Discourse, that he suppos'd I was protected by the said Prince *de* ———, nay, the Rogue said, he was sure I was in his Lodgings at *Versailles; for he never had so much as the least Intimation of the Way I was really gone;* but that I was there, he was certain, and certain that the Merchant was privy to it: The Merchant bade him Defiance; however, he gave him a great deal of Trouble, and put him to a great Charge, and had like to have brought him in for a Party to my Escape, in which Case he would have been oblig'd to have produc'd me, and that in the Penalty of some capital Sum of Money.

But the Merchant was too-many for him another Way; for he brought an Information against him for a Cheat, wherein, laying down the whole Fact, How he intended falsly to accuse the Widow of the Jeweller, for the supposed Murther of her Husband; that he did it purely to get the Jewels from her; and that he offer'd to bring him (*the Merchant*) in, to be *Confederate* with him, and to share the Jewels between them; proving also, his Design to get the Jewels into his Hands, and then to have dropp'd the Prosecution, upon Condition of my quitting the Jewels to him; upon this Charge he got him laid by the Heels; so he was sent to the *Concergerie,* that is to say, to *Bridewell,* and the Merchant clear'd: He got out of jayl in a little while, tho' not without the help of Money, and continued teizing the Merchant a long while; and at laſt threatening to assassinate and murther him; so the Merchant, who having buried his Wife about two Months before, was now a single Man, and not knowing what such a Villain might do, thought fit to quit *Paris*, and came away to *Holland* also.

It is moſt certain that, speaking of Originals, I was the Source and Spring of all that Trouble and Vexation to this honeſt Gentleman; and as it was afterwards in my Power to have made him full Satisfaction, and did not, I cannot say but I added Ingratitude to all the reſt of my Follies; but of that I shall give a fuller Account presently.

I was surpriz'd one Morning, when, being at the Merchant's House, whom he had recommended me to, in *Rotterdam*, and being busie in his Counting-House managing my Bills, and preparing to write a Letter to him, to *Paris*, I heard a Noise of Horses at the Door; which is not very common in a City, where every-body passes by Water; but he had, it seems, ferry'd over the *Maas* from *Wil-liamſtadt*, and so came to the very Door; and I looking towards the Door, upon hearing the Horses, saw a Gentleman alight, and come in at the Gate, I knew nothing, and expected nothing, to be sure, of the Person, but, as I say, was surpriz'd, and indeed more than ordinarily surpriz'd, when coming nearer to me, I saw it was my Merchant of *Paris*; my Benefactor; and indeed my Deliverer.

I confess, it was an agreeable Surprize to me, and I was exceeding glad to see him, who was so honourable, and so kind to me, and who indeed, had sav'd my Life: As soon as he saw me, he ran to me, took me in his Arms, and kiss'd me with a Freedom that he never offer'd to take with me before; *Dear Madam* ———, *says he, I am glad to see you safe in this Country; if you had stay'd two Days longer in* Paris, *you had been undone:* I was so glad to see him, that I could not speak a good-while, and I burst out into Tears, without speaking a Word for a Minute; but I recover'd that Disorder, and said, *The more, Sir, is my Obligation to you, that sav'd my Life;* and added, *I am glad to see you here, that I may consider how to ballance an Account, in which I am so much your Debtor.*

You and I will adjust that Matter easily, *says he*, now we are so near together; pray where do you Lodge? *says he.*

In a very honest good House, *said I*, where that Gentleman, your Friend, recommended me; pointing to the Merchant in whose House we then were.

And where you may Lodge too, Sir, *says the Gentleman,* if it suits with your Business and your other Conveniency.

With all my Heart, *says he*; then, madam, *adds he*, turning to me, I shall be near you, and have Time to tell you a Story, which will be very long, and yet many ways very pleasant to you, how troublesome that devilish Fellow, the *Jew*, has been to me, on your Account; and what a hellish Snare he had laid for you, if he could have found you.

I shall have Leisure too, Sir, *said I*, to tell you all my Adventures since that; which have not been a few, I assure you.

In short, he took up his Lodgings in the same house where I lodg'd, and the Room he lay in, open'd as he was wishing it wou'd, just opposite to my Lodging-room; so we could almost call out of Bed to one another, and I was not at all shy of him on that Score, for I believ'd him perfectly honest, and so indeed, he was; and if he had not, that Article was at present, no Part of my Concern.

It was not till two or three Days, and after his firſt
Hurries of Business were over, that we began to enter into the Hiſtory of our Affairs on every side, but when we
began, it took up all our conversation for almoſt a Fortnight: Firſt I gave him a particular Account of everything
that happen'd material upon my Voyage, and how we
were driven into *Harwich* by a very terrible Storm; how I
had left my Woman behind me, so frighted with the Danger she had been in, that she durſt not venture to set her
Foot into a Ship again any more; and that I had not come
myself, if the Bills I had of him had not been payable in
Holland, but that Money, he might see, wou'd make a
woman go anywhere.

He seem'd to laugh at all our womanish Fears upon
the Occasion of the Storm; telling me, it was nothing but
what was very ordinary in those Seas; but that they had
Harbours on every Coaſt, so near that they were seldom
in Danger of being loſt indeed; for, *says he*, if they cannot
fetch one Coaſt, they can always ſtand away for another,
and run afore it, *as he called it*, for one side or other: But
when I came to tell him what a crazy Ship it was, and how,
even when they got into *Harwich*, and into smooth Water,
they were fain to run the Ship on Shore or she wou'd
have sunk in the very harbour; and when I told him that
when I look'd out at the Cabin-Door I saw the *Dutchmen*,
one upon his Knees here, and another there, at their
Prayers, then indeed he acknowledg'd I had reason to be
alarm'd; but smiling, *he added*, But you, Madam, *says he*,
are so good a Lady, and so pious, you wou'd but have
gone to Heaven a little the sooner, the Difference had not
been much to you.

I confess, when he said this, it made all the Blood turn
in my Veins, and I thought I should have fainted; poor

Gentleman! thought I, you know little of me; what wou'd
I give to be really what you really think me to be! He perceiv'd the Disorder, but said nothing till I spoke; when,
shaking my Head, O *Sir*, said I, *Death in any Shape has
some Terror in it*, but in the frightful Figure of a Storm at
sea, and a sinking Ship, it comes with a double, a trebble,
and indeed an inexpressible Horrour; and if I were that
Saint you think me to be, which, God knows, I am not,
'tis still very dismal; I desire to die in a Calm if I can: He
said a great many good things, and very prettily order'd
his Discourse, between serious Reflection and Compliment; but I had too much Guilt to relish it as it was
meant, so I turn'd it off to something else, and talk'd of
the Necessity I had on me to come to *Holland*, but I
wish'd myself safe on Shore in *England* again.

He told me, he was glad I had such an Obligation upon me to come over into *Holland*, however, but hinted;
that he was so interested in my Wellfare, and besides,
had such further Designs upon me, that if I had not so
happily been found in *Holland*, he was resolv'd to have
gone to *England* to see me; and that it was one of the principal Reasons of his leaving *Paris*.

I told him I was extremely oblig'd to him for so far interesting himself in my Affairs; but that I had been so
far his Debtor before, that I knew not how anything
could encrease the Debt; for I owed my Life to him already, and I could not be in debt for anything more valuable than that.

He answer'd in the most obliging Manner possible,
that he wou'd put it in my Power to pay that Debt, and all
the Obligations besides, that ever he had or should be
able to lay upon me.

I began to understand him now, and to see plainly,

that he resolv'd to *make love to me*; but I would by no means seem to take the Hint, and besides I knew that he had a Wife with him in *Paris*, and I had, *juſt then, at leaſt,* no Guſt to any more intriguing; however, he surpriz'd me into a sudden Notice of the thing a little-while after, by saying something in his Discourse, that he did, *as he said,* in his Wife's Days; I ſtarted at that word. *What mean you by that, Sir?* said I; *Have you not a Wife at* Paris? No, Madam, indeed, *said he,* my Wife died the beginning of *September* laſt; which, it seems, was but a little after I came away.

We liv'd in the same house all this while; and as we lodg'd not far off of one-another, Opportunities were not wanting of as near an Acquaintance as we might desire; nor have such Opportunities the leaſt Agency in vicious Minds, to bring to pass even what they might not intend at firſt.

However, tho' he courted so much at a diſtance, yet his Pretensions were very honourable; and as I had before found him a moſt disintereſted Friend, and perfeCtly honeſt in his Dealings, even when I truſted him with all I had; so now I found him ſtriCtly virtuous; till I made him otherwise myself, even almoſt whether he wou'd or no, as you shall hear.

It was not long after our former Discourse, when he repeated what he had insinuated before, namely, that he had yet a Design to lay before me, which, if I would agree to his Proposals, wou'd more than ballance all Accounts between us: I told him I cou'd not reasonably deny him any-thing, and *except one thing, which I hop'd and believ'd he would not think of,* I should think myself very ungrateful, if I did not do everything for him that lay in my Power.

He told me what he should desire of me, wou'd be fully in my Power to grant, or else he shou'd be very unfriendly to offer it, and still, all this while he declined making the Proposal, *as he call'd it*, and so, for that time, we ended our Discourse, turning it off to other things; so that, *in short*, I began to think he might have met with some Disaster in his Business, and might have come away from *Paris* in some Discredit, or had had some Blow on his Affairs in general; And as really I had Kindness enough to have parted with a good Sum to have help'd him, and was in Gratitude, bound to have done so, *he having so effectually sav'd to me all I had*, so I resolv'd to make him the offer, the first time I had an Opportunity, which two or three Days after offer'd itself, very much to my Satisfaction.

He told me at large, *tho' on several Occasions*, the Treatment he had met with from the *Jew*, and what Expence he had put him to; how at length he had cast him, *as above*, and had recover'd good Damage of him, but that the Rogue was unable to make him any considerable Reparation; he had told me also, how the Prince de ——'s Gentleman had resented his Treatment of his Master; and how he had caus'd him to be used upon the *Pont Neuf, &c., as I have mention'd above*, which I laugh'd at most heartily.

It is pity, *said I*, that I should sit here, and make that Gentleman no Amends; if you wou'd direct me, Sir, *said I*, how to do it, I wou'd make him a handsome Present, and acknowledge the Justice he had done to me, as well as to the Prince his Master: He said he would do what I directed in it; so I told him I would send him 500 Crowns; *that's too much*, said he, *for you are but half interested in the Usage of the Jew; it was on his Master's Account he corrected*

him, not on yours: Well, however, we were oblig'd to do
nothing in it, for neither of us knew how to direct a Letter to him, or to direct any-body to him; so I told him I
wou'd leave it till I came to *England,* for that my Woman,
Amy corresponded with him, and that he had made Love
to her.

Well, but, Sir, *said I,* as in requital for his generous
Concern of me I am careful to think of him; it is but just,
that what Expense you have been oblig'd to be at, which
was all on my Account, shou'd be repaid you; and therefore, *said I,* let me see——— and there I paus'd, and began
to reckon up what I had observ'd from his own Discourse,
it had cost him in the several Disputes, and Hearings
which he had with that *Dog of a Jew,* and I cast them up
at something above 2130 Crowns; so I pull'd out some
Bills which I had upon a Merchant in *Amsterdam,* and a
particular Account in Bank, and was looking on them in
order to give them to him.

When he seeing evidently what I was going about, interrupted me with some Warmth, and told me he wou'd
have nothing of me on that Account, and desir'd I would
not pull out my Bills and Papers on that Score; that he
had not told me the Story on that Account, or with any
such View; that it had been his Misfortune first to bring
that ugly Rogue to me, which tho' it was with a good Design, yet he would punish himself with the Expence he
had been at, for his being so unlucky to me; that I cou'd
not think so hard of him, as to suppose he would take
Money of me, a *Widow,* for serving me, and doing Acts
of Kindness to me in a strange Country, and in Distress
too; but, *he said,* he would repeat what he had said before, that he kept me for a deeper reckoning, and that, as
he had told me, he would put me into a Posture to Even

all that Favour, as I call'd it, *at once,* so we shou'd talk it over another time and ballance all together.

Now I expected it wou'd come out, but still he put it off, as before, from whence I concluded, it could not be a Matter *of Love,* for that those things are not usually delay'd in such a manner, and therefore it must be a Matter of Money; upon which Thought, I broke the Silence and told him, that as he knew I had, by Obligation, more Kindness for him, than to deny any Favour to him that I could grant, and that he seem'd backward to mention his Case, I begg'd Leave of him to give me Leave to ask him, whether any-thing lay upon his Mind, with respect to his Business and Effects in the World? that if it did, he knew what I had in the World, as well as I did; and that if he wanted Money, I would let him have any Sum for his Occasion, as far as five or six thousand Pistoles, and he shou'd pay me as his own Affairs wou'd permit; and that, if he never paid me, I would assure him that I wou'd never give him any Trouble for it.

He rose up with Ceremony, and gave me Thanks, in Terms that sufficiently told me, he had been bred among People more polite, and more courteous, than is esteem'd the ordinary Usage of the *Dutch*; and after his Compliment was over, he came nearer to me, and told me, that he was oblig'd to assure me, tho' with repeated Acknowledgments of my kind Offer, that he was not in any want of Money; that he had met with no Uneasiness in any of his Affairs, not, not of any Kind whatever, except that of the Loss of his Wife, and one of his Children, which indeed, had troubled him much; but that this was no Part of what he had to offer me, and by granting which I should ballance all Obligations; but that, in short, it was that seeing Providence had (as it were for that Purpose) taken his Wife from him, I would make up the Loss to him; and with that, he held me faſt in his Arms, and kissing me, wou'd not give me leave to say No, and hardly to Breathe.

At length, having got room to speak, I told him that, as I had said before, I could deny him but one thing in the World; I was very sorry he shou'd propose *that thing only* that I cou'd not grant.

I could not but smile however, to myself that he should make so many Circles and round-about Motions to come at a Discourse which had no such rarity at the Bottom of it, if he had known all: But there was another reason why I resolv'd not to have him, when, at the same time, if he had courted me in a Manner less honeſt or virtuous, I believe I should not have denied him; but I shall come to that part presently.

He was, as I have said, long a-bringing it out, but when he had brought it out he pursued it with such Importunities as would admit of no Denial, *at leaſt he intended they shou'd not;* but I resiſted them obſtinately, and yet with Expressions of the utmoſt Kindness and Respeɛt for him that could be imagin'd; often telling him there was nothing else in the World that I cou'd deny him, and showing him all the Respeɛt, and upon all occasions treating him with Intimacy and Freedom as if he had been my Brother.

He tried all the Ways imaginable to bring his Design to pass, but I was inflexible; At laſt he thought of a Way which, he flatter'd himself, would not fail; nor would he have been miſtaken perhaps, in any other Woman in the World, *but me;* this was to try if he could take me at an Advantage and get to-Bed to me, and then, *as was moſt rational to think,* I should willingly enough marry him afterwards.

We were so intimate together, that nothing but Man and Wife could, or at least ought to be, more; but still our Freedoms kept within the Bounds of Modesty and Decency: But one Evening, above all the rest, we were very merry, and I fancy'd he push'd the Mirth to watch for his Advantage, and I resolv'd that I wou'd, at least, feign to be as merry as he; and that, in short, if he offer'd anything, he shou'd have his Will easily enough.

About One a-clock in the Morning, for so long we sat-up together, I said, *Come*, 'tis One a-Clock, *I must go to bed;* Well, says he, *I'll go with you;* No, No, says I, *go to your own Chamber;* he said he would go to-Bed with me: *Nay,* says I, *if you will,* I don't know what to say; *if I can't help it, you must:* However, I got from him, left him, and went into my Chamber, but did not shut the Door; and as he cou'd easily see that I was undressing myself, he steps to his own Room, which was but on the same Floor, and in a few Minutes undresses himself also, and returns to my Door in his Gown and Slippers.

I thought he had been gone indeed, and so that he had been in jest; and, by the way, thought either he had no-mind to the thing, or that he never intended it; so I shut my Door, that is, latch'd it, for I seldom lock'd or bolted it, and went to-Bed. I had not been in-Bed a Minute but he comes in his Gown to the Door and opens it a little-way, but not enough to come in, or look in, and says softly, What, are you really gone to-Bed? *Yes, yes,* says I, *get you gone:* No indeed, says he, *I shall not begone, you gave me Leave before, to come to-Bed, and you shan't say get you gone now:* So he comes into my Room, and then turns about, and fastens the Door, and immediately comes to the Bed-side to me: I pretended to scold and struggle, and bid him begone, with more Warmth than before, but it was all one; He had not a Rag of Cloaths on, but his Gown and Slippers, and Shirt, so he throws off his Gown, and throws open the Bed, and came in at once.

I made a seeming Resistance, but it was no more indeed; for, *as above*, I resolv'd from the beginning he should Lye with me if he would, and for the rest, I left it to come after.

Well, he lay with me that Night, and the two next, and very merry we were all the three Days between; but the third Night he began to be a little more grave: Now, my Dear, says he, though I have push'd this matter further than ever I intended, or than I believe, you expected from me, who never made any Pretences to you but what were very honest; yet to heal it all up, and let you see how sincerely I meant at first, and how honest I will ever be to you, I am ready to marry you still, and desire you to let it be done to-Morrow Morning; and I will give you the same fair Conditions of Marriage as I would have done before.

This, it must be own'd, was a testimony that he was very honest, and that he lov'd me sincerely, but I construed it quite another Way, namely, that he aim'd at the Money: But how surpriz'd did he look! and how was he confounded, when he found me receive his Proposal with Coldness and Indifference! and still tell him, that it was the only thing I could not grant!

He was astonish'd. What, not take me now! *says he,* when I have been abed with you! I answer'd coldly, tho' respectfully still, *It is true,* to my shame be it spoken, says I, *that you have taken me by Surprize and have had your Will of me; but I hope you will not take it ill that I cannot consent to Marry, for all that; if I am with-Child,* said I, *Care must be taken to manage that as you shall direct; I hope you won't ex-*

pose me for my having expos'd myself to you, but I cannot go any further; And at that Point I stood, and wou'd hear of no Matrimony, by any means.

Now because this may seem a little odd, I shall state the matter clearly as I understood it myself; I knew that while I was a Mistress, it is customary for the Person kept, to receive from them that keep; but if I shou'd be a wife, all I had then, was given up to the Husband, and I was thenceforth to be under his Authority only; and as I had Money enough, and needed not fear being what they call a cast-off Mistress, so I had no need to give him twenty Thousand Pounds to marry me, which had been buying my Lodging too dear a great deal.

Thus his Project of coming to-Bed to me, was a Bite upon himself, while he intended it for a Bite upon me; and he was no nearer his Aim of marrying me, than he was before; all his Arguments he could urge upon the Subject of Matrimony, were at an End, for I positively declin'd marrying him; and as he had refus'd the thousand Pistoles which I had offered him in Compensation for his Expences and Loss, at *Paris*, with the *Jew*, and had done it upon the Hopes he had of marrying me; so when he found his *Way* difficult still, he was amaz'd, and, I had some Reason to believe, repented that he had refus'd the money.

But thus it is when Men run into wicked Measures to bring their Designs about; I that was infinitely oblig'd to him before, began to talk to him as if I had ballanc'd Accounts with him now; and that the Favour of Lying with a Whore, was equal, not to the thousand Pistoles only, but to all the Debt I ow'd him for saving my Life, and all my Effects.

But he drew himself into it, and tho' it was a dear Bargain, yet it was a Bargain of his own making; he cou'd not say I had trick'd him into it; but as he projected and drew me in to lye with him, depending that it was a sure Game in order to a Marriage, so I granted him the Favour, as he called it, to ballance the Account of Favours receiv'd from him, and keep the thousand Pistoles with a good Grace.

He was extremely disappointed in this Article, and knew not how to manage for a great-while; and, as I dare say, if he had not expected to have made it an Earnest for marrying me, he would never have attempted me the other way; so, I believed, if it had not been for the Money, which he knew I had, he wou'd never have desir'd to marry me after he had lain with me: For where is the Man that cares to marry a Whore, tho' of his own making? And as I knew him to be no Fool, so I did him no Wrong, when I suppos'd that, but for the Money, he wou'd not have had any Thoughts of me that Way; especially after my yielding as I had done; in which it is to be remember'd that I made no Capitulation for marrying him, when I yielded to him, but let him do just what he pleas'd, without any previous Bargain.

Well, hitherto we went upon Guesses at one another's Designs; but as he continued to importune me to marry, tho' he had lain with me, and still did lie with me as often as he pleas'd, and I continued to refuse to marry him, tho' I let him lie with me whenever he desir'd it; I say, as these two Circumstances made up our Conversation, it could not continue long thus but we must come to an Explanation.

One Morning, in the middle of our unlawful Freedoms, that is to say, when we were in Bed together; he sigh'd and told me, he desir'd my Leave to ask me one

Question, and that I wou'd give him an Answer to it with the same ingenuous Freedom and Honesty, that I had us'd to treat him with; I told him I wou'd: Why, then, his Question was, why I wou'd not marry him, seeing I allow'd him all the Freedom of a Husband? *Or, says he, my Dear, since you have been so kind as to take me to your Bed, why will you not make me your Own, and take me for good-and-all, that* we may enjoy ourselves, *without any Reproach to one-another?*

I told him, that as I confess'd it was the only thing I could not comply with him in, so it was the only thing in all my Actions, that I could not give him a Reason for; that it was true, I had let him come to-Bed to me, which was suppos'd to be the greatest Favour a Woman could grant; but it was evident, and he might see it, that as I was sensible of the Obligation I was under to him, for saving me from the worst Circumstance it was possible for me to be brought to, I could deny him nothing; and if I had had any greater Favour to yield him, I should have done it, *that of Matrimony only excepted*, and he cou'd not but see that I lov'd him to an extraordinary Degree, in every Part of my Behaviour to him; but that as to marry-ing, which was giving up my Liberty, it was what once he knew I had done, and he had seen how it had hurried me up and down in the World, and what it had expos'd me to; that I had an Aversion to it, and desir'd he would not insist upon it; he might easily see I had no Aversion to him; and that if I was with-Child by him, he shou'd see a testimony of my Kindness to the Father, for that I wou'd settle all I had in the World upon the Child.

He was mute a good-while; at last, *says he*, Come, my Dear, you are the first Woman in the World that ever lay with a Man, and then refus'd to marry him, and therefore

there muſt be some other Reason for your Refusal; and I
have therefore, one other Requeſt, and that is, if I guess
at the true reason and remove the Objeƈtion, will you then
yield to me? I told him if he remov'd the Objeƈtion, I
muſt needs comply, for I shou'd certainly do every-thing
that I had no Objeƈtion againſt.

Why then, my Dear, it muſt be, that either you are already engag'd and marry'd to some other Man, or you
are not willing to dispose of your Money to me, and ex-
peƈt to advance yourself higher with your Fortune; Now
if it be the firſt of these, my Mouth will be ſtopp'd, and I
have no more to say; but if it be the laſt, I am prepared
effeƈtually to remove the Objeƈtion and answer all you
can say on that Subjeƈt.

I took him up short at the firſt of these; telling him he
muſt have base Thoughts of me indeed, to think that I
could yield to him in such a Manner as I had done, and
continue it with so much Freedom, as he found I did, if I
had a Husband, or were engag'd to any other Man; and
that he might depend upon it, that was not my Case, nor
any Part of my Case.

Why then, *said he*, as to the other, I have an Offer to
make to you, that shall take off all the Objeƈtion, *viz.*
That I will not touch one Piſtole of your Eſtate, more,
than shall be with your own voluntary Consent; neither
now, nor at any other time, but you shall settle it as you
please, for your Life, and upon whom you shall please
after your Death; that I shou'd see he was able to maintain me without it; and that it was not for that that he follow'd me from *Paris*.

I was indeed surpriz'd at that Part of his Offer, and he
might easily perceive it; it was not only what I did not ex-
peƈt, but it was what I knew not what Answer to make to;

He had indeed, remov'd my principal Objeƈtion, nay, all my Objeƈtions, and it was not possible for me to give any Answer; for if upon so generous an Offer I shou'd agree with him, I then did as good as confess, that it was upon the Account of my Money that I refus'd him; and that tho' I could give up my Virtue, and expose myself, yet I would not give up my Money, which, though it was true, yet was really too gross for me to acknowledge, and I cou'd not pretend to marry him upon that Principle neither; then as to having him, and make over all my Eƒtate out of his Hands, so as not to give him the Management of what I had, I thought it would be not only a little Gothick and Inhumane, but would be always a Foundation of Unkindness between us, and render us suspeƈted one to another; so that, upon the whole, I was oblig'd to give a new Turn to it, and talk upon a kind of an elevated Strain, which really was not in my Thoughts at firƒt, at-all; for I own, *as above*, the diveƒting myself of my Eƒtate, and putting my Money out of my Hand, was the Sum of the Matter, that made me refuse to marry; but, I say, I gave it a new Turn, upon this Occasion, as follows:

I told him, I had, perhaps differing Notions of Matrimony, from what the receiv'd Cuƒtom had given us of it; that I thought a Woman was a free Agent, as well as a Man, and was born free, and, cou'd she manage herself suitably, might enjoy that Liberty to as much Purpose as the Men do; that the Laws of Matrimony were indeed, otherwise, and Mankind at this time, aƈted quite upon other Principles; and those such, that a Woman gave herself entirely away from herself, in Marriage, and capitulated only to be, at beƒt, but *an Upper-Servant,* and from the time she took the Man, she was no better or worse than the Servant among the *Israelites,* who had his Ears bor'd, *that is,* nail'd to the Door-Post; who by that Act, gave himself up to be a Servant during Life.

That the very Nature of the Marriage-Contract was, in short, nothing but giving up Liberty, Estate, Authority, and every-thing to the Man, and the Woman was indeed, a mere Woman ever after, that is to say, a Slave.

He reply'd that though in some Respects it was as I had said, yet I ought to consider, that as an Equivalent to this, the Man had all the Care of things devolv'd upon him; that the Weight of Business lay upon his Shoulders, and as he had the Trust, so he had the Toil of Life upon him, his was the Labour, his the Anxiety of Living; that the Woman had nothing to do, but to eat the Fat, and drink the Sweet; to sit still, and look round her; be waited on, and made much of; be serv'd and lov'd and made easie; *especially if the Husband acted as became him;* and that, in general, the Labour of the Man was appointed to make the Woman live quiet and unconcern'd in the World; that they had the Name of Subjection without the Thing; and if in inferior Families, they had the Drudgery of the House, and Care of the Provisions upon them; yet they had indeed, much the easier Part; for in general, the Women had only the Care of managing, that is, spending what their Husbands get; and that a Woman had the Name of Subjection indeed, but that they generally commanded not the Men only, but all they had; manag'd all for themselves, and where the Man did his Duty, the Woman's Life was all Ease and Tranquillity; and that she had nothing to do but to be easie and to make all that were about her both easie and merry.

I return'd that while a Woman was single, she was a Masculine in her politic Capacity; that she had then the full Command of what she had, and the full Direction of

what she did; that she was a Man in her separated Capacity, to all Intents and Purposes that a Man cou'd be so to
himself; that she was controll'd by none because account-
able to none, and was in Subjection to none; so I sung
these two Lines of Mr. ——'s:

> Oh! 'tis pleasant to be free,
> The sweetest M I s s is Liberty.

I added, that whoever the Woman was, that had an
Estate, and would give it up to be the Slave of a *Great
Man*, that Woman was a Fool, and must be fit for nothing
but a Beggar; that it was my Opinion, a Woman was as
fit to govern and enjoy her own Estate, without a Man, as
a Man was, without a Woman; and that, if she had a-mind
to gratify herself as to Sexes, she might entertain a Man,
as a man does a Mistress; that while she was thus single;
she was her own, and if she gave away that Power, she
merited to be as miserable as it was possible that any Creature could be.

All he cou'd say, could not answer the Force of this, as
to Argument; only this, that the other Way was the ordinary Method that the World was guided by; that he had
Reason to expect I shou'd be content with that which all
the World was contented with; that he was of the Opinion
that a sincere Affection between a Man and his Wife answer'd all the Objections that I had made about the being
a Slave, a Servant, *and the like*; and where there was a mutual Love, there cou'd be no Bondage; but that there was
but one Interest; one Aim; one Design; and all conspir'd
to make both very happy.

Ay, said I, *that is the Thing I complain of;* the Pretence
of Affection, takes from a Woman everything that can be

call'd *herself*; she is to have no Interest; no Aim; no View; but all in the Interest, Aim, and View of the Husband; she is to be the passive Creature you spoke of, *said I*; she is to lead a Life of perfect Indolence, and living by Faith (not in God, but) in her Husband, she sinks or swims as he is either Fool or wise Man; unhappy or prosperous; and in the middle of what she thinks is her Happiness and Prosperity she is ingulfed in Misery and Beggary, which she had not the least Notice, Knowledge, or Suspicion of: How often have I seen a Woman living in all the Splendour that a plentiful Fortune ought to allow her? with her Coaches and Equipages; her Family, and rich Furniture; her Attendants and Friends; her Visiters, and good Company, all about her to-Day; to-Morrow surpriz'd with a Disaster; turn'd out of all by a Commission of Bankrupt; stripp'd to the Cloaths on her Back; her Jointure, *suppose she had it*, is sacrificed to the Creditors so long as her Husband liv'd, and she turn'd into the Street and left to live on the Charity of her Friends, *if she has any*, or follow the Monarch her Husband, into the *Mint*, and live there on the Wreck of his Fortunes till he is forc'd to run away from her, even there; and then she sees her Children starve; herself miserable; breaks her Heart, and cries herself to Death! This, *says I*, is the State of many a Lady that has had ten Thousand Pounds to her Portion.

He did not know how feelingly I spoke this, and what Extremities I had gone thro' of this Kind; how near I was to the very last Article above, *viz. crying myself to Death*; and how I really starv'd for almost two Years together.

But he shook his Head and said, Where had I lived? and what dreadful Families had I liv'd among, that had frighted me into such terrible Apprehensions of things? that these things indeed, might happen where Men ran

into hazardous things in Trade, and without Prudence
or due Consideration launch'd their Fortunes in a Degree beyond their Strength, grasping at Adventures beyond their Stocks, *and the like;* but that, as he was stated
in the World, if I wou'd embark with him, he had a Fortune equal with mine; that together, we should have no
Occasion of engaging in Business any more; but that in
any Part of the World where I had a-mind to live, whether *England, France, Holland,* or where I would, we might
settle, and live, as happily as the World could make any
one live; that if I desir'd the Management of our Estate,
when put together, if I wou'd not trust him with mine, he
would trust me with his; that we wou'd be upon one Bottom, and I shou'd steer. Ay, *says I,* you'll allow me to
steer, *that is,* hold the Helm, but you'll conn the Ship, *as*
they call it; that is, as at Sea, a boy Serves to Stand at the
Helm, but he that gives him the Orders is Pilot.

He laugh'd at my Simile; No, *says he,* you shall be Pilot
then, you shall conn the Ship; ay, *says I,* as long as you
please, but you can take the Helm out of my Hand when
you please, and bid me go spin; It is not you, *says I,* that I
suspect, but the Laws of Matrimony puts the Power into
your Hands; bids you do it; commands you to command;
and binds me, forsooth, to obey; you, that are now upon
even Terms with me, and I with you, *says I,* are the next
Hour set up upon the Throne, and the humble Wife
plac'd at your Footstool; all the rest, all that you call One-
ness of Interest, Mutual Affection, *and the like,* is Curtesie
and Kindness then, and a Woman is indeed, infinitely
oblig'd where she meets with it; but can't help herself
where it fails.

Well, he did not give it over yet, but came to the serious
Part, and there he thought he should be too many for me;

he first hinted that Marriage was decreed by Heaven; that it was the fix'd State of Life which God had appointed for Man's Felicity, and for establishing a legal Posterity; that there cou'd be no legal Claim of Estates by Inheritance, but by Children born in Wedlock; that all the rest was sunk under Scandal and Illegitimacy; and very well he talk'd upon that Subject, indeed.

But it would not do; I took him short there; Look you Sir, *said I*, you have an Advantage of me there indeed, in my particular Case, but it would not be generous to make use of it; I readily grant, that it were better for me to have marry'd you than to admit you to the Liberty I have given you; but as I cou'd not reconcile my Judgment to Marriage, for the Reasons above, and had Kindness enough for you, and Obligation too much on me, to resist you, I suffer'd your Rudeness, and gave up my Virtue; But I have two things before me to heal up that Breach of Honour, without that desperate one of Marriage, and those are, Repentance for what is past, and putting an End to it for Time to come.

He seem'd to be concern'd to think that I shou'd take him in that manner; he assur'd me that I mis-understood him; that he had more Manners, as well as more Kindness for me; and more Justice, than to reproach me with what he had been the Aggressor in, and had surpriz'd me into; That what he spoke, referr'd to my Words above; that the Woman, if she thought fit, might entertain a Man, as the Man did a Mistress; and that I seem'd to mention that way of Living as justifiable, and setting it as a lawful thing, and in the Place of Matrimony.

Well, we strain'd some Compliments upon those Points, not worth repeating; and I added, I suppos'd when he got to-Bed to me, he thought himself sure of me;

and indeed in the ordinary Course of things, after he had lain with me, he ought to think so; but that, upon the same foot of Argument which I had discours'd with him upon, it was just the contrary; and when a Woman had been weak enough to yield up the last Point before Wedlock, it wou'd be adding one Weakness to another, to take the Man afterwards; to pin down the Shame of it upon herself all Days of her Life, and bind herself to live all her Time with the only Man, that cou'd upbraid her with it; that in yielding at first, she must be a Fool, but to take the Man, is to be sure to be call'd Fool; that to resist a Man, is to act with Courage and Vigour, and to cast off the Reproach, which, in the Course of things, drops out of Knowledge and dies; the man goes one-way and the Woman another, as Fate and the Circumstances of Living direct; and if they keep one another's Council, the Folly is heard no more of; but to take the Man, *says I*, is the most preposterous thing in Nature, and (saving your Presence) is to befoul one's-self and live always in the Smell of it; *No, no*, added I, after a Man has lain with me *as a Mistress*, he ought never to lye with me *as a Wife*; that's not only preserving the Crime in Memory, but it is recording it in the Family; if the woman marries the Man afterwards, she bears the Reproach of it to the last Hour; if her Husband is not a Man of a hundred Thousand, he sometime or other upbraids her with it; if he has Children, they fail not one way or other, to hear of it; if the Children are virtuous, they do their Mother the Justice to hate her for it; if they are wicked, they give her the Mortification of doing the like, and giving her for the example: On the other-hand, if the Man and the Woman part, there is an End of the Crime, and an End of the Clamour; Time wears out the Memory of it; or a Woman may remove but a few Streets, and she soon out-lives it, and hears no more of it.

He was confounded at this Discourse, and told me, he cou'd not say but I was right in the Main; that as to that Part relating to managing Eſtates, it was arguing *à la Cavalier*; it was in some Sence right, if the Women were able to carry it on so, but that in general, the Sex were not capable of it, their Heads were not turn'd for it, and they had better choose a Person capable, and honeſt, that knew how to do them Juſtice, as Women, as well as to love them; and that then the Trouble was all taken off their Hands.

I told him, it was a dear Way of purchasing their Ease; for very often when the Trouble was taken off their Hands, so was their Money too; and that I thought it was far safer for the Sex not to be afraid of the Trouble, but to be really afraid of their Money; that if no-body was truſted, no-body would be deceiv'd, and the Staff in their own Hands was the beſt Security in the World.

He replied that I had ſtarted a new thing in the World; that however I might support it by subtle reasoning, yet it was a way of arguing that was contrary to the general Praćtice, and that he confess'd he was much disappointed in it; that had he known I wou'd have made such a Use of it, he would never have attempted what he did, which he had no wicked Design in, resolving to make me Reparation, and that he was very sorry he had been so unhappy; that he was very sure he shou'd never upbraid me with it hereafter, and had so good an Opinion of me, as to believe I did not suspećt him; but seeing I was positive in refusing him, notwithſtanding what had pass'd, he had nothing to do but to secure me from Reproach, by going back again to *Paris*, that so, according to my own way of arguing, it might die out of Memory, and I might never meet with it again to my Disdavantage.

I was not pleas'd with this part at-all, for I had no-mind to let him go neither; and yet I had no-mind to give him such hold of me as he wou'd have had; and thus I was in a kind of suspence, irresolute, and doubtful what Course to take.

I was in the House with him, as I have observ'd, and I saw evidently that he was preparing to go back to *Paris*, and particularly I found he was remitting Money to *Paris*, which was, as I understood afterwards, to pay for some Wines which he had given Order to have bought for him, at *Troyes* in *Champagne;* and I knew not what course to take; and besides that, I was very loath to part with him. I found also that I was with-Child by him, which was what I had not yet told him of; and sometimes I thought not to tell him of it at-all; but I was in a strange Place, and had no Acquaintance, tho' I had a great deal of Substance, which indeed, having no Friends there, was the more dangerous to me.

This oblig'd me to take him one Morning, when I saw him, as I thought, a little anxious about his going and ir-resolute; says I to him, *I fancy you can hardly find in your Heart to leave me now: The more unkind is it in you*, said he, *severely unkind, to refuse a Man that knows not how to part with you.*

I am so far from being unkind to you, *said I*, that I will go all over the World with you, if you desire me, except to *Paris*, where you know I can't go.

It is a pity so much Love, *said he*, on both Sides, shou'd ever separate.

Why then, *said I*, do you go away from me?

Because, *said he*, you won't take me.

But if I won't take you, *said I*, you may take me any-where, but to *Paris*.

He was very loath to go any-where, he said, without me, but he muſt go to *Paris* or to the *Eaſt Indies*.

I told him I did not use to court, but I durſt venture myself to the *Eaſt-Indies* with him, if there was a Neces-sity of his going.

He told me, God be thank'd, he was in no Necessity of going any-where, but that he had a tempting Invita-tion to go to the *Indies*.

I answer'd I wou'd say nothing to that, but that I de-sir'd he would go any-where but to *Paris*; because there he knew I muſt not go.

He said he had no Remedy, but to go where I cou'd not go, for he could not bear to see me, if he must not have me.

I told him, that was the unkindeſt thing he cou'd say of me, and that I ought to take it very ill, seeing I knew how very well to oblige him to ſtay, without yielding to what he knew I cou'd not yield to.

This amaz'd him, and he told me I was pleas'd to be myſterious; but that he was sure it was in no-body's Pow-er to hinder him going, if he resolv'd upon it, except me; who had Influence enough upon him to make him do any-thing.

Yes, *I told him*, I cou'd hinder him, because I knew he cou'd no more do an unkind thing by me, than he cou'd do an unjuſt one; and to put him out of his Pain, I told him I was with-Child.

He came to me, and, taking me in his Arms, and kiss-ing me a Thousand times almoſt, said, Why wou'd I be so unkind not to tell him that before?

I told him '*twas hard, that,* to have him ſtay, I shou'd

be forc'd do as Criminals do to avoid the Gallows, *plead my Belly*, and that I thought I had given him Testimonies enough of an Affection equal to that of a Wife; if I had not only lain with him, been with-Child by him; shown myself unwilling to part with him; but offer'd to go to the *East-Indies* with him; and except One Thing, that I could not grant, what cou'd he ask more?

He stood mute a good-while, but afterwards told me he had a great-deal more to say, if I cou'd assure him that I would not take ill what-ever Freedom he might use with me in his Discourse.

I told him he might use any Freedom in Words with me; for a Woman who had given Leave to such other Freedoms, as I had done, had left herself no room to take any-thing ill, let it be what it wou'd.

Why then, *he said*, I hope you believe, Madam, I was born a Christian, and that I have some Sence of Sacred Things upon my Mind; When I first broke-in upon my own Virtue and assaulted yours; when I surpriz'd and, as it were, forc'd you to that which neither you intended, nor I design'd but a few Hours before, it was upon a Presumption that you wou'd certainly marry me, if once I cou'd go that Length with you; and it was with an honest Resolution to make you my Wife.

But I have been surpriz'd with such a Denial, that no Woman in such Circumstances ever gave to a Man; for certainly it was never known, that any Woman refus'd to marry a Man that had first lain with her, much less a Man that had gotten her with-Child; but you go upon different Notions from all the World; and though you reason up-on it so strongly, that a Man knows hardly what to an-swer, yet I must own, there is something in it shocking to Nature, and something very unkind to yourself; but above all, it is unkind to the Child that is yet unborn; who, if we marry, will come into the World with Advantage enough, but, if not, is ruin'd before it is born; muſt bear the eternal Reproach of what it is not guilty of; muſt be branded from its Cradle with a Mark of Infamy; be loaded with the Crimes and Follies of its Parents, and suffer for Sins that it never committed: This I take to be very hard, and indeed cruel to the poor Infant not yet born, whom you cannot think of, with any Patience, if you have the common Affection of a Mother, and not do that for it, which shou'd at once place it on a Level with the reſt of the World; and not leave it to curse its Parents for what also we ought to be asham'd of: I cannot, therefore, *says he*, but beg and entreat you, as you are a Christian, and a Mother, not to let the innocent Lamb you go with, be ruin'd before it is born, and leave it to curse and reproach us hereafter for what may be so easily avoided.

Then, dear Madam, said he with a World of Tenderness, (and I thought I saw Tears in his Eyes), allow me to repeat it, that I am a Chriſtian, and consequently I do not allow what I have rashly, and without due Consideration, done; I say, I do not approve of it as lawful; and therefore tho' I did, with a View I have mention'd, one unjuſtifiable Action, I cannot say, that I could satisfy myself to live in a continual Practice of what, in Judgment we muſt both condemn; And tho' I love you above all the Women in the World, and have done enough to convince you of it, by resolving to marry you after what has pass'd between us, and by offering to quit all Pretensions to any Part of your Eſtate, so that I shou'd, as it were, take a Wife after I had lain with her, and without a Farthing Portion, which, as my Circumſtances are, I need not do; I say, notwithſtanding my Affection to you, which is inexpressible, yet I cannot give up Soul as well as Body, the Interest of this World, and the Hopes of another; and you cannot call this my Disrespect to you.

If ever any Man in the World was truly valuable for the strictest honesty of Intention, *this was the Man*; and if ever Woman in her Sences rejected a *Man of Merit* on so trivial and frivolous a Pretence, *I was the Woman*; but surely it was the most preposterous thing that ever Woman did.

He would have taken me as a Wife, but would not entertain me as a Whore; was ever Woman angry with any Gentleman on that head? And was ever Woman so stupid to choose to be a Whore where she might have been an honest Wife? But Infatuations are next to being possess'd of the Devil; I was inflexible, and pretended to argue upon the Point of a Woman's Liberty, as before; but he took me short, and with more Warmth than he had yet us'd with me, tho' with the utmost respect, reply'd, Dear Madam, you argue for Liberty at the same time that you restrain yourself from that Liberty, which God and Nature has directed you to take; and, to supply the Deficiency, propose a vicious Liberty, which is neither honourable nor religious; will you propose Liberty at the expense of Modesty?

I return'd that he mistook me; I did not propose it; I only said that those that cou'd not be content without concerning the Sexes in that Affair might do so indeed; might entertain a Man as Men do a Mistress if they thought fit, but he did not hear me say I wou'd do so, and tho' by what had pass'd he might well censure me in that Part, yet he should find, for the future, that I should freely converse with him without any Inclination that way.

He told me, he cou'd not promise that for himself, and

thought he ought not to trust himself with the Opportunity; for that, as he had fail'd already, he was loath to
lead himself into the Temptation of offending again; and
that this was the true Reason of his resolving to go back
to *Paris*; not that he cou'd willingly leave me, and would
be very far from wanting my Invitation; but if he could
not stay upon Terms that became him, either as an honest
Man or a Christian, what cou'd he do? And he hop'd, *he
said*, I could not blame him, that he was unwilling anything that was to call him Father, should upbraid him
with leaving him in the World to be call'd Bastard; adding that he was astonish'd to think how I could satisfie
myself to be so cruel to an innocent Infant, not yet born;
profess'd he could neither bear the thoughts of it, much
less bear to see it, and hop'd I would not take it ill that he
cou'd not stay to see me Deliver'd, for that very Reason.

I saw he spoke this with a disturb'd Mind and that it
was with some Difficulty that he restrain'd his Passion; so
I declin'd any further Discourse upon it; only said I
hop'd he would consider of it. *O, Madam!* says he, *Do not
bid me consider, 'tis for you to consider;* And with that he
went out of the Room, in a strange kind of Confusion, as
was easie to be seen in his Countenance.

If I had not been one of the foolishest, as well as wick-
edest Creatures upon Earth, I cou'd never have acted
thus; I had one of the honestest, compleatest Gentlemen
upon Earth, at my hand; he had in one Sence sav'd my
Life, but he had sav'd that Life, from Ruin in a most re-
markable Manner; he lov'd me even to Distraction, and
had come from *Paris* to *Rotterdam*, on purpose to seek
me; he had offer'd me Marriage, even after I was with-
Child by him, and had offer'd to quit all his Pretensions
to my Estate, and give it up to my own Management,

having a plentiful Eſtate of his own: Here I might have
settled myself out of the reach even of Disaſter itself; his
Eſtate and mine, wou'd have purchas'd even then above
Two Thousand Pounds a Year, and I might have liv'd
like a Queen, nay, far more happy than a Queen; and
which was above all, I had now an Opportunity to have
quitted a Life of Crime and Debauchery, which I had
been given up to for several Years, and to have sat down
quiet in Plenty and Honour, and to have set myself apart
to the Great Work, which I have since seen so much Necessity of, and Occasion for; I mean that of Repentance.

But my Measure of Wickedness was not yet full; I
continued obſtinate againſt Matrimony, and yet I cou'd
not bear the Thoughts of his going away neither; As to
the Child, I was not very anxious about it; I told him I
wou'd promise him that it shou'd never come to him to
upbraid him with its being illegitimate; that if it was a Boy
I would breed it up like the Son of a Gentleman, and use
it well for his sake; and after a little more such Talk as
this, and seeing him resolv'd to go, I retir'd, but could
not help letting him see the Tears run down my Cheeks;
he came to me, and kiss'd me, entreated me, conjur'd me
by the Kindness he had shown me in my Diſtress; by the
Juſtice he had done me in my Bills and Money Affairs;
by the Respeƈt which made him refuse a Thousand Pistoles from me for his Expenses with that Traytor the
Jew; by the Pledge of our Misfortunes, *so he call'd it*,
which I carry'd with me; and by all that the sincereſt Affeƈtion cou'd propose to do, that I wou'd not drive him
away.

But it would not do; I was ſtupid and sensless, deaf to
all his Importunities, and continued so to the laſt; so we
parted, only desiring me to promise that I would write

him word when I was Deliver'd, and how he might give me an Answer; and this I engag'd my Word I would do; and upon his desiring to be inform'd which Way I intended to dispose of myself, I told him I resolv'd to go directly to *England* and to *London*, where I propos'd to Lye-in; but since he resolv'd to leave me, I told him, I suppos'd it would be of no Consequence to him, what became of me.

He lay in his Lodgings that Night, but went away early in the Morning, leaving me a Letter in which he repeated all he had said; recommended the Care of the Child, and desir'd of me that as he had remitted to me the Offer of a Thousand Pistoles, which I wou'd have given him for the Recompense of his Charges and Trouble with the *Jew*, and had given it me back; so he desir'd I wou'd allow him to oblige me to set apart that Thousand Pistoles, with its Improvement, for the Child and for its Education; earnestly pressing me to secure that little Portion for the abandon'd Orphan when I shou'd think fit, *as he was sure I would*, to throw away the rest upon something as worthless as my sincere Friend at *Paris*; he concluded with moving me to reflect with the same Regret as he did, on our Follies we had committed together; ask'd me Forgiveness for being the Aggressor in the Fact, and forgave me every-thing, *he said*, but the Cruelty of refusing him, which he own'd he could not forgive me so heartily as he shou'd do, because he was satisfied it was an injury to myself; would be an Introduction to my Ruin, and that I wou'd seriously repent of it; he foretold some fatal things, which, *he said*, he was well assur'd I should fall into; and that, at last I would be ruin'd by a bad Husband; bid me be the more wary, that I might render him a False Prophet; but to remember, that if ever I came into Distress I had a fast-Friend at *Paris*, who wou'd not upbraid me with the unkind things past, but wou'd be always ready to return me Good for Evil.

This Letter stunn'd me; I cou'd not think it possible for any-one that had not dealt with the Devil, to write such a Letter; for he spoke of some particular things which afterwards were to befal me, with such an Assurance that it frighted me beforehand; and when those things did come to pass, I was perswaded he had some more than humane Knowledge; in a word, his Advices to me to repent, were very affectionate; his Warnings of Evil to happen to me, were very kind; and his Promises of Assistance, if I wanted him, were so generous, that I have seldom seen the like; and tho' I did not at first set much by that Part, because I look'd upon them as what might not happen, and as what was improbable to happen at that time; yet all the rest of his Letter was so moving, that it left me very melancholly, and I cry'd four and twenty Hours after, almost without ceasing, about it; and yet, even all this while, whatever it was that bewitch'd me, I had not one serious Wish that I had taken him; I wish'd heartily indeed that I cou'd have kept him with me; but I had a mortal Aversion to marrying him, or indeed any-body else, but form'd a thousand wild Notions in my Head, that I was yet gay enough, and young, and handsome enough to please a Man of Quality; and that I wou'd try my Fortune at *London*, come of it what wou'd.

Thus blinded by my own Vanity, I threw away the only Opportunity I then had, to have effectually settl'd my Fortunes, and secur'd them for this World; and I am a Memorial to all that shall read my Story, a standing Monument of the Madness and Distraction which Pride and Insinuations from Hell run us into; how ill our Passions guide us; and how dangerously we act, when we follow the Dictates of an ambitious Mind.

I was rich, beautiful and agreeable, and not yet old; I had known something of the Influence I had had upon the Fancies of Men, even of the highest Rank; I never forgot that the Prince de —— had said with an Ecstasie that I was the finest Woman in *France*; I knew I cou'd make a Figure at *London*, and how well I cou'd grace that Figure; I was not at a Loss how to behave, and having already been ador'd by Princes, I thought of nothing less than of being Mistress to the King himself: But I go back to my immediate Circumstances at that time.

I got over the Absence of my honest Merchant but slowly at first; It was with infinite Regret that I let him go at-all, and when I read the Letter he left, I was quite confounded; as soon as he was out of Call, and irrecoverable, I wou'd have given half I had in the World, for him back again; my Notions of things chang'd in an Instant, and I call'd myself a thousand Fools, for casting myself upon a Life of Scandal and Hazard; when after the Shipwreck of Virtue, Honour, and Principle, and sailing at the utmost Risque in the stormy Seas of Crime, and abominable Levity, I had a safe Harbour presented and no Heart to cast-Anchor in it.

His Predictions terrify'd me; his Promises of Kindness if I came to Distress, melted me into Tears, but frighted me with the Apprehensions of ever coming into such Distress, and fill'd my Head with a thousand Anxieties and Thoughts, how it shou'd be possible for me, who had now such a Fortune, to sink again into Misery.

Then the dreadful Scene of my Life, when I was left with my five Children, &c., as I have related, represented itself again to me, and I sat considering what Measures I might take to bring myself to such a State of Desolation again, and how I shou'd act to avoid it.

But these things wore off gradually; as to my Friend, the Merchant, he was gone, and gone irrecoverably, for I durst not follow him to *Paris*, for the Reasons mention'd above; again, I was afraid to write to him to return, lest he shou'd have refus'd, as I verily believ'd he wou'd; so I sat and cry'd intollerably, for some Days, nay, I may say, for some Weeks; but I say, it wore off gradually; and as I had a great deal of Business for managing my Effects, the Hurry of that particular Part, serv'd to divert my Thoughts, and in part to wear out the Impressions which had been made upon my Mind.

I had sold my Jewels, all but the fine Diamond Ring, which my Gentleman, the Jeweller us'd to wear, and this, at proper times, I wore myself; as also the Diamond Necklace, which the Prince had given me, and a pair of extra-ordinary Ear-Rings, worth about 600 Pistoles; the other, which was a fine Casket he left with me at his going to *Versailles*, and a small Case with some Rubies and Emeralds, &c. I say, I sold them at The *Hague* for 7600 Pistoles; I had receiv'd all the Bills which the Merchant had help'd me to at *Paris*, and with the Money I brought with me, they made up 13900 Pistoles more; so that I had in Ready-Money, and in Account in the Bank at *Amsterdam*, above One and twenty Thousand Pistoles, besides Jewels; and how to get this Treasure to *England*, was my next Care.

The Business I had had now with a great many People, for receiving such large Sums, and selling Jewels of such considerable Value, gave me Opportunity to know and converse with several of the best Merchants of the Place, so that I wanted no Direction now how to get my

Money remitted to *England*; applying therefore to several Merchants, that I might neither risque it all on the Credit of one Merchant, nor suffer any single Man to know the Quantity of Money I had; I say, applying myself to several Merchants, I got bills of Exchange, payable in *London*, for all my Money; the first Bills I took with me; the second Bills I left in Trust (in case of any Disaster at Sea) in the Hands of the first Merchant, him to whom I was recommended by my Friend from *Paris*.

Having thus spent nine Months in *Holland*, refus'd the best Offer ever Woman in my Circumstances had; parted unkindly, and indeed, barbarously with the best Friend, and honestest Man in the World; got all my Money in my Pocket, and a Bastard in my Belly, I took Shipping at the *Briel*, in the Packet-Boat, and arriv'd safe at *Harwich*, where my Woman, *Amy*, was come, by my Direction, to meet me.

I wou'd willingly have given ten Thousand Pounds of my Money to have been rid of the Burthen I had in my Belly, as above; but it cou'd not be, so I was oblig'd to bear with that Part, and get rid of it by the ordinary Method of Patience and a hard Travel.

I was above the contemptible Usage that Women in my Circumstances oftentimes meet with; I had considered all that before-hand; and having sent *Amy* before-hand; and remitted her Money to do it, she had taken me a very handsome House in ⸺ *Street* near *CharingCross*, had hir'd me two Maids, and a Footman, whom she had put in a good Livery, and having hir'd a Glass Coach and four Horses, she came with them and the Man Servant, to *Harwich*, to meet me, and had been there near a Week before I came; so I had nothing to do, but to go-away to *London*, to my own House, where I arriv'd in very good

Health, and where I passed for a *French* Lady by the title of——.

My firſt Business was to get all my Bills accepted; which, to cut thc Story short, was all both accepted, and currently paid; and I then resolv'd to take me a Country-Lodging somewhere near the Town, to be *Incognito*, till I was brought to-Bed; which, appearing in such a Figure and having such an Equipage, I easily manag'd without any-body's offering the usual insults of Parish-Enquiries: I did not appear in my new House for some time, and afterwards I thought fit, for particular Reasons, to quit that House and not come to it at-all, but take handsome large Apartments in the Pall-mall, in a House, out of which was a private Door into the King's Garden, by the Permission of the Chief Gardener, who had lived in the House.

I had now all my Effeſts secur'd; but my Money being my great Concern at that time, I found it a Difficulty how to dispose of it, so as to bring me in an annual Intereſt; however, in some time I got a subſtantial safe Mortgage for 14000 Pound, by the Assiſtance of the famous Sir *Robert Clayton*, for which I had an Eſtate of 1800 Pounds a Year bound to me; and had 700 Pounds *per Annum* Intereſt for it.

This with some other Securities, made me a very handsome Eſtate of above 1000 Pounds a Year; enough one wou'd think, to keep any Woman in *England* from being a Whore.

I Lay in at ——, about four Miles from *London*, and brought a fine Boy into the World; and, according to my Promise, sent an Account of it to my Friend at *Paris*, the Father of it; and in the Letter, told him how sorry I was for his going away, and did as good as intimate, that if he

would come once more to see me, I should use him better
than I had done; He gave me a very kind and obliging
Answer, but took not the least Notice of what I had said
of his coming Over, so I found my Interest lost there for
ever: He gave me Joy of the Child, and hinted, that he
hop'd I would make good what he had begg'd for the
poor Infant, as I had promis'd; and I sent him word
again, that I would fulfil his Order to a Tittle; and such a
Fool, and so weak I was in this last Letter, notwithstanding what I have said of his not taking Notice of my Invita-
tion, as to ask his Pardon almost, for the Usage I gave
him at *Rotterdam*, and stoop'd so low as to expostulate
with him for not taking Notice of my inviting him to
come to me again, as I had done; and which was still more
went so far as to make a second sort of an Offer to him,
telling him almost in plain Words, that if he wou'd come
over now, I wou'd have him; but he never gave me the
least Reply to it at all, which was as absolute a Denial to
me, as he was ever able to give; so I sat down, I cannot
say contented, but vex'd heartily that I had made the Offer at-all; for he had, as I may say, his full Revenge of me,
in scorning to answer, and to let me twice ask that of him,
which he with so much Importunity begg'd of me before.

I was now up-again, and soon came to my City Lodgings in the *Pall mall*; and here I began to make a Figure
suitable to my Estate, which was very great; and I shall
give you an Account of my Equipage in a few Words,
and of myself too.

I paid 60 l. a Year for my new Apartments, for I took
them by the Year; but then, they were handsome Lodgings indeed, and very richly furnish'd. I kept my own
Servants to clean and look after them; found my own
Kitchen-Ware, and Firing; my Equipage was handsome,

but not very great: I had a Coach, a Coachman, a Footman, my Woman *Amy*, who I now dress'd like a Gentlewoman, and made her my Companion, and three Maids;
and thus I liv'd for a time: I dress'd to the height of every
Mode, went extremely rich in Cloaths, and as for Jewels,
I wanted none; I gave a very good Livery lac'd with Silver, and as rich as any-body below the Nobility, could be
seen with: And thus I appear'd, leaving the World to
guess who or what I was, without offering to put myself
forward.

I walk'd sometimes in the Mall with my Woman,
Amy, but I kept no Company and made no Acquaintances,
only made as gay a Show as I was able to do, and that upon all Occasions: I found, however, the World was not
altogether so unconcern'd about me, as I seemed to be
about them; and first, I understood that the Neighbours
began to be mighty inquisitive about me; as who I was?
and what my Circumstances were?

Amy was the only Person who cou'd answer their Curiosity, or give any Account of me, and she a tattling Woman, and a true Gossip, took Care to do that with all the
Art that she was Mistress of; she let them know that I
was the widow of a Person of Quality in *France*; that I
was very rich; that I came over hither to look after a
Estate that fell to me by some of my Relations who died
here; that I was worth 40,000 l. all in my own Hands,
and the like.

This was all wrong in *Amy*, and in me too, though we
did not see it at first; for this recommended me indeed,
to those sort of Gentlemen they call *Fortune-Hunters*, and
who always besieg'd Ladies, *as they call'd it*, on purpose
to take them Prisoners, *as I call'd it*; that is to say, to marry the Women, and have the spending of their Money;

But if I was wrong in refusing the honourable Proposals of the *Dutch Merchant*, who offered me the Disposal of my whole Estate, and had as much of his own to maintain me with; I was right now, in refusing those Offers which came generally from Gentlemen of good Families, and good Estates, but who, living to the Extent of them, were always needy and necessitous, and wanted a Sum of Money to make themselves easie, *as they call it*; that is to say, to pay off Incumbrances, Sisters' Portions, *and the like*; and then the Woman is Prisoner for Life, and may live as they please to give her Leave: This Life I had seen into clearly enough, and therefore I was not to be catch'd that way; however, as I said, the Reputation of my Money brought several of those sort of Gentry about me, and they found means, by one Stratagem or other, to get access to my Ladyship; but, in short, I answer'd them all well enough; *that I liv'd single, and was happy;* that *as I had no Occasion to change my Condition for an Estate,* so I did not see, *that by the best Offer that any of them cou'd make me, I cou'd mend my fortune; that I might be honour'd with* Titles indeed, and in time rank on public Occasions with the Peeresses; I mention that, because one that offer'd at me was the eldest Son of a Peer; *But that I was as well without the Title, as long as I had the Estate;* and *while I had* 2000 l. *a Year of my own, I was happier than I cou'd be in being Prisoner of State to a Nobleman*; for I took the Ladies of that Rank to be little better.

As I have mention'd Sir *Robert Clayton*, with whom I had the good Fortune to become acquainted, on account of the Mortgage which he help'd me to, it is necessary to take Notice, that I had much Advantage in my ordinary Affairs by his Advice, and therefore I call it my good Fortune; for as he paid me so considerable an annual income

as 700 l. a Year, so am I to acknowledge myself much a
Debtor, not only to the Juſtice of his Dealings with me,
but to the Prudence and Conduꝗ which he guided me to,
by his Advice, for the Management of my Eſtate; and as
he found I was not inclin'd to marry, he frequently took
Occasion to hint how soon I might raise my Fortune to a
prodigious Height, if I would but order my Family-
Economy so far within my Revenue, as to lay-up every
year something, to add to the Capital.

I was convinc'd of the Truth of what he said, and
agreed to the Advantages of it; you are to take it as you
go, that Sir *Robert* suppos'd by my own Discourse, and
especially, by my Woman *Amy*, that I had 2000l. a Year
income; he judg'd, as he said, by my way of Living, that I
cou'd not spend above one Thousand; and so, he added,
I might prudently lay by 1000 l. every Year, to add to the
Capital; and by adding every Year the additional Intereſt, or Income of the Money to the Capital, he prov'd to
me that in ten Year, I shou'd double the 1000 l. *per Annum* that I laid by; and he drew me out a Table, as he
call'd it, of the Encrease, for me to judge by; and by
which, he said, if the Gentlemen of *England* would but
aꝗ so, every Family of them would encrease their Fortunes to a great Degree, juſt as Merchants do by
Trade; whereas now, *says Sir Robert*, by the Humour of
living up to the Extent of their Fortunes, and rather beyond, the Gentlemen, *says he*, ay, and the Nobility too,
are, almoſt all of them, Borrowers, and all in necessitous
Circumſtances.

As Sir *Robert* frequently visited me, and was (if I may
say so from his own Mouth) very well pleas'd with my
way of conversing with him, for he knew nothing, nor so
much as guess'd at what I had been; I say, as he came

often to see me, so he always entertain'd me with this Scheme of Frugality; and one time he brought another Paper, wherein he shew'd me, much to the same Purpose as the former, to what Degree I shou'd increase my Estate if I wou'd come into his Method of contracting my Expenses; and by this Scheme of his, it appear'd that laying up a Thousand Pounds a Year, and every Year adding the Interest to it, I shou'd in twelve Years' time have in Bank, One and twenty Thousand, and Fifty eight Pounds; after which, I might lay-up two Thousand Pounds a Year.

I objected, that I was a young Woman; that I had been us'd to live plentifully, and with a good Appearance, and that I knew not how to be a Miser.

He told me, that if I thought I had enough, it was well; but if I desired to have more, this was the Way; that in another twelve Year, I shou'd be too rich, so that I shou'd not know what to do with it.

Ay Sir, says I, you are contriving how to make me a rich Old Woman, but that won't answer my End; I had rather have 20,000 l. now than 60,000 l. when I am fifty Year old.

Then, Madam, says he, *I suppose your Honour has no Children?*

None, *Sir Robert*, said I, *but what are provided for;* so I left him in the dark, as much as I found him: However, I consider'd his scheme very well, tho' I said no more to him at that time, and I resolv'd, tho' I would make a very good Figure,—I say I resolv'd to abate a little of my Expence and draw in, live closer, and save something, if not so much as he propos'd to me: It was near the End of the Year that Sir *Robert* made this Proposal to me, and when the Year was up, I went to his House in the City, and

there I told him, I came to thank him for his Scheme of
Frugality; that I had been ſtudying much upon it; and
tho' I had not been able to mortifie myself so much as to
lay-up a Thousand Pounds a Year; yet, as I had not come
to him for my Intereſt half-yearly, as was usual, I was
now come to let him know, that I had resolved to lay up
that seven Hundred a year and never use a Penny of it;
desiring him to help me to put it out to Advantage.

Sir *Robert*, a Man thoroughly vers'd in arts of improv-
ing Money, but thoroughly honeſt, *said to me*, Madam, I
am glad you approve of the Method that I propos'd to
you; but you have begun wrong; you should have come
for your Intereſt at the Half-Year, and then you had had
the Money to put out; now you have loſt half a Year's Intereſt of 350 l., which is 9 l., for I had but *5 per Cent.* on
the Mortgage.

Well, well, Sir, *says I*, can you put this out for me now?

Let it lie, Madam, *says he*, till the next Year, and then
I'll put our your 1400 l. together, and in the meantime I'll
pay you intereſt for the 700 l. So he gave me his Bill for
the Money, which he told me shou'd be no less than 6 l.
per Cent. Sir *Robert Clayton*'s Bill was what no-body would
refuse; so I thank'd him and let it lie; and next Year I did
the same, and the third Year Sir *Robert* got me a good
mortgage for 2200 l. at 6 *per cent*. Intereſt: So I had 132 l.
a Year added to my Income; which was a very satisfying
Article.

But I return to my Hiſtory: As I have said, I found
that my Measures were all wrong, the Poſture I set up in,
expos'd me to innumerable Visitors of the Kind I have
mention'd above; I was cry'd up for a vaſt Fortune, and
one that Sir *Robert Clayton* manag'd for; and Sir *Robert
Clayton* was courted for me, as much as I was for myself;

But I had given Sir *Robert* his Cue; I had told him my Opinion of Matrimony, in juſt the same Terms as I had done my Merchant, and he came into it presently; he own'd that my Observation was juſt, and that if I valued my Liberty, as I knew my Fortune and that it was in my own Hands, I was to blame if I gave it away to anyone.

But Sir *Robert* knew nothing of my Design; that I aimed at being a kept Miſtress, and to have a handsome Maintenance; and that I was ſtill for getting Money, *and Laying it up too*, as much as he cou'd desire me, only by a worse Way.

However, Sir *Robert* came seriously to me one Day, and told me he had an Offer of Matrimony to make to me, that was beyond all that he had heard had offer'd themselves, and this was a Merchant; Sir *Robert* and I agreed exactly in our Notions of a Merchant; Sir *Robert* said, and I found it to be true, that a true-bred Merchant is the beſt Gentleman in the Nation; that in Knowledge, in Manners, in Judgment of things, the Merchant outdid many of the Nobility; that having once maſter'd the World, and being above the Demand of Business, tho' no real Eſtate, they were then superior to moſt Gentlemen, even in Eſtate; that a Merchant in flush Business, and a capital Stock is able to spend more Money than a Gentleman of 5000 l. a Year Eſtate; that while a Merchant spent, he only spent what he got, and not that; and that he laid up great Sums every Year.

That an Eſtate is a Pond, but that a Trade was a Spring; that if the firſt is once mortgag'd it seldom gets clear, but embarrass's the Person for ever; but the Merchant had his Eſtate continually flowing; and upon this, he nam'd me Merchants who liv'd in more real Splendour, and spent more Money than most of the Noblemen in *England* could singly expend, and that they still grew immensely rich.

He went on to tell me, that even the Tradesmen in *London*, speaking of the better sort of Trades, could spend more Money in their Families, and yet give better Fortunes to their Children, than, generally speaking, the Gentry of *England* from 1000 l. a Year downward cou'd do, and yet grow rich too.

The Upshot of all this was to recommend to me, rather the bestowing my Fortune upon some eminent Merchant, who liv'd already in the first Figure of a Merchant, and who, not being in Want or Scarcity of Money, but having a flourishing Business and a flowing Cash, wou'd at the first word, settle all my Fortune on myself and Children and maintain me like a Queen.

This was certainly right; and had I taken his Advice I had been really happy; but my Heart was bent upon an Independency of Fortune; and I told him, I knew no State of Matrimony, but what was at best, a State of Inferiority, if not of Bondage; that I had no Notion of it, that I liv'd a Life of absolute Liberty now; was free as I was born, and, having a plentiful Fortune, I did not understand what Coherence the words *Honour* and *Obey* had with the Liberty of a *Free Woman*; that I knew no Reason the Men had to engross the whole Liberty of the Race and make the Women, notwithstanding any disparity of Fortune, be subject to the Laws of Marriage, of their own making; that it was my misfortune to be a woman; but I was resolv'd it should not be made worse by the Sex; and seeing Liberty seemed to be the Men's Property, I wou'd be a *Man-Woman*; for as I was born free, I wou'd die so.

Sir Robert smil'd, and told me, I talk'd a kind of *Amazonian* Language; that he found few Women of my Mind, or that if they were, they wanted Resolution to go on with it; that notwithstanding all my Notions, which he could not but say had once some Weight in them, yet he understood I had broke-in upon them and had been marry'd; I answer'd I had so, but he did not hear me say, that I had any Encouragment from what was past, to make a second Venture; that I was got well out of the Toil, and if I came in again I should have nobody to blame but myself.

Sir *Robert* laugh'd heartily at me but gave over offering any more Arguments, only told me, he had pointed me out for some of the best Merchants in *London*, but since I forbad him, he wou'd give me no Disturbance of that Kind; he applauded my way of managing my Money, and told me, I shou'd soon be monstrous rich; but he neither knew, nor mistrusted, that with all this Wealth, I was yet a Whore, and was not averse to adding to my Estate at the further Expence of my Virtue.

But to go on with my Story as to my way of living; I found, as above, that my living as I did would not answer; that it only brought the *Fortune-Hunters* and Bites about me, as I have said before, to make a Prey of me and my Money; and, in short, I was Harass'd with Lovers, *Beaus*, and *Fops* of Quality in abundance; but it wou'd not do; I aim'd at other things, and was possess'd with so vain an Opinion of my own Beauty, that nothing less than the King himself was in my Eye; and this Vanity was rais'd by some Words *let fall* by a Person I convers'd with, who was, perhaps, likely enough to have brought such a thing to pass, had it been sooner; *but that Game began to be pretty well over at Court:* However, the having mention'd such a thing, it seems, a little too publickly, it brought abundance of People about me, upon a wicked Account too.

And now I began to act in a new Sphere; the Court was exceeding gay and fine, tho' fuller of Men than of Women, the Queen not affecting to be very much in publick; on the other hand, it is no Slander upon the Courtiers, *to say*, they were as wicked as any-body in reason could desire them: The KING had several Mistresses, who were prodigious fine, and there was a glorious show on that Side indeed: If the Sovereign gave himself a Loose, it cou'd not be expected the rest of the Court shou'd be all saints; so far was it from that, tho' I would not make it worse than it was, that a Woman that had any-thing agreeable in her Appearance, could never want Followers.

I soon found myself thronged with Admirers; and I receiv'd visits from some Persons of very great Figure, who always introduc'd themselves by the help of an old Lady or two who were now become my Intimates; and one of them, I understood afterwards, was set to work on purpose to get into my Favour, in order to introduce what follow'd.

The Conversation we had was generally courtly, but civil; at length, some gentlemen propos'd to Play, and made what they call'd a Party; this, it seems, was a Contrivance of one of my Female hangers-on, *for, as I said, I had two of them*, who thought this was the way to introduce People, as often as she pleas'd, and so indeed it was; They play'd high and stay'd late, but begg'd my Pardon, only ask'd Leave to make an Appointment for the next Night; I was as gay, and as well-pleas'd as any of them, and one night, told one of the Gentlemen, my Lord——, that seeing they were doing me the Honour of diverting themselves at my Apartment, and desir'd to be there sometimes, I did not keep a Gaming-Table, but I would give them a little Ball the next day, if they pleas'd, which they accepted very willingly.

Accordingly in the Evening the Gentlemen began to come, where I let them see, that I understood very well what such things meant; I had a large Dining-Room in my Apartments, with five other Rooms on the same Floor, all which I made Drawing-Rooms for the Occasion, having all the Beds taken down for the Day; in three of these I had Tables plac'd, cover'd with Wine and Sweetmeats; the fourth had a green Table for Play, and the fifth was my own Room, where I sat, and where I receiv'd all the Company that came to pay their Compliments to me: I was dress'd, you may be sure, to all the Advantage possible, and had all the Jewels on, that I was Mistress of: My Lord ———, to whom I had made the invitation, sent me a Sett of fine Musick from the Play-House, and the Ladies danc'd and we began to be very merry; when about eleven a-Clock I had Notice given me, that there were some Gentlemen coming in Masquerade.

I seem'd a little surpris'd and began to apprehend some Disturbance; when my Lord ———, perceiving it, spoke to me to be easie, for that there was a Party of the Guards at the Door, which shou'd be ready to prevent any Rudeness; and another Gentleman gave me a Hint as if the KING was among the Masks; I colour'd as red as Blood itself cou'd make a Face look, and expressed a great Surprize; however, there was no going back, so I kept my Station in my Drawing-Room, but with the Folding-Doors wide open.

A-while after, the Masks came in and began with a Dance *à la Comique*, performing wonderfully indeed;

while they were dancing, I withdrew, and left a Lady to answer for me that I would return immediately; in less than half an Hour I return'd, dressed in the Habit of a *Turkish Princess*; the Habit I got at *Leghorn*, when my *Foreign Prince* bought me a *Turkish* Slave, as I have said —the *Maltese* Man-of-War had, it seems, taken a *Turkish* Vessel going from *Constantinople* to *Alexandria*, in which were some Ladies bound for *Grand Cairo* in *Egypt*; and as the Ladies were made Slaves, so their fine Cloaths were thus expos'd; and with this *Turkish* Slave, I bought the rich Cloaths too: The dress was extraordinary fine indeed, I had bought it as a Curiosity, having never seen the like; the Robe was a fine *Persian* or *India* Damask; the Ground white, and the Flowers blue and gold, and the Train held five Yards; the Dress under it, was a Vest of the same, embroider'd with Gold, and set with some Pearl in the Work and some *Turquois* Stones; to the Vest, was a Girdle five or six inches wide, after the *Turkish* Mode, and on both Ends where it join'd or hook'd was set with Diamonds for eight inches either way, only they were not true Diamonds; but nobody knew that but myself.

The Turban or Head-Dress, had a Pinacle on the top, but not above five Inches, with a Piece of loose Sarcenet hanging from it; and on the Front, just over the Forehead, was a good Jewel, which I had added to it.

This Habit, as above, cost me about sixty Pistoles in *Italy*, but cost much more in the Country from whence it came; and little did I think, when I bought it, that I shou'd put it to such a Use as this, tho' I had dress'd myself in it many times by the help of my little *Turk*, and afterwards between *Amy* and I, only to see how I looked in it: I had sent her up before, to get it ready, and when I came up, I had nothing to do but slip it on, and was down in my Drawing-Room in a little more than a quarter of an Hour; when I came there the room was full of Company, but I order'd the Folding-Doors to be shut for a Minute or two, till I had receiv'd the Compliments of the Ladies that were in the Room, and had given them a full View of my Dress.

But my Lord ———, who happen'd to be in the Room, slipp'd out at another Door, and brought back with him one of the Masks, a tall well-shap'd Person, but who had no Name, *being all Mask'd*, nor would it have been allow'd to ask any Person's Name on such an Occasion; The Person spoke in *French* to me, that it was the finest Dress he had ever seen; and ask'd me if he should have the Honour to dance with me? I bow'd, as giving my Consent, but said as I had been a Mohametan I could not dance after the Manner of this Country; I suppos'd their Musick would not play *à la Moresque*. He answer'd merrily I had a Christian's face, and he'd venture it that I cou'd dance like a Christian; adding that so much beauty could not be Mohametan: Immediately the Folding-Doors were flung open, and he led me into the Room. The Company were under the greatest Surprize imaginable; the very Musick stopped awhile to gaze; for the Dress was indeed, exceedingly surprizing, perfectly new, very agreeable, and wonderful rich.

The Gentleman, *whoever he was*, for I never knew, led me only a Courant, and then ask'd me if I had a mind to dance an Antick, that is to say, whether I wou'd dance the Antick as they had danc'd in Masquerade, or any-thing by myself. I told him, anything else rather, if he pleas'd; so we danc'd only two *French* Dances, and he led me to the Drawing-Room Door, when he retired to the rest of the

Masks: When he left me at the Drawing-Room Door I did not go in, as he thought I wou'd have done, but turn'd about and shew'd myself to the whole Room, and, calling my Woman to me, gave her some Directions to the Musick, by which the Company presently understood that I would give them a Dance by myself: Immediately all the House rose up, and paid me a kind of a Compliment by removing back every way to make me room, for the Place was exceeding full: the Musick did not at first hit the Tune that I directed, which was a *French* Tune, so I was forc'd to send my woman to 'em again, standing all this while at my Drawing-Room Door; but as soon as my Woman spoke to them again, they play'd it right, and I, to let them see it was so, stepp'd forward to the middle of the Room; then they began it again, and I danc'd by myself a Figure which I learnt in *France*, when the Prince de —— desir'd I would dance for his Diversion; it was indeed, a very fine Figure, invented by a famous Master at *Paris*, for a Lady or a Gentleman to dance single, but being perfectly new, it pleas'd the Company exceedingly, and they all thought it had been *Turkish*; nay, one Gentleman had the Folly to expose himself so much, as to say, *and I think swore too*, that he had seen it danc'd at *Constantinople*; which was ridiculous enough.

At the finishing the Dance the Company clapp'd and almost shouted; and one of the Gentlemen cried out, *Roxana! Roxana!* by ——, with an Oath, upon which foolish Accident I had the Name of *Roxana* presently fix'd upon me all over the Court End of Town, as effectually as if I had been Christen'd *Roxana*: I had, it seems, the Felicity of pleasing every-body that Night, to an Extreme; and my Ball, but especially my Dress, was the Chat of the Town for that Week, and so the name *Roxana* was the Toaſt at and about the Court; no other Health was to be nam'd with it.

Now things began to work as I wou'd have them, and I began to be very popular, as much as I cou'd desire: The Ball held till (as well as I was pleas'd with the show) I was sick of the Night; the gentlemen Mask'd, went off about three a'-Clock in the Morning; the other Gentle-- men sat down to Play; the Music held it out; and some of the Ladies were dancing at six in the Morning.

But I was mighty eager to know who it was danced with me; some of the lords went so far as to tell me, I was very much honour'd in my Company; one of them spoke so broad, as almoſt to say it was the KING, but I was con- vinc'd afterwards, it was not; and another reply'd, If he had been His Majeſty he shou'd have thought it no dis- honour to Lead-up a *Roxana*; but to this Hour I never knew positively who it was; and by his Behaviour I thought he was too young, His Majeſty being at that time in an Age that might be discover'd from a young Person, even in his Dancing.

Be that as it wou'd, I had 500 Guineas sent me the next Morning, and the Messenger was order'd to tell me, that the Persons who sent it desir'd a Ball again at my Lodg- ings on the next *Tuesday*, but that they wou'd have my Leave to give the Entertainment themselves: I was mighty well pleas'd with this, (to be sure) but very in- quisitive to know who the Money came from; but the Messenger was silent as Death, as to that Point; and, bowing always at my Enquiries, begg'd me to ask no Queſtions which he could not give an obliging Answer to.

I forgot to mention that the Gentlemen that play'd gave a Hundred Guineas to the Box, *as they call'd it*, and at the End of their Play, they ask'd my Gentlewoman of the Bed-Chamber, as they called her (Mrs. *Amy*, for-sooth), and gave it her; and gave twenty Guineas more among the Servants.

These magnificent Doings equally both pleas'd and surpriz'd me, and I hardly knew where I was; but especi-ally that Notion of the K I N G being the Person that danc'd with me puff'd me up to that Degree, that I not only did not know anybody else, but indeed was very far from knowing myself.

I had now the next *Tuesday* to provide for the like Com-pany; but, alas! it was all taken out of my Hand. Three Gentlemen, who yet were, it seems, but Servants, came on the *Saturday*, and bringing sufficient Testimonies that they were right, for one was the same who brought the five hundred Guineas; I say three of them came, and brought Bottles of all sorts of Wines, and Hampers of Sweet-Meats to such a Quantity, it appear'd they de-sign'd to hold the Trade on more than once, and that they wou'd furnish everything to a Profusion.

However, as I found a Deficiency in two things, I made Provision of about twelve Dozen of fine Damask Napkins, with Table-cloaths of the same, sufficient to cover all the Tables, with three Table-cloaths upon every Table, and Side-boards in Proportion; also, I bought a handsome Quantity of Plate, necessary to have serv'd all the Side-boards, but the Gentlemen would not suffer any of it to be us'd; telling me they had brought fine *China* Dishes and Plates for the whole Service; and that in such public Places they cou'd not be answerable for the Plate; so it was set all up in large Glass-Cupboard in the room I sat in, where it made a very good show indeed.

On *Tuesday* there came such an Appearance of Gentle-men and Ladies, that my Apartments were by no means able to receive them; and those who in particular appear'd as Principals gave Order below to let no more Company come up; the street was full of Coaches with Coronets, and fine Glass Chairs; and, in short, it was impossible to receive the Company; I kept my little Room, as before, and the Dancers fill'd the great Room; all the Drawing-Rooms also were fill'd, and three Rooms below-Stairs which were not mine.

It was very well that there was a strong Party of the Guards brought to keep the Door, for without that, there had been such a promiscuous Crowd, and some of them scandalous too, that we should have been all Disorder and Confusion; but the three Head-Servants manag'd all that, and had a Word to admit all the Company by.

It was uncertain to me, and is to this Day, who it was that danc'd with me the *Wednesday* before, when the Ball was my own; but that the K - - - was at this Assembly, was out of Question with me, by Circumstances that I suppose I cou'd not be deceiv'd in; and particularly, that there were five Persons who were not Mask'd, three of them had blue Garters, and they appear'd not to me till I came out to dance.

This Meeting was manag'd just as the first, tho' with much more Magnificence, because of the Company; I plac'd myself (exceedingly rich in Cloaths and Jewels) in the middle of my little Room, as before, and made my Compliments to all the Company, as they pass'd me, as I did before; but my Lord ——, who had spoken openly to me the first Night, came to me and, unmasking, told me the Company had order'd him to tell me they hop'd they should see me in the Dress I had appear'd in the first Day, which had been so acceptable, that it had been the Occasion of this new Meeting; and, Madam, *says he,*

there are some in this Assembly whom it is worth your
while to oblige.

I bowed to my Lord —— and immediately withdrew;
While I was above, a-dressing in my new Habit, two
Ladies, perfectly unknown to me, were convey'd into my
Apartment below, by the Order of a Noble Person who,
with his Family, had been in *Persia*; and here indeed, I
thought I shou'd have been out-done, or perhaps baulk'd.

One of these Ladies was dress'd most exquisitely fine
indeed, in the Habit of a Virgin Lady of Quality of *Geor-
gia*, and the other in the same Habit of *Armenia*, with each
of them a Woman-Slave to attend them.

The Ladies had their Petticoats short, to their Ancles,
but pleated all round, and before them short Aprons, but
of the finest Point that cou'd be seen; their Gowns were
made with long Antick Sleeves hanging down behind,
and a Train let down; they had no Jewels, but their
Heads and Breasts were dress'd up with Flowers, and
they both came in veil'd.

Their Slaves were *bare-headed*; but their long black
Hair was breeded in Locks hanging down behind, to their
Wastes, and tied up with Ribbons; they were dress'd
exceedingly rich, and were as beautiful as their Mistresses; for none of them had any Masks on: They waited in my Room till I came down, and all paid their Respects to me after the *Persian* manner, and sat down on a
Safra, that is to say, almost cross-legg'd on a Couch made
up of Cushions laid on the Ground.

This was admirably fine, and I was indeed, startled at
it; they made their compliments to me in *French* and I reply'd in the same Language; when the Doors were open'd
they walk'd into the Dancing-Room, and danc'd such a
Dance as indeed nobody there had ever seen, and to an in-

ſtrument like a Guittar with a small low-sounding Trum-
pet, which indeed, was very fine, and which my Lord
—— had provided.

They danc'd three times all-alone, for nobody indeed
cou'd dance with them: The Novelty pleas'd truly, but
yet there was something wild and *Bizarre* in it, because
they really acted to the Life the barbarous Country
whence they came; but as mine had the *French* Behaviour
under the *Mohametan* Dress, it was every way as new, and
pleas'd much better, indeed.

As soon as they had shown their *Georgian* and *Armenian*
Shapes, and danc'd, as I have said, three times, they withdrew, paid their Compliments to me (for I was Queen of
the Day), and went off to undress.

Some Gentlemen then danc'd with Ladies all in Masks,
and when they ſtopp'd no-body rose up to dance, but all
call'd out, *Roxana, Roxana*; in the Interval my Lord ——
had brought another mask'd Person into my Room,
whom I knew not, only that I cou'd discern it was not the
same Person that led me out before: This noble Person
(for I afterwards underſtood it was the Duke of ——)
after a short Compliment, led me out into the middle of
the Room.

I was dress'd in the same Veſt and Girdle as before;
but the Robe had a Mantle over it, which is usual in the
Turkish Habit, and it was of Crimson and Green, the
Green brocaded with Gold; and my *Tyhaiai*, or *Head-
Dress*, vary'd a little from that I had before, as it ſtood
higher, and had some Jewels about the rising Part; which
made it look like a Turban crown'd.

I had no mask, neither did I Paint, and yet I had the
Day of all the Ladies that appear'd at the Ball, I mean, of
those that appear'd with Faces on; as for those Mask'd,

nothing could be said of them, no doubt there might be many finer than I was; it mu&t be confess'd that the Habit was infinitely advantageous to me, and every-body look'd at me with a kind of Pleasure, which gave me great Advantage too.

After I had danc'd with that noble Person, I did not offer to dance by myself, as I had before; but they all call'd out *Roxana* again; and two of the Gentlemen came into the Drawing-Room, to intreat me to give them the *Turkish* Dance, which I yielded to, readily; so I came out and danc'd, ju&t as at fir&t.

While I was dancing, I perceiv'd five Persons &tanding all together, and among them, one only with his Hat on; it was an immediate Hint to me who it was, and had at fir&t, almo&t put me into some Disorder; but I went on, receiv'd the Applause of the House, as before, and retir'd into my own Room; When I was there, the five Gentlemen came cross the Room to my Side, and coming in, follow'd by a Throng of Great Persons, the Person with his Hat on said, Madam *Roxana you perform to Admiration*: I was prepar'd, and offer'd to kneel to kiss his Hand, but he declin'd it, and salut'd me, and so, passing back again thro' the Great Room, went away.

I do not say here, who this was, but I say, I came afterwards to know something more plainly; I wou'd have withdrawn, and disrob'd, being somewhat too thin in that Dress, unlac'd and open-brea&ted, as if I had been in my Shift; but it cou'd not be, and I was oblig'd to dance afterwards with six or eight Gentlemen, mo&t, if not all of them, of the Fir&t Rank; and I was told afterwards that one of them was the D— of M——th.

About two or three a'-Clock in the Morning, the Company began to decrease, the Number of Women especially, dropp'd away Home, some and some at a time; and the Gentlemen retir'd down-Stairs, where they unmask'd and went to Play.

Amy waited at the Room where they Play'd, sat up all-Night to attend them; and in the Morning, when they broke-up, they swept the Box into her Lap, when she counted out to me, sixty-two Guineas and a half; and the other Servants got very well too: *Amy* came to me when they were all gone. *Law, Madam!* says *Amy*, with a long gaping Cry, what shall I do with all this Money? And indeed the poor Creature was half mad with Joy.

I was now in my Element; I was as much talk'd of as any-body cou'd desire, and I did not doubt but some thing or other wou'd come of it, but the Report of my being so rich, rather was a Balk to my View, than any-thing else; for the Gentlemen, that wou'd perhaps have been troublesome enough otherwise, seem'd to be kept off, for *Roxana* was too high for them.

There is a Scene which came in here, which I must cover from human Eyes or Ears; for three Years and about a Month, Roxana liv'd retir'd, having been oblig'd to make an Excursion, in a Manner, and with a Person which Duty, and private Vows oblige her not to reveal, at least not yet.

At the End of this Time I appear'd again; but I must add that as I had in this Time of Retreat *made Hay, &c.*, so I did not come Abroad again with the same Lustre, or shine with so much Advantage as before; for as some People had got at least, a Suspicion of where I had been, and who had had me all the while, it began to be publick that *Roxana* was, in short, a mere *Roxana*, neither better nor worse, and not that Woman of Honour and Virtue that was at first suppos'd.

You are now to suppose me about seven Years come to

Town, and that I had not only suffer'd the old Revenue, which I hinted was manag'd by Sir *Robert Clayton*, to grow, as was mention'd before; but I had laid-up an incredible Wealth, the time considered; and had I yet had the least Thought of reforming, I had all the Opportunity to do it with Advantage, that ever Woman had, for the common Vice of all Whores, I mean money; was out of the Question, nay, even Avarice itself seem'd to be glutted; for, including what I had saved in reserving the Interest of 14,000 l. which, as above, I had left to grow, and including some very good Presents I had made to me, in meer Compliment, upon these shining masquerading Meetings, which I held up for about two Years, and what I made of three Years of the most glorious Retreat, *as I call it,* that ever Woman had, I had fully doubled my first Substance, and had near 5000 Pounds in Money, which I kept at-home; besides abundance of Plate, and Jewels, which I had either given me, or had bought to set myself out for Public Days.

In a word, I had now five and thirty Thousand Pounds Estate; and as I found Ways to live without wasting either Principal or Interest, I laid-up 2000 l. every Year at least, out of the meer Interest, adding it to the Principal; and thus I went on.

After the End of what I may call my Retreat, and out of which I brought a great deal of Money, I appear'd again, but I seem'd like an old Piece of Plate that has been hoarded up some Years, and comes out tarnish'd and discolour'd; so I came out blown, and looked like a *cast-off Mistress,* nor indeed, was I any better, tho' I was not at-all impair'd in Beauty, except that I was a little fatter than I was formerly, and always granting that I was four Years older.

However; I preserv'd the Youth of my Temper; was always bright, pleasant in Company, and agreeable to every-body, or else every-body flatter'd me; and in this Condition I came abroad to the World again; and tho' I was not so popular as before, and indeed, did not seek it, because I knew it cou'd not be, yet I was far from being without Company, and that of the greatest Quality, *of Subjects I mean*, who frequently visited me, and sometimes we had Meetings for Mirth, and Play at my Apartments, where I failed not to divert them in the most agreeable Manner possible.

Nor cou'd any of them make the least particular Application to me, from the Notion they had of my excessive Wealth, which, as they thought, plac'd me above the meanness of a Maintenance, and so left no room to come easily about me.

But at last I was very handsomely attack'd by a Person of Honour, and (which recommended him particularly to me) a Person of a very great Estate; he made a long Introduction to me upon the Subject of my Wealth: Ignorant Creature! *said I to myself*, considering him as a L O R D; was there ever Woman in the World that cou'd stoop to the Baseness of being a Whore, and was above taking the Reward of her Vice? *No, no, depend upon it, if your Lordship obtains any-thing of me, you must pay for it; and the Notion of my being so rich, serves only to make it cost you the dearer, seeing you cannot offer a small matter to a Woman of* 2000 l. *a Year Estate.*

After he had harangu'd upon that Subject a good-while, and had assur'd me he had no Design upon me; that he did not come to make a Prize of me, or to pick my Pocket, which, (by the way) I was in no fear of, for I took too much Care of my Money, to part with any of it that way; he then turn'd his Discourse to the Subject of Love; a Point so ridiculous to me, without the main thing, I mean the Money, that I had no Patience to hear him make so long a Story of it.

I receiv'd him civilly, and let him see I cou'd bear to hear a wicked Proposal, without being affronted, and yet I was not to be brought into it too easily: He visited me a long-while, and, in short, courted me as closely and assiduously, as if he had been wooing me to Matrimony; he made me several valuable Presents, which I suffer'd myself to be prevail'd with to accept, but not without great Difficulty.

Gradually I suffer'd also his other Importunities, and when he made a Proposal of a Compliment, or Appointment to me, for a Settlement, *he said*, That tho' I was rich, yet there was not the less due from him, to acknowledge the Favours he receiv'd; and that if I was to be his, I shou'd not live at my own Expence, *cost what it wou'd*: I told him I was far from being Extravagant, and yet I did not live at the Expence of less than 500 l. a Year out of my own Pocket; that, however, I was not covetous of settled Allowances, for I look'd upon that as a kind of *Golden Chain*, something like Matrimony; that tho' I knew how to be true to a Man of Honour, as I knew his Lordship to be, yet I had a kind of Aversion to the Bonds; and tho' I was not so rich as the World talk'd me up to be, yet I was not so poor as to bind myself to Hardships, for a Pension.

He told me, he expected to make my Life perfectly easie, and intended to so; that he knew of no Bondage there cou'd be in a private Engagement between us; that the Bonds of Honour, he knew, I wou'd be ty'd by, and think them no Burthen; and for other Obligations, he scorn'd to expect any-thing from me, but what he knew, as a Woman of Honour, I cou'd grant; then as to Maintenance, he told me he wou'd soon show me that he valued me infinitely above 500 l. a year; and upon this foot we began.

I seem'd kinder to him after this Discourse, and as Time and Private Conversation made us very intimate, we began to come nearer to the main Article, *namely*, the 500l. a Year. He offer'd that at first Word; and to acknowledge it as an infinite Favour to have it be accepted of; and I, that thought it was too much by all the Money, suffer'd myself to be master'd or prevail'd with, to yield, even on but a bare Engagement upon Parole.

When he had obtain'd his End that way, I told him my Mind: Now you see, my Lord, *said I*, how weakly I have acted, *namely*, to yield to you without any Capitulation, or any-thing secur'd to me, but that which you may cease to allow, when you please; if I am the less valued for such a Confidence, I shall be injur'd in a Manner that I will endeavour not to deserve.

He told me that he wou'd make it evident to me, that he did not seek me by way of Bargain, as such things were often done; that as I had treated him with a generous Confidence, so I shou'd find I was in the Hands of a Man of Honour, and one that knew how to value the Obligation; and upon this, he pull'd out a Goldsmith's Bill for 300 l. which, putting it into my Hand, he said he gave me as a Pledge, that I shou'd not be a Loser by my not having made a Bargain with him.

This was engaging indeed, and gave me a good idea of our future Correspondence; and in short, as I could not refrain treating him with more Kindness than I had done before, so one thing begetting another, I gave him several Testimonies that I was entirely his own, by Inclination, as well as by the common Obligation of a Mistress; and this pleas'd him exceedingly.

Soon after this private Engagement I began to consider, whether it were not more suitable to the Manner of Life I now led, to be a little less publick; and as I told my Lord it wou'd rid me of the Importunities of others, and of continual Visits from a sort of People who he knew of, and who, by the way, having now got the Notion of me which I really deserv'd, began to talk of the old Game, Love and Gallantry, and to offer at what was rude enough; things as nauseous to me now, as if I had been married; and as virtuous as other People: The Visits of these People began indeed, to be uneasie to me, and particularly, as they were always very tedious and impertinent; nor cou'd my Lord - - - - be pleas'd with them at all, if they had gone on: It wou'd be diverting to set down here, in what manner I repuls'd these sort of People; how in some I resented it as an Affront, and told them, that I was sorry they shou'd oblige me to vindicate myself from the Scandal of such Suggeſtions, by telling them, that *I cou'd see them no more*, and by desiring them not to give themselves the trouble of visiting me, who, tho' I was not willing to be uncivil, yet thought myself oblig'd never to receive any Visit from any Gentleman, after he had made such Proposals as those to me: But these things would be too tedious to bring in here; it was on this Account I propos'd to his Lordship my taking new Lodgings for Privacy; besides, I consider'd that as I might live very handsomely, and yet not so publicly, so I need not spend so much Money, by a great deal; and if I made 500 l. a Year of this generous Person, it was more than I had any Occasion to spend, by a great deal.

My Lord came readily into this Proposal, and went further than I expeĉted; for he found out a Lodging for me in a very handsome House where yet he was not known; I suppose he had employ'd somebody to find it out for him; and where he had a convenient Way to come into the Garden, by a Door that open'd into the Park; a thing very rarely allow'd in those Times.

By this Key he cou'd come in at what time of Night or Day he pleas'd, and as we had also a little Door in the lower Part of the House, which was always left upon a Lock, and his was the Master-Key, so if it was twelve, one, or two a-Clock at Night, he cou'd come directly into my Bed-Chamber. *N.B.*—I was not afraid I shou'd be found a-Bed with anybody else, for, in a word, I convers'd with nobody at-all.

It happen'd pleasantly enough one Night; his Lordship had staid late, and I, not expecting him that Night, had taken *Amy* to-Bed with me, and when my Lord came into the Chamber we were both fast asleep; I think it was near three a-Clock when he came in, and a little merry, but not at all fuddl'd or what they call in Drink; and he came at once into the Room.

Amy was frighted out of her Wits, and cry'd out; *I said Calmly*, indeed, my Lord, I did not expect you to-Night, and we have been a little frighted to-Night with Fire: *O!* *says he*, I see you have got a Bedfellow with you; I began to make an Apology, *No, no, says my Lord*, you need no Excuse, 'tis not a Man-Bedfellow I see; but then, talking merrily enough, he caught his Words back; but hark-ye, *says he*, now I think on't, how shall I be satisfied it is not a Man-Bedfellow? O, *says I*, I dare say your Lordship is satisfy'd 'tis poor *Amy*. Yes, says he, 'tis Mrs. *Amy*, but how do I know what *Amy* is? It may be Mr. *Amy* for aught I know; I hope you'll give me Leave to be satisfy'd: I told him, Yes, by all means I wou'd have his lordship satisfy'd, but I suppos'd he knew who she was.

Well, he fell foul of poor *Amy*, and indeed I thought once he would have carry'd the Jest on before my Face, as was once done in a like Case; but his Lordship was not so hot neither; but he would know whether *Amy* was Mr. *Amy* or Mrs. *Amy*, and so I suppose he did; and then being satisfy'd in that doubtful Case, he walk'd to the further end of the room and went into a little Closet, and sat down.

In the meantime *Amy* and I got up, and I bid her run and make the Bed in another Chamber for my Lord, and I gave her Sheets to put into it; which she did immediately, and I put my Lord to Bed there; and when I had done, at his Desire, went to-Bed to him: I was backward at first, to come to-Bed to him, and made my Excuse, because I had been in-bed with *Amy*, and had not shifted me, but he was past those Niceties at that time; and as long as he was sure it was Mrs. *Amy*, and not Mr. *Amy*, he was very well satisfy'd, and so the Jest pass'd over; but *Amy* appear'd no more all that Night or the next Day, and when she did, my Lord was so merry with her upon his *Ecclairicissiment*, as he call'd it, that *Amy* did not know what to do with herself.

Not that *Amy* was such a nice Lady in the main, if she had been fairly dealt with, as has appear'd in the former Part of this Work; but now she was surpriz'd and a little hurried, that she scarce knew where she was; and besides she was, as to his Lordship, as nice a Lady as any in the World, and, for any-thing he knew of her, she appear'd as such; the rest was to us only that knew of it.

I held this wicked Scene of Life out eight Years, reckoning from my first coming to England; and though my Lord found no Fault, yet I found, without much examining that any-one who look'd in my Face, might see I was

above twenty Years old, and yet, without flattering myself, I carried my Age, which was above Fifty, very well
too.

I may venture to say that no Woman ever liv'd a Life
like me, of six and twenty Years of Wickedness, without
the least Signals of Remorse; without any Signs of Repentance; or without so much as a Wish to put an End to
it; I had so long habituated myself to a Life of Vice, that
really it appear'd to be no Vice to me; I went on smooth
and pleasant; I wallow'd in Wealth, and it flow'd in upon
me at such a Rate, having taken the frugal Measures that
the good Knight directed, so that I had at the End of the
eight Years, two Thousand eight Hundred Pounds coming Yearly in, of which I did not spend one Penny, being
maintain'd by my Allowance from my Lord ———, and
more than maintain'd, by above 200 l. per *Annum*; for
tho' he did not contract for 500 l. a year, as I made dumb
Signs to have it be, yet he gave me Money so often, and
that in such large Parcels, that I had seldom so little as
seven to eight Hundred Pounds a Year of him, one Year
with another.

I must go back here, after telling openly the wicked
things I did, to mention something which, however, had
the Face of doing good; I remember'd that when I went
from *England*, which was fifteen Years before, I had left
five little Children, turn'd out, as it were, to the wide
World, and to the Charity of their Father's Relations;
the Eldest was not six Years old, for we had not been
marry'd full seven Years when their Father went away.

After my coming to *England* I was greatly desirous to
hear how things stood with them; and whether they were
all alive or not; and in what Manner they had been maintain'd; and yet I resolv'd not to discover myself to them,

in the leaſt; or to let any of the People that had the breeding of them up, know that there was such a-body left in
the World, as their Mother.

Amy was the only-body I could truſt with such a Commission, and I sent her into *Spittle-Fields*, to the old Aunt,
and to the poor Woman, that was so inſtrumental in disposing the Relations to take some Care of the Children,
but they were both gone, dead and buried some Years; the
next Enquiry she made, was at the house where she carry'd the poor Children and turn'd them in at the Door;
when she came there, she found the House inhabited by
other People, so that she cou'd make little or nothing of
her Enquiries, and came back with an Answer, that indeed, was no answer at me, for it gave me no Satisfaction
at all: I sent her back to enquire in the Neighbourhood,
what was become of the Family, that lived in that House?
and if they were remov'd, where they liv'd? and what Circumſtances they were in, and withal, if she cou'd, what
became of the poor Children, and how they liv'd and
where? how they had been treated? *and the like.*

She brought me back word, upon this second going;
that she heard as to the Family, that the husband who
tho' but Uncle-in-Law to the Children, had yet been
kindest to them, was dead; and that the Widow was left
but in mean Circumſtances, that is to say, she did not
want, but that she was not so well in the World as she was
thought to be when her Husband was alive.

That as to the poor Children, two of them, it seems,
had been kept by her, that is to say, by her Husband,
while he liv'd, for that it was againſt her Will, that we all
knew; but the honeſt Neighbours pity'd the poor Children, *they said*, heartily; for that their Aunt us'd them
barbarously and made them little better than Servants in

the House, to wait upon her and her Children, and scarce allow'd them Cloaths fit to wear.

These were, it seems, my Eldeſt, and third, which were Daughters; the Second was a Son, the Fourth a Daughter, and the Youngeſt a Son.

To finish the melancholy Part of this Hiſtory of my two unhappy Girls, she brought me word, that as soon as they were able to go out, and get any Work, they went from her; and some said, she had turn'd them out of Doors, but it seems she had not done so, but she us'd them so cruelly that they left her; and one of them went to Service to a Neighbour's a little-way off, who knew her, an honeſt, subſtantial Weaver's Wife, to whom she was Chamber-Maid, and in a little time she took her Siſter out of the *Bridewell* of her Aunt's House and got her a Place too.

This was all melancholly and dull; I sent her then to the Weaver's House, where the Eldeſt had liv'd, but found that her Miſtress being dead, she was gone, and no-body knew there, whither she went; only that they heard she had liv'd with a great Lady at the other end of the Town, but they did not know who that Lady was.

These Enquiries took us up three or four Weeks, and I was not one Jot the better for it, for I cou'd hear nothing to my Satisfaction; I sent her next to find out the honeſt Man, who, as in the Beginning of my Story I obſerv'd, made them be entertain'd, and caus'd the youngeſt to be fetch'd from the Town where we liv'd, and where the Parish Officers had taken Care of him: This Gentleman was ſtill alive; and there she heard that my youngeſt Daughter and eldeſt Son were dead also; but that my youngeſt Son was alive and was at that time, about 17 Years old, and that he was put out Apprentice, by the kindness and Charity of his Uncle, but to a mean Trade, and at which he was oblig'd to work very hard.

Amy was so curious in this Part, that she went immediately to see him, and found him all-dirty, and hard at-work; she had no remembrance at all of the Youth, for she had not seen him since he was about two Years old, and it was evident he cou'd have no Knowledge of her.

However, she talk'd with him and found him a good, sensible, mannerly Youth; that he knew little of the Story of his Father or Mother, and had no View of any-thing but to work hard for his Living; and she did not think fit to put any great things into his Head, lest it shou'd take him off his Business, and perhaps make him turn giddy-headed and be good for nothing; but she went and found out that Kind Man, his Benefactor, who had put him out; and finding him a plain, well-meaning, honest, and kind-hearted Man, she opened her Tale to him the easier: She made a long Story, how she had a prodigious Kindness for the Child because she had the same for his Father and Mother; told him, that she was the Servant-Maid that brought all of them to their Aunt's Door, and ran away and left them; that their poor Mother wanted Bread; and what came of her after, she wou'd have been glad to know; she added, that her Circumstances had happen'd to mend in the World; and that, as she was in Condition, so she was dispos'd to show some Kindness to the Children if she cou'd find them out.

He receiv'd her with all the Civility that so kind a Proposal demanded; gave her an Account of what he had done for the Child; how he had maintain'd him, fed and cloath'd him; put him to School, and at last put him out to a Trade; *she said*, he had indeed, been a Father to the

Child; but, Sir, *says she*, 'tis a very laborious, hard-work-
ing Trade, and he is but a thin weak Boy; that's true, *says
he*, but the Boy chose the Trade, and I assure you I gave
20 l. with him, and am to find him Cloaths all his Appren-
ticeship; and as to its being a hard Trade, *says he*, that's
the Fate of his Circumstances, poor Boy; I could not well
do better for him.

Well, Sir, as you did all for him in Charity, *says she*, it
was exceeding well; but as my Resolution is to do something for him, I desire you will if possible, take him away
again, from that Place where he works so hard, for I cannot bear to see the Child work so very hard for his Bread,
and I will do something for him, that shall make him live
without such hard Labour.

He smil'd at that; I can indeed, *says he*, take him away,
but then I must lose my 20 l. that I gave with him.

Well, sir, said *Amy*, I'll enable you to lose that 20l. immediately; and so she puts her Hand in her Pocket, and
pulls out her Purse.

He began to be a little amaz'd at her, and look'd her
hard in the Face, and that so very much, that she took
Notice of it, and said, Sir, I Fancy by your looking at me,
you think you know me, but I am assur'd you do not, for
I never saw your Face before; I think you have done
enough for the Child, and that you ought to be acknowledg'd as a Father to him, but you ought not to lose by
your kindness to him, more than the Kindness of bringing him up obliges you to; and therefore there's the twenty Pound, *added she*, and pray let him be fetch'd away.

Well, Madam, says he, I will thank you for the Boy, as
well as for my self; but will you please to tell me, what I
must do with him.

Sir, says *Amy*, as you have been so Kind to keep him so

many Years, I beg you will take him home again oneYear more, and I'll bring you an hundred Pound more, which I will desire you to lay out in Schooling and Cloaths for him, and to pay you for his Board; perhaps I may put him in a Condition to return your Kindness.

He look'd pleas'd, but surpriz'd very much, and enquired of *Amy*, but with very great Respect, what he should go to school to learn? and what trade she would please to put him out to?

Amy said, he should put him to learn a little *Latin*, and then Merchants' Accounts; and to write a good Hand, for she would have him be put to a *Turkey*-Merchant.

Madam, *says he*, I am glad for his sake, to hear you talk so; but do you know that a *Turkey* Merchant will not take him under 4 or 500 Pounds?

Yes, Sir, says *Amy, I know it very well.*

And, *says he*, that it will require as many Thousands to set him up?

Yes, Sir, *says Amy*, I know that very well too; and resolving to talk very big, *she added*, I have no Children of my own, and I resolve to make him my Heir, and if ten Thousand Pounds be requir'd to set him up, he shall not want it; I was but his Mother's Servant when he was born, and I mourn'd heartily for the Disaster of the Family; and I always said, if ever I was worth anything in the World, I wou'd take the Child for my own, and I'll be as good as my Word now, tho' I did not then foresee that it wou'd be with me, as it has been since: And so *Amy* told him a long Story, how she was troubled for me; and what she wou'd give to hear whether I was dead or alive, and what Circumstances I was in; that if she cou'd but find me, if I was ever so poor, she would take Care of me, and make a Gentlewoman of me again.

He told her, that as to the Child's Mother, she had been reduc'd to the laſt Extremity, and was oblig'd (as he suppos'd she knew) to send the Children all among her Husband's Friends; and if it had not been for him, they had all been sent to the Parish; but that he oblig'd the other Relations to share the Charge among them; that he had taken two, whereof he had loſt the eldeſt, who died of the Small-Pox; but that he had been as careful of this, as of his own, and had made very little Difference in their breeding up; only that when he came to put him out, he thought it was beſt for the Boy to put him to a Trade which he might set-up in without a Stock; for otherwise his Time wou'd be loſt; and that as to his Mother, he had never been able to hear one Word of her, no, not tho' he had made the utmoſt Enquiry after her; that there went a Report, that she had drown'd herself; but that he cou'd never meet with any-body that cou'd give him a certain Account of it.

Amy counterfeited a Cry for her poor Miſtress; told him, she wou'd give anything in the World to see her, if she was alive; and a great deal more such-like Talk they had about that; then they returned to speak of the Boy.

He enquir'd of her why she did not seek after the Child before, that he might have been brought up from a younger Age, suitable to what she design'd to do for him.

She told him, she had been out of *England*, and was but newly return'd from the *Eaſt-Indies*; that she had been out of *England*, and was but newly return'd, was true, but the latter was false, and was put in to blind him, and provide againſt further Enquiries, for it was not a ſtrange thing for young Women to go away poor to the *Eaſt-Indies*, and come home vaſtly Rich; so she went on with Dire¢tions about him; and both agreed in this, that the

Boy should by no means be told what was intended for him, but only that he should be taken home again to his Uncle's; that his Uncle thought the Trade too hard for him, *and the like.*

About three Days after this, *Amy* goes again, and carry'd him the hundred Pound she promis'd him, but then *Amy* made quite another Figure than she did before; for she went in my Coach with two Footmen after her, and dress'd very fine also, with Jewells and a Gold Watch; and there was indeed, no great Difficulty to make *Amy* look like a Lady, for she was a very handsome, well-shap'd Woman, and genteel enough; the Coachman and Servants were particularly order'd to show her the same Respect as they wou'd to me, and to call her Madam *Collins*, if they were ask'd any questions about her.

When the Gentleman saw what a Figure she made, it added to the former Surprize, and he entertain'd her in the most respectful Manner possible; congratulated her Advancement in Fortune, and particularly rejoyc'd that it should fall to the poor Child's Lot to be so provided for, contrary to all Expectation.

Well, *Amy* talk'd big, but very free and familiar; told them she had no Pride in her good Fortune; (and that was true enough, for to give *Amy* her due, she was far from it, and was as good-humour'd a Creature as ever liv'd), that she was the same as ever, and that she always lov'd this Boy, and was resolv'd to do something extraordinary for him.

Then she pull'd out her Money, and paid him down an hundred and twenty Pounds, which, she said, she paid him, that he might be sure he should be no Loser by taking him Home again, and that she would come and see him again, and talk further about things with him, that so all might be settled for him, in such a Manner, as the Accidents, such as Mortality or any-thing else, should make no Alteration to the Child's Prejudice.

At this Meeting, the Uncle brought his Wife out, a good motherly, comely, grave Woman, who spoke very tenderly of the Youth, and, as it appear'd, had been very good to him, tho' she had several Children of her own: After a long Discourse she put in a Word of her own; Madam, *says she*, I am heartily glad of the good Intentions you have for this poor Orphan, and I rejoice sincerely in it, for his sake, but, Madam, you know (I suppose) that there are two Sisters alive too, may we not speak a Word for them? *Poor Girls, says she*, they have not been so kindly us'd as he has; and are turn'd out to the wide World.

Where are they, Madam? *says Amy.*

Poor Creatures, *says the Gentlewoman*, they are out at Service, no-body knows where but themselves; their Case is very hard.

Well, Madam, *says Amy*, though, if I cou'd find them, I would assist them; yet my Concern is for my Boy, *as I call him*, and I will put him into a Condition to take Care of his Sisters.

But, Madam, *says the good compassionate Creature*, he may not be so charitable perhaps, by his own inclination, for Brothers are not Fathers; and they have been cruelly us'd already, poor Girls; we have often reliev'd them, both with Victuals and Cloaths too, even while they were pretended to be kept by their barbarous Aunt.

Well, madam, *says Amy*, what can I do for them; they are gone, it seems, and cannot be heard of? When I see them, 'tis time enough.

She press'd *Amy* then to oblige their Brother, out of

the plentiful Fortune he was like to have, to do something for his Sisters when he should be able.

Amy spoke coldly of that still, but said, she would consider of it, and so they parted for that time; they had several Meetings after this, for *Amy* went to see her adopted Son, and order'd his Schooling, Cloaths, and other things, but enjoin'd them not to tell the Young-Man any-thing, but that they thought the Trade he was at, too hard for him, and they wou'd keep him at-home a little longer, and give him some Schooling, to fit him for better Business; and *Amy* appear'd to him as she did before, only as one that had known his Mother, and had some Kindness for him.

Thus this Matter pass'd on for near a Twelve-month, when it happen'd that one of my Maid-Servants having ask'd *Amy* Leave, for *Amy* was Mistress of the Servants, and took, and put-out such as she pleas'd; I say, having ask'd Leave to go into the City to see her Friends, came Home crying bitterly, and in a most grievous Agony she was, and continued so several Days, till *Amy* perceiving the Excess, and that the Maid would certainly cry herself Sick, she took an Opportunity with her and examin'd her about it.

The Maid told her a long Story, that she had been to see her Brother, the only Brother she had in the World, and that she knew he was put-out Apprentice to a -----, but there had come a Lady in a Coach, to his Uncle ----, who had brought him up, and made him take him Home again; and so the Wench run-on with the whole Story, just as 'tis told above, till she came to that Part that belong'd to herself; and there, *says she*, I had not let them know where I liv'd, and the Lady wou'd have taken me, and they say, wou'd have provided for me too, as she has done for my Brother, but no-body cou'd tell where to find me, and so I have lost it all, and all the Hopes of being any-thing, but a poor Servant all my Days; and then the Girl fell a-crying again.

Amy said, what's all this Story? who could this Lady be? It must be some trick sure? No, *she said*, it was not a Trick, for she had made them take her Brother home from Apprentice, and bought him new Cloaths, and put him to have more Learning; and the Gentlewoman said she wou'd make him her Heir.

Her Heir! says *Amy*; what does that amount to; it may be she had nothing to leave him; she might make any-body her Heir.

No, no, *says the girl*, she came in a fine Coach and Horses, and I don't know how many Footmen to attend her, and brought a great bag of Gold, and gave it to my Uncle - - - - -, he that brought up my Brother, to buy him Cloaths and to pay for his Schooling and Board.

He that brought up your Brother! *says Amy;* why did not he bring you up too, as well as your Brother? Pray, who brought you up then?

Here the poor Girl told a melancholly Story, how an Aunt had brought-up her and her Sister, and how bar-barously she had us'd them, as we have heard.

By this time *Amy* had her Head full enough, and her Heart too; and did not know how to hold it, or what to do, for she was satisfied that this was no other than my own Daughter; for she told her all the History of her Father and Mother; and how she was carried by their Maid to her Aunt's Door, just as is related in the beginning of my Story.

Amy did not tell me this Story for a great-while, nor did she well know what Course to take in it; but as she had Authority to manage everything in the Family, she took Occasion some time after, without letting me know any-thing of it, to find some Fault with the Maid and turn her away.

Her reasons were good, tho' at firſt I was not pleas'd when I heard of it, but I was convinc'd afterwards, that she was in the right; for if she had told me of it, I shou'd have been in great Perplexity, between the Difficulty of concealing myself from my own Child, and the Inconvenience of having my Way of Living be known among my Firſt Husband's Relations, and even to my Husband himself; for as to his being dead at *Paris*, *Amy* seeing me resolv'd againſt marrying any-more, had told me that she had form'd that Story only to make me easie when I was in *Holland*, if any-thing should offer to my liking.

However, I was too tender a Mother ſtill, notwithſtanding what I had done, to let this poor Girl go about the World drudging, as it were, for Bread, and slaving at the Fire and in the Kitchen as a Cook-Maid; besides, it came into my Head, that she might perhaps marry some poor Devil of a Footman or a Coachman, or some such thing, and be undone that way; or, which was worse, be drawn in to lie with some of that coarse cursed Kind and be with-Child, and be utterly ruin'd that way; and in the midſt of all my Prosperity this gave me great Uneasiness.

As to sending *Amy* to her, there was no doing that now; for as she had been Servant in the House, she knew *Amy*, as well as *Amy* knew me; and no doubt, tho' I was much out of her Sight, yet she might have had the Curiosity to have peep'd at me, and seen me enough to know me again, if I had discover'd myself to her; so that, in short, there was nothing to be done that way.

However, *Amy*, a diligent, indefatigable Creature,

found out another Woman, and gave her her Errand, and sent her to the honeſt Man's House in *Spittle-Fields*, whither she suppos'd the Girl wou'd go, after she was out of her Place, and bade her talk with her, and tell her at a diſtance, that as something had been done for her Brother, so something wou'd be done for her too; and that she shou'd not be discourag'd, she carried her 20 l to buy her Cloaths, and bade her not to go to Service any more, but think of other things; that she shou'd take a Lodging in some good Family, and that she should soon hear farther.

The Girl was overjoyed with this News, you may be sure, and at firſt a little too much elevated with it, and dress'd herself very handsomely indeed, and, as soon as she had done so, came and paid a Visit to Madam *Amy* to let her see how fine she was: *Amy* congratulated her, and wish'd it might be all as she expeĉted, but admonish'd her not to be elevated with it too much; told her, Humility was the beſt Ornament of a Gentlewoman; and a great deal of good Advice she gave her, but discover'd nothing.

All this was aĉted in the firſt Years of my setting up my new Figure here in Town, and while the Masks and Balls were in Agitation; and *Amy* carried on the Affair of setting-out my Son into the World, which we were assiſted in by the sage Advice of my faithful Counsellor, Sir *Robert Clayton*, who procur'd us a Maſter for him, by whom he was afterwards sent Abroad to *Italy*, as you shall hear in its place; and *Amy* manag'd my Daughter too, very well, tho' by a third hand.

THE END OF THE FIRST VOLUME